Eighteenth Century Drama:

Afterpieces

Eighteenth Century Drama:
Afterpieces

EDITED WITH AN INTRODUCTION BY
RICHARD W. BEVIS

OXFORD UNIVERSITY PRESS
LONDON   OXFORD   NEW YORK
1970

Oxford University Press

LONDON OXFORD NEW YORK
GLASGOW TORONTO MELBOURNE WELLINGTON
CAPE TOWN SALISBURY IBADAN NAIROBI LUSAKA DAR ES SALAAM ADDIS ABABA
BOMBAY CALCUTTA MADRAS KARACHI LAHORE DACCA
KUALA LUMPUR SINGAPORE HONG KONG TOKYO

First published as an Oxford University Press
paperback by Oxford University Press, London, 1970

PRINTED IN GREAT BRITAIN
BY RICHARD CLAY (THE CHAUCER PRESS) LTD
BUNGAY SUFFOLK

Contents

Introduction   vii

Suggestions for Further Reading   xvii

The Historical Register for the Year 1736 (1737),
   by Henry Fielding   1

A Will and No Will (1746), *by Charles Macklin*   37

Miss in Her Teens (1747), *by David Garrick*   77

The Kept Mistress (1756)   109

Polly Honeycombe (1760), *by George Colman*   135

The Upholsterer (1758–1763), *by Arthur Murphy*   163

The Way to Keep Him (1760), *by Arthur Murphy*   197

The Commissary (1765), *by Samuel Foote*   243

To B. H. B.

Introduction

Afterpieces were short, usually humorous playlets which followed the five-act main attraction and concluded the theatrical evening in the eighteenth and nineteenth centuries. During the Georgian heyday far more comedies were written as afterpieces than as 'mainpieces', some of them by the most talented comic authors of the day, and over its whole life span the afterpiece was an integral part of English theatre. The custom of presenting afterpieces has long since passed, stranding such hulks as *Tom Thumb* and *The Critic*, but now that the 'entertainment world' has made such compact forms of drama familiar again, many of these afterpieces seem curiously modern in their means and ends, their strengths and weaknesses.

I

The history of the rise and fall of the afterpiece is inseparable from the stories of those who produced and patronized it. The earliest known double bill in England[1] occurred in mid-winter 1676–7. For a companion piece to his translation of Racine's *Bérénice*, the tragedian Thomas Otway brought out Molière's *Les Fourberies de Scapin* as *The Cheats of Scapin*. The experiment was not repeated, however, until November 1696, when Thomas Betterton's company at Lincoln's Inn Fields put on a mainpiece plus a farce for six nights running. Betterton and a group of fellow actors and actresses had left Drury Lane Theatre after a squabble with its manager, Christopher Rich, in 1695; the extraordinary programme was an attempt to undercut Rich by luring his customers away. Inter-playhouse rivalry was to be a major factor in establishing the afterpiece on a regular basis in the eighteenth century.

Meanwhile, other relevant pressures were building up. The influence of French neoclassical criticism, with its insistence on the strict separation and purity of genres, was growing in England. As early as 1668, Dryden made the Francophile Lisideius protest, in the essay *Of Dramatic Poesy*,

There is no theatre in the world has anything so absurd as the English tragicomedy; 'tis a drama of our own invention, and the fashion of it is enough to proclaim it so; here a course of mirth, there another of sadness and passion, a third of honour, and fourth a duel; thus, in two hours and a half we run through

---

[1] The afterpiece was established on the French stage by 1650, and the satyr-play provides a classical precedent.

all the fits of Bedlam. The French affords you as much variety on the same day, but they do it not so unseasonably, or *mal a propos*, as we: our poets present you the play and the farce together ... but are not mirth and compassion things incompatible?

Note that his objection is not to farce *per se*, but to the *mixing* of farce with serious drama. This position militated for just such a division into 'play' and 'farce' as finally came about.

Another support for the afterpiece – this one wholly native in origin and based on quite different premises – came from the spectators. Many observers noted the changing composition of theatre audiences in the late seventeenth century, especially after the 'Glorious Revolution' of 1688 ousted the free-living Stuart court. The licentious drama it had encouraged was discredited; in the reign of William and Mary a sterner moral code was diffused from court to theatre than had been the case since the Restoration. The new sovereigns, in fact, viewed the stage with suspicion, and this affected the whole complex of dramatists, actors, theatregoers, and critics. Gradually the courtiers were supplanted as the drama's chief patrons by bourgeois merchants and businessmen, most of whom lacked literary education and were in no way attached to tradition, dramatic or otherwise. They were perfectly willing to countenance any theatrical novelty, including the afterpiece, so long as it afforded them light and reasonably innocent entertainment—too willing, in the opinion of most critics. John Dennis deplored the arrival of the middle class in the playhouse, commenting glumly in 1702[2] that 'the English were never sunk so miserably low in their taste, as they are at present'.

The altered audience also figured in an important financial innovation. In March 1692 Thomas Killigrew complained to a Court of Chancery that Alexander Davenant, his fellow-patentee at the Theatre Royal, was monopolizing the 'after-money': a reduced rate allowed those who came in after the second act of a three-act, or the third of a five-act play. But why this concession to latecomers, who (the circumstances suggest) must have been numerous? Killigrew and Davenant had inherited from the early Restoration period a tradition of matinee performances: the leisured courtiers of Charles II's day preferred a 2 P.M. curtain. But as more working men came to plays, this hour created a problem, and although gradually the curtain rose later— five o'clock in the early eighteenth century, six in Garrick's day—in the late seventeenth century it was still too early for many members of the working and business classes. They evidently protested against receiving only half value for their money, and the patentees' answer was to accept 'after-money'. For a while this sufficed (becoming in the eighteenth century

[2] In his 'Large Account of the Taste in Poetry'.

the 'half-price' custom), but as greater numbers of the audience entered late, they grew more insistent in their demands for a full evening's entertainment. The obvious answer was the afterpiece, even though this lengthened the theatrical programme to four or five hours over-all.

Thus by about 1700 a set of conditions existed in London favourable to the establishment of the afterpiece custom, but the use of double bills was still sporadic. The major watershed was November 1714, when the entrepreneur John Rich opened Lincoln's Inn Fields Theatre in competition with Drury Lane. Rich at once hit upon the afterpiece as a means of wooing an audience, and staged at least forty-six in his short first season. Drury Lane replied in kind, and the two houses produced over 225 afterpieces in the first full season of competition (1715–16). By the mid-twenties the phase of struggling for a place on the programme was over; from this time on an afterpiece with each full-length play was virtually *de rigueur*. The *petites pièces* were popular with both spectators and playwrights. In the mid-eighteenth century, writes Lynch, the afterpiece was often 'a greater attraction for the audience than the regular drama it accompanied',[3] and a visitor to England in 1791 noticed that the playhouses were fuller during the second half of the evening's entertainment.

Afterpieces were played regularly in London until well on in Victoria's reign. Scholars differ whether the fast suburban train or the later dinner hour of society ended the afterpiece custom, but most agree that its disappearance was due to the shortening of the theatrical evening about the end of the third quarter of the nineteenth century. From its inception the afterpiece had been closely connected with the working man and the half-price custom, and when the theatre once again became 'fashionable' in format, its exit was inevitable.[4]

II

Of the assorted types of afterpiece drama, farce is the oldest; it had its origins in the anti-stage legislation of the Commonwealth period (1642–60). Numerous ordinances of the Puritan Parliament in those years forbade the acting of 'publike Stage-playes'. These edicts snapped the continuity of English dramatic traditions, as well as bedevilling a generation of actors, but never, as Hotson has shown, did they completely stifle theatrical activity: 'even during the height of the war, plays were given with remarkable frequency at the regular playhouses in London . . . the actors went on performing in defiance of the ordinance against them.'[5] They played

---

[3] *Box, Pit and Gallery* (1953), p. 238.
[4] By the end of the nineteenth century the process had come full circle, and a polite theatrical clientele was again enjoying matinees without afterpieces.
[5] *The Commonwealth and Restoration Stage* (1928), pp. 16–17.

both at impromptu theatres in private houses and at tenacious public theatres such as the Red Bull. At the latter especially they were subject to frequent raids and property confiscations which cut heavily into their already thin margin of profit. In these trying times they hit upon the droll (from 'the droll humours of . . .') or farce ('stuffing'): a brief, amusing selection from a larger play, which could be slipped into the programme along with some lawful entertainment, cost little to produce, and lent itself to a quick getaway. Francis Kirkman, a Commonwealth actor, later explained:

When the publique Theatres were shut up . . . then all that we could divert ourselves with were these humours and pieces of Plays, which passing under the Name of a merry conceited Fellow, called *Bottom the Weaver*, *Simpleton the Smith*, *John Swabber*, or some such title, were only allowed us, and that but by stealth too, and under pretence of Rope-dancing, or the like; and these being all that was permitted us, great was the confluence of the Auditors; and these small things were as profitable, and as great get-pennies to the Actors as any of our late famed Plays. I have seen the Red Bull Play-House, which was a large one, so full, that as many went back for want of room as had entred; and as meanly as you may think of these Drols, they were then Acted by the best Comedians then and now in being . . .[6]

Born as a desperate evasion of oppressive authority, English farce might well have died when that authority was removed and legitimate drama returned to the London stage, but it did not. A demand had been created, at least among the lower and middle classes, during the interregnal years, and after the Restoration the farce or droll lived on in the booths of the fairs and among the strolling troupes. As yet there was no place for it in the regular theatre, but this may have been a disguised blessing. English farce 'grew up' in the half-century between Davenant and John Rich; in the relative privacy of obscure provincial workshops it experimented with forms and with materials, learned from French and Italian farce and *commedia*, and developed its own actors. When the call came in the early eighteenth century, there existed already a few good native farces and the authorial and histrionic traditions necessary to produce more at once.

Of the other genres which the afterpiece custom fostered, we are concerned here only with those which had some basis in English comic traditions: the dramatic satire and the short comedy. The former traces its independent existence back to Old and Jonsonian Comedy on one hand, and on the other to *The Knight of the Burning Pestle* (1607) and *The Rehearsal* (1671), burlesques on the theatrical absurdities of their day. Fielding in the 1730s and Foote in the 1750s and '60s, finding welcome freedom from convention in the afterpiece, developed the *short* dramatic satire into a potent

[6] *The Wits, or Sport Upon Sport* (1672), quoted in Hotson, p. 48.

weapon, simultaneously amusing and trenchant. The type is easily recognized by its subjugation of character and form to satiric purpose, and by its casual disregard of the comic essentials of reconciliation and a love match at the end. The dramatic satire is represented in this volume by *The Historical Register for 1736*, *Polly Honeycombe*, and *The Commissary*.

It is often difficult, however, to distinguish the short or *petite* comedy from farce. The eighteenth century was no clearer than we as to where the dividing line fell in practice, though its theories sound confident enough. Here, for example, is Joseph Reed, a farce-writer of the time:

> The Bard, whose hopes on Comedy depend,
> Must strive instruction with delight to blend,
> While he, who bounds his less-aspiring views
> To Farce, the Combrush of the Comic Muse,
> With pleasantry alone may fill the scene;
> His business chiefly this—to cure the spleen:
> To raise the pensive mind from grave to gay,
> And help to laugh a thoughtful hour away.[7]

This treatment is typical as far as it goes, but incomplete. The critical consensus has usually been that comedy must emphasize character, remain within the bounds of probability, combine the instructive with the humorous, and evoke, however faintly, in its closing *saturnalia* of feasts and weddings, echoes of its origins in the spring fertility rituals of the Greeks. Farce, on the other hand, whose only purpose is to raise a laugh, may utilize improbable incidents, slapstick, or whatever else serves its end. Despite such attempts at definition, most of the plays in this volume were given two or three different labels in their time, as various criteria—length, nature, position in the programme—were applied by various writers. Only *The Way to Keep Him* is beyond doubt a pure short comedy; although *Miss in Her Teens* seems another example of this type, it was called a farce in the eighteenth century. The two benefit[8] plays, *A Will and No Will* and *The Kept Mistress*, as well as *The Upholsterer*, were usually designated as farces, but each of the latter two combines a short comedy with a satiric plot, leaving Macklin's play the only undisputed farce here.

The idea of the shortened comedy came from France. English translations and imitations were introduced in London by Garrick and James Miller in the 1730s and '40s and the form was subsequently developed by Colman, Foote, and Murphy. Its peak period was very brief: at most the twenty-five years following *Miss in Her Teens*. After the passing of the generation of

---

[7] Prologue to *The Register Office* (1761), unpublished Larpent MS.

[8] A performance whose receipts (after house charges) went to the actor, actress, author, or theatre employee whose 'night' it was.

pioneers, all departed by 1777, the farce and short comedy both tended to lapse into sentiment, melodrama, and vaudeville.

In fact, aside from the tradition-based forms, the roster of afterpiece drama is undistinguished. Rich's pantomimes[9] threatened to monopolize the afterpiece entirely on occasion after 1717, remaining popular into the nineteenth century. As the theatre rivalries continued and audience demand grew, the supply of dramatic novelties used as afterpieces came to include animal and other circus acts, comic and ballad operas and musical farces, burlettas,[10] melodramas, pastorals, preludes, 'sketches', scenic spectacles, and every other conceivable species of theatrical exhibition. The breakdown of the classical dramatic genres—comedy and tragedy—begun in the seventeenth century was complete by the middle of the eighteenth, and the modern 'entertainment world' was born, largely in the afterpiece. The crucial development of Georgian drama was, not sentiment, but the proliferation of this irregular, many-faceted 'minor theatre' (which we usually think of as a Victorian phenomenon). The number of non-traditional, comic-type plays written and produced increased with each season; by 1776 they constituted the largest single bloc of performances in the repertoire, dominating everything else—tragedy, laughing and sentimental comedy, farce.

Drama naturally ceased to be written for the afterpiece when the custom lost its *raison d'être* and died of neglect late in the nineteenth century. The short comedy had lost its vitality much earlier; its demise was overdue. Of the thousands of afterpieces extant, very few are in editions accessible to the general reader, and almost all have disappeared from the stage: our theatre-going habits do not allow leisure for afterpieces, and these plays were not meant to be produced alone. Yet now the whirligig of taste has enabled the once-dependent 'afterpiece' to set up on its own: as the situation comedy or satirical sketch of television, the night-club ensemble skit, and the terse one-act of contemporary legitimate theatre. A genre, once created, is not destroyed—only transmuted.

III

The first question to ask about any artifact is: what was it *intended* to do? The query is especially pertinent to afterpiece comedy. If we approach it on other than its own terms, we will not only be disappointed, but will be missing the whole point—and the pleasure appropriate to the genre.

First of all, then, the reader or spectator must not expect to find in the

---

[9] An operetta, usually on a mythical subject, interspersed with a mimed farce of Harlequin and Columbine (often satirizing the operetta plot), and adorned with spectacular scenery.

[10] Comic operas had original music, while ballad operas used old airs; musical farces were shorter and had fewer songs than either. The burletta narrated a mythological or *commedia* story with the aid of music.

afterpiece Shakespearian, or any other, *romantic* comedy, attended with poetry, ritual, and plural levels of meaning. The eighteenth century inherited rather the satiric Jonsonian type via Restoration manners comedy, and was, like the latter, always in prose. Thus *Every Man in His Humour*, not *As You Like It*, is the correct 'standard of beauty' against which to judge these afterpieces. Caricature rather than character, wit rather than humour, ingenuity in devising minor incidents rather than broader imaginative powers, satire on corrupt manners rather than sympathetic or profound understanding of human failings, and conventional verisimilitude rather than any transcendence of the naturalistic surface: these are the reasonable expectations in afterpiece comedy. These qualities were what the all-powerful Georgian audience demanded in their curtain-dropper, and what the sensible dramatist therefore gave them.

Secondly, the art of the afterpiece is *stereotypic*: this is the essential point, and failure to grasp it will be fatal to enjoyment. A very few plots and character-types serve as the constants in an equation whose variables are the particular situations and incidents (the *lazzi* or 'turns' of the *commedia*) which the individual playwright invents. It is an error to look deeper than the surface for anything new; the afterpiece, like a sentimental scene in Dickens or a melodrama, is stylized, and any stylized form derives its power and profundity from the time-tested cliché slightly varied, the ritual incantation run through for the ten-thousandth time. The opening cadences of an heroic-formulaic poem, the introductory progressions of an instrumental blues, the first scene of a farce, all invite us into an artistic medium in which the building materials are known quantities, and the interest is: what will be done with them this time? The afterpiece invites comparison with the *commedia dell'arte* (one of its progenitors), or with its descendants the comic strip, the animated cartoon, and the cinema farce. From the first glimpse of each familiar pair of standard constants—Harlequin and Columbine, Laurel and Hardy, Dagwood and Blondie, heavy father and witty servant—there is much we can safely assume: character (or role) is a 'given', the number of possible outcomes is severely limited, and the type of resolution may be predicted. The charm lies in seeing *how* the contriver will reach the inevitable goal.

Finally there is the *caveat*, necessary though vain, that an extraordinary effort of histrionic and historical imagination is required to visualize the afterpiece on the stage, and that even then we can touch only a small part of what the play was actually like. This is true chiefly because the actors used the text merely as a starting-point. Heirs to a double tradition of improvisation—the *commedia* and the early English farce—afterpiece players ad-libbed shamelessly, stumbled upon or deliberately invented new bits of stage business, and in general showed a high degree of independence of the printed page. As a result of this perpetual experimentation and serendipity, afterpieces evolved autonomously, like living organisms responding to their environments. *The Upholsterer* is one example, and Garrick's *Lethe* ran through seven editions in twenty-five years, not in order that the author might legislate alterations, but simply to keep abreast of the changes wrought in the play by the nightly moulding and grinding of performance. Each text, then, is only a frame in the moving picture of afterpiece comedy.

IV

There was more creative activity in the afterpiece than in the mainpiece throughout the eighteenth century. As a rule critics have conceded the afterpiece 'greater vitality', but it is still a surprise to learn just how dominant it really was. In performances, of course, the two were numerically almost equal, but of the plays received by the Licenser between 1737 and 1777 nearly 80 per cent were afterpieces of one type or another; the short comedies and farces alone outnumbered mainpiece comedies by more than two to one. The major comic playwrights of the Garrick era produced three-quarters of their work in three acts or less. Though most people looked down on the afterpiece as an inferior form, it did not suffer from the stagnancy that beset regular comedy and tragedy for most of the century.

Afterpiece and mainpiece traded plays briskly back and forth. The commoner procedure was for an unsuccessful or worn-out mainpiece to be reduced to an afterpiece, but movement in the other direction was not unknown. When *The Historical Register* drew large crowds as an afterpiece Fielding simply moved it unaltered to the first billing; after *The Way to Keep Him* succeeded in three acts, Murphy expanded it to five with few changes in the original material. Mainpieces reworked as afterpieces, however, were not only truncated but 'farcicalized'—made more dependent on stage business, more readily laughable.

Naturally all this traffic begot influence. As Nettleton wrote long ago, the afterpiece 'may be said to exercise a real, though not definitely determinable, influence on regular drama'.[11] Today we are in a position to determine the nature of this influence, and it must be admitted that much of it was bad. The '*illegitimi*' helped to break down comedy into numerous sub-types, and indulged their audiences' penchant for unreflective laughter with spectacle, intrigue, and incident; inexorably their 'greater vitality' caused their tone, their devices, and their level of conduct to flow into the relative vacuum of mainpiece comedy, with unfortunate results.

Against this tendency to degrade, however, must be balanced the seminal function of the traditional comedies and farces. In the same sense that early

---

[11] *English Drama 1642–1780* (1914), p. 249.

Elizabethan drama prepared for Shakespeare, early Georgian minor comedy culminated in Goldsmith and Sheridan. *The Rivals* has debts to five afterpieces; eight of Foote's plays were pilfered for mainpiece material; the Colman-Garrick *Clandestine Marriage* is based in part on Townley's farce *False Concord*, etc. Though obscure to us, these afterpieces were well known in their own time, and affected regular comedy significantly.

Now that the volumes of *The London Stage* have shown the statistical insignificance of sentimental comedy in the repertory, 'we may be inclined to wonder,' as Allardyce Nicoll once wrote, 'whether, after all, it was not sentimentalism which was the fashion insecurely planted on the theatre. . . .'[12] Admittedly sentiment looms larger in drama *written* in the eighteenth century, but *only* in the mainpiece: the afterpiece remained a bastion of the older, 'laughing' tradition,[13] and herein lies its chief historical importance. Critics of the time upheld the separation of the serious and the funny into before and after, repeating the insistence of neoclassical criticism (mentioned above) that such fundamentally different modes as 'mirth and compassion' be compartmentalized. But since 'grave Morality' was already established in the mainpiece, the refuge of laughter and licence was a foregone conclusion. 'In many of our farces are to be found some of the strongest comic situations, and the most genuine wit and humour that grace our stage,' declared one critic in 1785.

The extent to which audiences demanded this division is startling. Oliver Goldsmith had considerable difficulties finding a theatre manager who would take *She Stoops to Conquer* in 1773 because of the prevailing taste for sentiment. Garrick turned him down flat; Colman accepted only after some hesitation. In his dedicatory letter to Johnson published with the play Goldsmith wrote: 'The undertaking a comedy not merely sentimental was very dangerous; and Mr. Colman, who saw this piece in its various stages, always thought it so.' Obviously he means that a non-sentimental *five-act* comedy was thought 'dangerous', for many unsentimental *afterpiece* comedies were popular with this same audience, and neither Goldsmith nor Colman displayed any qualms about being associated with them. The originality and achievement of Sheridan and Goldsmith lay not in *reviving* traditional comedy, but in restoring it to the mainpiece.

Modern critics have generally recognized the existence of this dichotomy, but what has been overlooked is the importance it gives to the general obscurity of these afterpieces, owing to the low proportion which were published. In Garrick's time only one mainpiece in eight, but one of every

---

[12] *A History of English Drama 1660–1900*, III (3rd ed., rev., 1952), 171.

[13] Of over a hundred afterpieces between 1738 and 1777, only six could be termed sentimental, while over three-fourths were comic in the traditional sense. About half of the new mainpiece comedies in the same period were sentimental.

three afterpieces, failed to achieve publication.[14] This fact has sweepingly affected posterity's 'image' of eighteenth-century comedy, by preserving disproportionate numbers of the more widely sentimentalized mainpiece, while the afterpiece, the main carrier of traditional laughing comedy, ran a higher risk of perishing at the end of its stage career. What we have inherited is, in fact, the published or readers' theatre: parallel to, but different from, the transitory acted theatre. The 'disappearance of the comic tradition' in Georgian drama was *only* apparent.

V

The plays in this volume were chosen to represent the major types of 'legitimate' (traditional) afterpiece comedy in its most flourishing period, 1735–75. These types are discussed above, and the headnote to each play will clarify the reasons for including it. Some arguments against wider boundaries have already been suggested; an idea of afterpiece drama outside these generic and chronological limits can be gained from Leo Hughes's *Ten English Farces*, from chapters 24 and 25 of Dickens's *Nicholas Nickleby*, and from some of the shorter comedies in the volume *Nineteenth Century Plays*, edited by George Rowell.

This is a critical edition; thus the typographic eccentricities of the originals have been retained only in some of the peripheral material, such as prologues. An editorial policy of silent 'modernization' has been adopted elsewhere in the text, in the belief that more is thus gained in ease of reading and in due emphasis on the essential modernity of these plays than is lost in 'period flavour'. Spelling, capitalization, and italics, then, are silently modernized. Punctuation has been treated with more caution, and left unaltered where this does not produce a confusing conflict with modern usage. (Since eighteenth-century playwrights often used the comma and the dash to indicate speech rhythms rather than syntactical relationships, their retention may be helpful in reading or acting.)

I am indebted to the University of California, Berkeley, and to the American University of Beirut for material assistance on this project; to the staffs of the Henry E. Huntington Library and Art Gallery, San Marino, California, and the Jafet Library, American University, Beirut, for their co-operation; and to Richard Brain and Judith Osborne of the Oxford University Press, London, for astute guidance.

Beirut, 1969   RICHARD W. BEVIS

---

[14] My own computation, based on 50 comic mainpieces and 100 afterpieces, 1738–77.

Suggestions for Further Reading

Frederick S. Boas, *An Introduction to Eighteenth Century Drama, 1700–1780* (Oxford, 1953).

V. C. Clinton-Baddeley, *All Right on the Night* (London, 1954). Georgian theatre.

Comedy, edited by Wylie Sypher (New York, 1956). Essays by Bergson, Meredith, and Sypher.

Leslie Hotson, *The Commonwealth and Restoration Stage* (Cambridge, Mass., 1928).

Leo Hughes, *A Century of English Farce* (Princeton, N.J., 1956).

The London Stage 1660–1800, edited by G. W. Stone and others (Carbondale, Ill., 1960–). Five parts. A reference work.

James J. Lynch, *Box, Pit and Gallery* (Berkeley and Los Angeles, Cal., 1953). Georgian theatre.

George H. Nettleton, *English Drama 1642–1780* (New York, 1914).

Allardyce B. Nicoll, *A History of English Drama 1660–1900* (3rd ed., rev., Cambridge, 1952), 6 vols.

Harry W. Pedicord, *The Theatrical Public in the Time of Garrick* (New York, 1954).

Ashley H. Thorndike, *English Comedy* (New York, 1929).

THE
HISTORICAL REGISTER

for the Year 1736

Henry Fielding

1707–1754

The novelist Henry Fielding needs no introduction, but Fielding the play-wright is more obscure—undeservedly so, since he was scarcely less important in his sphere. For several years before he turned to prose fiction Fielding was the leading satirist of the London stage during a period of lively expansion. John Gay's *The Beggar's Opera* (1728) and Fielding's *Tom Thumb*, *The Author's Farce*, and *The Coffee-House Politician* (all 1730) and *The Grub Street Opera* (1731) gave great impetus and popularity to dramatic satire, and the genre burgeoned season by season. Politics were a favourite target, especially the venal administration of Sir Robert Walpole, the Whig Prime Minister and reputed author of the saying, 'Every man has his price.' Fielding and many of his distinguished contemporaries felt that the age 'cried out for satire'. Each year his attacks grew bolder: *Don Quixote in England* (1734), *Pasquin* (1736), *Eurydice*, *Eurydice Hissed*[1], and *The Historical Register* (all 1737). The theatre was in ferment—in the spring of 1737 there were fourteen new plays at Fielding's New Haymarket Theatre alone—but the Government was alarmed and watchful. In attempts to strengthen dramatic censorship, which had existed in England in some form since 1554, 'playhouse bills' were read in Parliament in 1733 and 1735, but failed. *Pasquin*[2] revived the issue, however, and the next year Walpole finally got the bill he wanted. Some say that *The Historical Register*, which opened at the 'Hay' on 21 March and was so popular that it was made a mainpiece before its run of 37 performances was half over, brought on the Licensing Act; others blame *The Golden Rump*, a scurrilous satire carried to Walpole by one of Fielding's rival managers in May of that year, and read aloud by Sir Robert in Parliament 'to great indig-

[1] Performed first in April 1737, and often throughout the rest of that spring in a double bill with *The Historical Register*. The title refers to the unsuccessful *Eurydice*, which had one performance in February.

[2] Fielding's *Pasquin; a Dramatick Satire of the Times* (1736) satirized Walpole and corruption in a rehearsal format.

nation'. (In 1740 Fielding accused the Prime Minister of 'rigging' the entire episode, while Horace Walpole later charged that the play was by Fielding.)

What is indisputable is the aftermath. On 24 May the Licensing Act (an amendment to a 1714 vagrancy statute) was read before Parliament. It was approved by both Houses and the King within a month; the only spirited opposition came from Lord Chesterfield. Its main provisions limited the legal theatres to those possessing patents (i.e., Covent Garden and Drury Lane); empowered the Lord Chamberlain to prohibit performances; and required that all new plays, additions to old ones, prologues, and epilogues be submitted to his office for inspection and licensing.[1]

The effects on Fielding's career and on theatre history were equally swift and violent. He disappeared from the stage completely for five years, and never again produced an unconventional or wholly new play. In 1741 he turned to prose fiction. The London stage, restricted quantitatively and qualitatively, lost momentum and potential talent; the number of new plays and of performances per season declined sharply. It did not begin to recover until 1760, and the restricting legislation, confirmed by the Theatres Act of 1843, remained in force until 1968.

The text is based on the first edition, 1737. *The Historical Register* has been admirably edited for the Regents Restoration Drama Series by William W. Appleton (London and Lincoln, Nebr., 1967).

---

[1] The only *positive* contribution of the office of Examiner of Plays to dramatic history has been the collection of acting MSS. thus obtained, e.g. the Larpent collection, 1737–1824, an important source for this volume.

THE
HISTORICAL REGISTER

For the Year 1736.

As it is Acted at the

NEW THEATRE

In the HAY-MARKET.

To which is added a very merry TRAGEDY, called,

EURYDICE HISS'D,

OR

A Word *to the* Wise.

Both written by the Author of *Pasquin.*

To these are prefixed a long *Dedication to the Publick,* and a *Preface* to that *Dedication.*

LONDON,

Printed: And sold by *J. Roberts*, near the *Oxford-Arms-Inn* in *Warwick-Lane.*

PREFACE
to the
DEDICATION

As no man hath a more stern and inflexible hatred to flattery than myself, it hath been usual with me to send most of my performances into the world without the ornament of those epistolary prefaces, commonly called *dedications*; a custom, however, highly censured by my bookseller, who affirms it a most unchristian practice. A patron is, says he, a kind of godfather to a book; and a good author ought as carefully to provide a patron to his works, as a good parent should a godfather to his children: he carries this very far, and draws several resemblances between those two offices (for having, in the course of his trade with dramatic writers, purchased, at a moderate computation, the fee-simple of one hundred thousand similes, he is perhaps the most expert in their application, and most capable of shewing likenesses, in things utterly unlike, of any man living). What, says he, does more service to a book, or raises curiosity in a reader, equal with—dedicated to his Grace the Duke of——or the Right Honourable the Earl of——in an advertisement? I think the patron here may properly be said *to give a name* to the book—and if he gives a present also, what doth he less than a godfather? Which present if the author applies to his own use, what doth he other than the parent? He proceeds to shew how a bookseller is a kind of dry nurse to our works, with other instance which I shall omit, having already said enough to prove the exact analogy between children and books, and of the method of providing for each; which I think affords a sufficient precedent for throwing the following piece on the public, it having been usual for several very prudent parents to act by their children in the same manner.

DEDICATION
to the
PUBLIC.

I hope you will pardon the presumption of this dedication, since I really did not know in what manner to apply for your leave; and since I expect no present in return (the reason, I conceive, which first introduced the ceremony of asking leave among dedicators), for surely it is somewhat absurd to ask a man leave to flatter him; and he must be a very impudent or simple fellow, or both, who will give it. Asking leave to dedicate, therefore, is asking whether you will pay for your dedication, and in that sense I believe it is understood by both authors and patrons.   8

But farther, the very candid reception which you have given these pieces, pleads my excuse. The least civility to an author or his works, hath been held, time immemorial, a just title to a dedication, which is perhaps no more than an honest return of flattery, and in this light, I am certain no one ever had so great (I may call it) an obligation as myself, seeing that you have honoured this my performance with your presence every night of its exhibition, where you have never failed shewing the greatest delight and approbation; nor am I less obliged to you for those eulogiums which you have been heard in all places to—but hold, I am afraid this is an ingenious way which authors have discovered to convey inward flattery to themselves, while outwardly they address it to their patron: wherefore I shall be silent on this head, having more reasons to give why I chose you to patronize these pieces. And,   20

first, the design with which they are writ; for, tho' all dramatic entertainments are properly calculated for the public, yet these, I may affirm, more particularly belong to you; as your diversion is not merely intended by them, their design being to convey some hints, which may, if you please, be of infinite service in the present state of that theatrical world whereof they treat, and which is, I think, at present, so far from flourishing as one could wish, that I have with much concern observed some steps lately taken, and others too justly apprehended, that may much endanger the constitution of the British theatre: for, tho' Mr. —— be a very worthy man, and my very good friend, I cannot help thinking his manner of proceeding somewhat too

29 the British theatre] In 1735, Sir John Barnard had read to Parliament a bill to restrict the liberty of the stage by licensing plays. It was rejected when Walpole tried to enlarge its scope, but *Pasquin* (see p. 1) had revived the issue, and an even stricter bill was now being discussed.

arbitrary, and his method of buying actors at exorbitant prices to be of very ill consequence: for the town must reimburse him these expenses, on which account those advanced prices so much complained of must be always continued; which, tho' the people, in their present flourishing state of trade and riches may very well pay, yet in worse times (if such can be supposed) I am afraid they may fall too heavy, the consequence of which I need not mention. Moreover, should any great genius produce a piece of most exquisite contrivance, and which would be highly relished by the public, tho' perhaps not agreeable to his own taste or private interest, if he should buy off the chief actors, such play, however excellent, must be unavoidably sunk, and the public lose all the benefit thereof. Not to trouble the reader with more inconveniences arising from this *Argumentum Argentarium*, many of which are obvious enough—I shall only observe, that corruption hath the same influence on all societies, all bodies, which it hath on corporeal bodies, where we see it always produce an entire destruction and total change: for which reason, whoever attempteth to introduce corruption into any community, doth much the same thing, and ought to be treated in much the same manner, with him who poisoneth a fountain, in order to disperse a contagion, which he is sure every one will drink of.   49

The last excuse I shall make for this presumption, is the necessity I have of so potent a patron to defend me from the iniquitous surmises of a certain anonymous dialogous author, who, in the *Gazetteer* of the 17th instant, has represented *The Historical Register*, as aiming, in conjunction with *The Miller of Mansfield*, the overthrow of the M———y. If this suggestion had been inserted in *The Craftsman* or *Common-Sense*, or any of those papers which nobody reads, it might have passed unanswered; but as it appears in a paper of so general a reception as *The Gazetteer*, which lies in the window of almost every post-house in England, it behoves me, I think, in the most serious manner, to vindicate myself from aspersions of so evil a tendency to my future prospects. And here I must observe, that had not mankind been either very blind or very dishonest, I need not have publicly informed them, that *The Register* is a Ministerial pamphlet, calculated to infuse into the minds of the people a great opinion of their Ministry, and thereby procure an employment for the author, who has been often promised one, whenever he would write on that side.   65

---

33 advanced prices] Both Charles Fleetwood, manager of Drury Lane, and John Rich, manager of Lincoln's Inn Fields and (after 1732) Covent Garden, made a practice of increasing prices when a pantomime was playing.   42 *Argumentum Argentarium*] Economic discussion.   52 the 17th instant] Actually the 7th May 1737. Appleton speculates that the author was Hervey. The *Daily Gazetteer* was a pro-Walpole paper; *The Craftsman* and *Common Sense* (l. 55) took the other side.   54 *The Miller of Mansfield*] *The King and the Miller of Mansfield* (1737), the best-known play of Robert Dodsley (1703–64), bookseller, was considered to have democratic and levelling tendencies.

And, *first*, can anything be plainer than the first stanza of the Ode?

> This is a *day, in days of yore,
> Our fathers never saw before;
> This is a day, 'tis one to ten,
> Our sons will never see again.

Plainly intimating that such times as these never were seen before, nor will ever be seen again; for which the present age are certainly obliged to their Ministry.
                                                                                          73
What can be meant by the scene of politicians, but to ridicule the absurd and inadequate notions, persons among us, who have not the honour to know 'em, have of the Ministry and their measures? Nay, I have put some sentiments into the mouths of these characters, which I was a little apprehensive were too low even for a conversation at an ale-house.—I hope *The Gazetteer* will not find any resemblance here, as I hope he will not make such a compliment to any M———y, as to suppose, that such persons have ever been capable of the assurance of aiming at being at the head of a great people, or to any nation, as to suspect 'em [of] contentedly living under such an administration.
                                                                                          83
The eagerness which these gentlemen express at applying all manner of evil characters to their patrons, brings to my mind a story I have somewhere read. As two gentlemen were walking the street together, the one said to the other, upon spying the figure of an ass hung out—Bob, Bob, look yonder, some impudent rascal has hung out your picture on a signpost: the grave companion, who had the misfortune to be extremely short-sighted, fell into a violent rage, and calling for the master of the house, threatened to prosecute him for exposing his features in that public manner: the poor landlord, as you may well conceive, was extremely astonished, and denied the fact; upon which the witty spark, who had just mentioned the resemblance, appeals to the mob now assembled together, who soon smoked the jest, and agreed with him, that the sign was the exact picture of the gentleman: at last, a good-natured man, taking compassion of the poor figure, whom he saw the jest of the multitude, whispered in his ear, Sir, I see your eyes are bad, and that your friend is a rascal, and imposes on you; the sign hung out is the sign of an ass, nor will your picture be here unless you draw it yourself.
                                                                                          99
But I ask pardon for troubling the reader with an impertinent story, which can be applied only, in the above-mentioned instance, to my present subject.

I proceed in my defence, to the scene of the patriots; a scene which I thought would have made my fortune, seeing that the favourite scheme of

---

* For *day*, in the first and third line, you may read *man*, if you please.

66 the Ode] Cf. Act I, sc. i, ll. 106-26.

turning patriotism into a jest, is so industriously pursued; and I will challenge all the Ministerial advocates to shew me, in the whole bundle of their writings, one passage where false patriotism (for I suppose they have not the impudence to mean any other) is set in a more contemptible and odious light than in the aforesaid scene. I hope, too, it will be remarked, that the politicians are represented as a set of blundering blockheads rather deserving pity than abhorrence, whereas the others are represented as a set of cunning self-interested fellows, who, for a little paltry bribe, would give up the liberties and properties of their country. Here is the danger, here is the rock on which our Constitution must, if it ever does, split. The liberties of a people have been subdued by the conquest of valour and force, and have been betrayed by the subtle and dexterous arts of refined policy; but these are rare instances; for geniuses of this kind are not the growth of every age, whereas, if a general corruption be once introduced, and those who should be the guardians and bulwarks of our liberty, once find, or think they find an interest in giving it up, no great capacity will be required to destroy it; on the contrary, the meanest, lowest, dirtiest fellow, if such a one should have ever the assurance, in future ages, to mimic power, and browbeat his betters, will be as able as Machiavel himself could have been, to root out the liberties of the bravest people. 123

But I am aware I shall be asked, who is this *Quidam*, that turns the patriots into ridicule, and bribes them out of their honesty? Who but the Devil could act such a part? Is not this the light wherein he is everywhere described in Scripture, and the writings of our best divines? Gold hath been always his favorite bait, wherewith he fisheth for sinners; and his laughing at the poor wretches he seduceth, is as diabolical an attribute as any. Indeed it is so plain, who is meant by this *Quidam*, that he who maketh any wrong application thereof, might as well mistake the name of Thomas for John, or old Nick for old Bob. 132

I think I have said enough to convince every impartial person of my innocence, against all malicious insinuations; and farther to convince them that I am a Ministerial writer (an honour I am highly ambitious of attaining), I shall proceed now to obviate an opinion entertained by too many, that a certain person is sometimes the author, often the corrector of the press, and always the patron of the *Gazetteer*. To shew the folly of this supposition I shall only insist, that all persons, tho' they should not afford him any extraordinary genius, nor any (the least) taste in polite literature, will grant me this *datum*, that the said certain person is a man of an ordinary capacity, and a moderate share of common sense: which, if allowed, I think it will follow

131 Thomas for John] Thomas Pelham-Holles, Duke of Newcastle, and John, Lord Hervey, were both supporters of Walpole ('old Bob'). 136 a certain person] i.e. *Quidam* (alias Walpole).

that it is impossible he should either write or countenance a paper written, not only without the least glimmering of genius, the least pretension to taste, but in direct opposition to all common sense whatever. If any one should ask me, how then it is carried on? I shall only answer with my politicians, I cannot tell, unless by the assistance of the old gentleman just before-mentioned, who would, I think, alone protect or patronize it, as I think, indeed, he is the only person who could invent some of the schemes avowed in that paper, which, if it does not immediately disappear, I do intend shortly to attempt conjuring it down, intending to publish a paper in defence of the M———y, against the wicked, malicious, and sly insinuations conveyed in the said paper.   153

You will excuse a digression so necessary to take off surmises, which may prove so prejudicial to my fortune; which, however, if I should not be able to accomplish, I hope you will make me some amends for what I suffer by endeavouring your entertainment. The very great indulgence you have shewn my performances at the little theatre, these two last years, have encouraged me to the proposal of a subscription for carrying on that theatre, for beautifying and enlarging it, and procuring a better company of actors. If you think proper to subscribe to these proposals, I assure you no labour shall be spared, on my side, to entertain you in a cheaper and better manner than seems to be the intention of any other. If Nature hath given me any talents at ridiculing vice and imposture, I shall not be indolent, nor afraid of exerting them while the liberty of the press and stage subsists, that is to say, while we have any liberty left among us. I am, to the public,   166

A most sincere friend,
and most devoted servant,

158 the little theatre] Fielding was lessee of the Little (or New) Theatre in the Haymarket for 1736-7.

Dramatis Personæ

MEN

Medley	Mr. Roberts
Sowrwit	Mr. Lacy
Lord Dapper	Mr. Ward
Ground-Ivy	Mr. Jones
Hen, the auctioneer	Mris. Charke
Apollo's bastard son	Mr. Blakes
Pistol	Mr. Davis
Quidam	Mr. Smith

Politicians {
Mr. Jones
Mr. Tepping
Mr. Woodburn
Mr. Smith
Mr. Machen

Patriots {
Mr. Topping
Mr. Machen
Mr. Pullen
Mr. Woodburn

Banter	Mr. Smith
Dangle	Mr. Lowther

WOMEN

Mris. Screen	Mris. Haywood
Mris. Barter	Miss Kawer

Ladies {
Mris. Charke
Mris. Haywood
Mris. Lacy
Miss Jones

Prompter, actors, etc.

[Players, Courtiers, Officers, Beaux, Gentleman]

THE
Historical Register
for the year 1736

ACT I. SCENE I.

Enter several Players.

1 Player. Mr. Emphasis, good-morrow, you are early at the rehearsal this morning.

Emph. Why, faith, Jack, our beer and beer sat but ill on my stomach, so I got up to try if I could not walk it off.

1 Play. I wish I had anything in my stomach to walk off; if matters do not go better with us shortly, my teeth will forget their office.

2 Play. These are poor times, indeed, not like the days of *Pasquin.*

1 Play. Oh! Name 'em not! Those were glorious days indeed, the days of beef and punch; my friends, when come there such again?

2 Play. Who knows what this new author may produce? Faith, I like my part very well.   11

1 Play. Nay, if variety will please the town, I am sure there is enough of it; but I could wish, methinks, the satire had been a little stronger, a little plainer.

2 Play. Now I think it is plain enough.

1 Play. Hum! Ay, it is intelligible; but I would have it downright; 'gad, I fancy I could write a thing to succeed, myself.

2 Play. Ay, prithee, what subject wouldst thou write on?

1 Play. Why, no subject at all, but I would have a humming deal of satire, and I would repeat in every page, that courtiers are cheats and don't pay their debts, that lawyers are rogues, physicians blockheads, soldiers cowards, and ministers—   22

2 Play. What, what, Sir?

1 Play. Nay, I'll only name 'em, that's enough to set the audience a-hooting.

2 Play. Zounds, Sir, here is wit enough for a whole play in one speech.

7 *Pasquin*] *Pasquin ; a Dramatick Satire of the Times,* a popular prototype of *The Historical Register.* See p. 1, n. 2.

1 Play. For one play, why, Sir, 'tis all I have extracted out of above a dozen.

2 Play. Who have we here?

1 Play. Some gentlemen, I suppose, come to hear the rehearsal.   30

Enter Sowrwit *and* Lord Dapper.

L. Dap. Pray, gentlemen, don't you rehearse the *Historical Register* this morning?

1 Play. Sir, we expect the author every minute.

Sowr. What is this *Historical Register*, is it a tragedy, or a comedy?

1 Play. Upon my word, Sir, I can't tell.

Sowr. Then I suppose you have no part in it.

1 Play. Yes, Sir, I have several, but—oh, here is the author himself, I suppose he can tell, Sir.

Sowr. Faith, Sir, that's more than I suppose.

Enter Medley.

Med. My Lord, your most obedient servant; this is a very great and unexpected favour indeed, my Lord. Mr. Sowrwit, I kiss your hands; I am very glad to see you here.   42

Sowr. That's more than you may be by-and-by, perhaps.

L. Dap. We are come to attend your rehearsal, Sir; pray when will it begin?

Med. This very instant, my Lord: gentlemen, I beg you would be all ready, and let the prompter bring me some copies for these gentlemen.

Sowr. Mr. Medley, you know I am a plain speaker, so you will excuse any liberties I take.

Med. Dear Sir, you can't oblige me more.

Sowr. Then I must tell you, Sir, I am a little staggered at the name of your piece; doubtless, Sir, you know the rules of writing, and I can't guess how you can bring the actions of a whole year into the circumference of four and twenty hours.   53

Med. Sir, I have several answers to make to your objection; in the first place, my piece is not of a nature confined to any rules, as being avowedly irregular, but if it was otherwise I think I could quote you precedents of plays that neglect them; besides, Sir, if I comprise the whole actions of the year in half an hour, will you blame me, or those who have done so little in that time? My *Register* is not to be filled like those of vulgar news-writers, with trash for want of news; and therefore, if I say little or nothing, you may thank those who have done little or nothing.   61

Enter Prompter *with books.*

Oh! Here are my books.

Sowr. In print already, Mr. Medley?

Med. Yes, Sir, it is the safest way; for if a man stays till he is damned, it is possible he may never get into print at all: the town is capricious, for which reason always print as fast as you write, that if they damn your play, they may not damn your copy too.

Sowr. Well, Sir, and pray what is your design, your plot?

Med. Why, Sir, I have several plots, some pretty deep, and some but shallow.   70

Sowr. I hope, Sir, they all conduce to the main design.

Med. Yes, Sir, they do.

Sowr. Pray, Sir, what is that?

Med. To divert the town, and bring full houses.

Sowr. Pshaw! You misunderstand me, I mean what is your moral, your, your, your—

Med. Oh! Sir, I comprehend you—Why, Sir, my design is to ridicule the vicious and foolish customs of the age, and that in a fair manner, without fear, favour, or ill-nature, and without scurrility, ill manners, or commonplace; I hope to expose the reigning follies, in such a manner, that men shall laugh themselves out of them before they feel that they are touched.   81

Sowr. But what thread or connection can you have in this history? For instance, how is your political connected with your theatrical?

Med. O very easily—when my politics come to a farce, they very naturally lead to the playhouse, where, let me tell you, there are some politicians too, where there is lying, flattering, dissembling, promising, deceiving and undermining, as well as in any court in Christendom.

Enter a Player.

Play. Won't you begin your rehearsal, Sir?

Med. Ay, ay, with all my heart, is the music ready for the prologue?

Sowr. Music for the prologue!   90

Med. Ay, Sir, I intend to have everything new, I had rather be the author of my own dullness, than the publisher of other men's wit; and really, Mr. Sowrwit, the subjects for prologues are utterly exhausted: I think the general method has been either to frighten the audience with the author's reputation, or to flatter them to give their applause, or to beseech them to it, and that, in a manner, that will serve for every play alike: now, Sir, my prologue will serve for no play but my own, and to that I think nothing can be better adapted, for as mine is the history of the year, what can be a properer prologue than an Ode to the New Year?

Sowr. An Ode to the New Year?   100

Med. Yes, Sir, an Ode to the New Year—come, begin, begin.

Enter Prompter.

B

Promp. Sir, the prologue is ready.

Sowr. Dear Medley, let me hear you read it, possibly it may be sung so fine I may not understand a word of it.

Med. Sir, you can't oblige me more.

ODE to the New Year.

This is a day, in days of yore,
Our fathers never saw before:
This is a day, 'tis one to ten,
Our sons will never see again.   110
   Then sing the day,
   And sing the song,
   And thus be merry
   All day long.
This is the day,
And that's the night,
When the sun shall be gay,
And the moon shall be bright.
   The sun shall rise,
   All in the skies;   120
   The moon shall go,
   All down below.
   Then sing the day,
   And sing the song;
   And thus be merry
   All day long.

Ay, ay, come on, and sing it away.

Enter singers, who sing the Ode.

Med. There, Sir, there's the very quintessence and cream of all the odes I have seen for several years last past.

Sowr. Ay, Sir, I thought you would not be the publisher of another man's wit?   131

Med. No more I an't, Sir, for the devil of any wit did I ever see in any of them.

Sowr. Oh! Your most humble servant, Sir.

Med. Yours, Sir, yours; now for my play. Prompter, are the politicians all ready at the table?

Promp. I'll go and see, Sir.   [*Exit.*

106–26 ODE to the New Year] Colley Cibber annually wrote such an ode.

Med. My first scene, Mr. Sowrwit, lies in the island of Corsica, being at present the first scene of politics of all Europe.

Enter Prompter.

Promp. Sir, they are ready.   140
Med. Then draw the scene, and discover them.

Scene draws, and discovers five Politicians *sitting at a table.*

Sowr. Here's a mistake in the print, Mr. Medley, I observe, the second politician is the first person who speaks.
Med. Sir, my first and greatest politician never speaks at all, he's a very deep man, by which you will observe I convey this moral, that the chief art of a politician is to keep a secret.
Sowr. To keep his politics a secret, I suppose you mean.
Med. Come, Sir, begin.
2 Polit. Is King Theodore returned yet?
3 Polit. No.   150
2 Polit. When will he return?
3 Polit. I cannot tell.
Sowr. This politician seems to me to know very little of the matter.
Med. Zounds, Sir, would you have him a prophet as well as a politician? You see, Sir, he knows what's past, and that's all he ought to know; 'sblood, Sir, would it be in the character of a politician to make him a conjurer? Go on, gentlemen: pray, Sir, don't interrupt their debates, for they are of great consequence.
2 Polit. These mighty preparations of the Turks are certainly designed against some place or other; now, the question is, what place are they designed against? And that is a question which I cannot answer.   161
3 Polit. But it behoves us to be upon our guard.
4 Polit. It does, and the reason is, because we know nothing of the matter.
2 Polit. You say right, it is easy for a man to guard against dangers which he knows of, but to guard against dangers which nobody knows of, requires a very great politician.
Med. Now, Sir, I suppose you think that nobody knows anything.
Sowr. Faith, Sir, it appears so.
Med. Ay, Sir, but there is one who knows; that little gentleman, yonder in the chair, who says nothing, knows it all.   171
Sowr. But how do you intend to convey this knowledge to the audience?

138–9 Corsica . . . all Europe] Corsica was at this time struggling for independence. Its revolt against Genoa in 1729 had finally been quelled by Austrian troops, and in 1736 it had accepted a Westphalian king.

Med. Sir, they can read it in his looks; 'sblood, Sir, must not a politician be thought a wise man without his giving instances of his wisdom?

5 Polit. Hang foreign affairs, let us apply ourselves to money.

Omnes. Ay, ay, ay.

Med. Gentlemen, that over again—and be sure to snatch hastily at the money; you're pretty politicians truly.

5 Polit. Hang foreign affairs, let us apply ourselves to money.

Omnes. Ay, ay, ay.   180

2 Polit. All we have to consider relating to money, is how we shall get it.

3 Polit. I think we ought first to consider whether there is any to be got, which if there be, I do readily agree that the next question is, how to come at it?

Omnes. Hum.

Sowr. Pray, Sir, what are these gentlemen in Corsica?

Med. Why, Sir, they are the ablest heads in the Kingdom, and consequently the greatest men, for you may be sure all well-regulated governments, as I represent this of Corsica to be, will employ in their greatest posts, men of the greatest capacity.   190

2 Polit. I have considered the matter, and I find it must be by a tax.

3 Polit. I thought of that, and was considering what was not taxed already.

2 Polit. Learning; suppose we put a tax upon learning.

3 Polit. Learning, it is true, is a useless commodity, but I think we had better lay it on ignorance, for learning being the property but of a very few, and those poor ones too, I am afraid we can get little among them; whereas ignorance will take in most of the great fortunes in the Kingdom.

Omnes. Ay, ay, ay.   [*Exeunt politicians.*

Sowr. Faith, 'tis very generous in these gentlemen to tax themselves so readily.   200

Med. Ay, and very wise too, to prevent the people's grumbling, and they will have it all among themselves.

Sowr. But what is become of the politicians?

Med. They are gone, Sir, they're gone; they have finished the business they met about, which was to agree on a tax, that being done—they are gone to raise it; and this Sir, is the full account of the whole history of Europe, as far as we know of it, comprised in one scene.

Sowr. The devil it is! Why, you have not mentioned one word of France, or Spain, or the Emperor.

Med. No, Sir, I turn those over to the next year, by which time we may possibly know something what they are about; at present our advices are so very uncertain, I know not what to depend on; but come, Sir, now you shall have a council of ladies.   213

Sowr. Does this scene lie in Corsica too?

Med. No, no, this lies in London—you know, Sir, it would not have been quite so proper to have brought English politicians (of the male kind I mean) on the stage, because our politics are not quite so famous; but in female politicians, to the honour of my countrywomen I say it, I believe no country can excel us; come, draw the scene, and discover the ladies.

Promp. Sir, they are not here; one of them is practising above stairs with a dancing-master, and I can't get her down.   221

Med. I'll fetch 'em, I warrant you.   [*Exit*.

Sowr. Well, my Lord, what does your Lordship think of what you have seen?

L. Dap. Faith, Sir, I did not observe it; but 'tis damned stuff, I am sure.

Sowr. I think so, and I hope your Lordship will not encourage it. They are such men as your Lordship, who must reform the age; if persons of your exquisite and refined taste will give a sanction to politer entertainments, the town will soon be ashamed of laughing at what they do now.

L. Dap. Really, this is a very bad house.   230

Sowr. It is not indeed so large as the others, but I think one hears better in it.

L. Dap. Pox of hearing, one can't see—one's self I mean; here are no looking-glasses, I love Lincoln's Inn-Fields, for that reason, better than any house in town.

Sowr. Very true, my Lord, but I wish your Lordship would think it worth your consideration, as the morals of a people depend, as has been so often and well proved, entirely on their public diversions, it would be of great consequence, that those of the sublimest kind should meet with your Lordship's and the rest of the nobility's countenance.   240

L. Dap. Mr. Sowrwit, I am always ready to give my countenance to anything of that kind, which might bring the best company together; for as one does not go to see the play, but the company, I think that's chiefly to be considered, and therefore I am always ready to countenance good plays.

Sowr. No one is a better judge what is so than your Lordship.

L. Dap. Not I, indeed, Mr. Sowrwit—but as I am one half of the play in the Green-Room, talking to the actresses, and the other half in the boxes, talking to the women of quality, I have an opportunity of seeing something of the play, and perhaps may be as good a judge as another.

Enter Medley.

Med. My Lord, the ladies cannot begin yet; if your Lordship will honour me in the Green-Room, where you will find it pleasanter than upon this cold stage.   252

234 Lincoln's Inn-Fields] Rich's theatre, lavishly decorated with mirrors on the stage, was noted for productions of pantomime and spectacle, and subsequently opera.

L. Dap. With all my heart—come, Mr. Sowrwit.

Sowr. I attend your Lordship.   [*Exeunt.*

Promp. Thou art a sweet judge of plays, indeed, and yet it is in the power of such sparks as these, to damn an honest fellow, both in his profit and reputation.   [*Exit.*

ACT II.   SCENE I.

Enter Medley, Lord Dapper, Sowrwit, *and* Prompter.

Med. Come, draw the scene, and discover the ladies in council; pray, my Lord, sit.

[*The scene draws, and discovers four* Ladies.]

Sowr. What are these ladies assembled about?

Med. Affairs of great importance, as you will see—please to begin all of you.   [*The* Ladies *all speak together.*

All Ladies. Was you at the opera, Madam, last night?

2 Lady. Who can miss an opera while Farinello stays?

3 Lady. Sure he is the charmingest creature.

4 Lady. He's everything in the world one could wish.

1 Lady. Almost everything one could wish.   10

2 Lady. They say there's a lady in the city has a child by him.

All Ladies. Ha, ha, ha!

1 Lady. Well, it must be charming to have a child by him.

3 Lady. Madam, I met a lady in a visit the other day, with three.

All Ladies. All Farinello's.

3 Lady. All Farinello's, all in wax.

1 Lady. Oh Gemini! Who makes them? I'll send and bespeak half a dozen tomorrow morning.

2 Lady. I'll have as many as I can cram into a coach with me.

Sowr. Mr. Medley, Sir, is this history? This must be invention.   20

Med. Upon my word, Sir, 'tis fact, and I take it to be the most extra-ordinary accident that has happened in the whole year, and as well worth recording. Faith, Sir, let me tell you, I take it to be ominous; for if we go on to improve in luxury, effeminacy and debauchery, as we have done lately, the next age, for aught I know, may be more like the children of squeaking Italians than hardy Britons.

7 Farinello] Carlo Broschi (1705–82), usually known as Farinelli, the most celebrated castrato singer of his day.

All Ladies. Don't interrupt us, dear Sir.

1 Lady. What mighty pretty company they must be?

2 Lady. Oh, the prettiest company in the world!

3 Lady. If one could but teach them to sing like their father.   30

4 Lady. I'm afraid my husband won't let me keep them, for he hates I should be fond of anything but himself.

All Ladies. O the unreasonable creature!

1 Lady. If my husband was to make any objection to my having 'em, I'd run away from him, and take the dear babies with me.

Med. Come, enter Beau Dangle.

Enter Dangle.

Dang. Fie upon it, ladies, what are you doing here? Why are not you at the auction? Mr. Hen has been in the pulpit this half hour.

1 Lady. Oh, dear Mr. Hen, I ask his pardon, I never miss him.

2 Lady. What's to be sold today?   40

1 Lady. Oh, I never mind that; there will be all the world there.

Dang. You'll find it almost impossible to get in.

All Ladies. Oh! I shall be quite miserable if I don't get in.

Dang. Then you must not lose a moment.

All Ladies. O! Not a moment for the world. [*Exeunt* Ladies [*with* Dangle].

Med. There they are gone.

Sowr. I am glad on't with all my heart.

L. Dap. Upon my word, Mr. Medley, that last is an exceeding good scene, and full of a great deal of politeness, good sense, and philosophy.

Med. 'Tis nature, my Lord, 'tis nature.   50

Sowr. Faith, Sir, the ladies are much obliged to you.

Med. Faith, Sir, 'tis more than I desire such ladies, as I represent here, should be; as for the nobler part of the sex, for whom I have the greatest honour, their characters can be no better set off, than by ridiculing that light, trifling, giddy-headed crew, who are a scandal to their own sex, and a curse on ours.

Promp. Gentlemen, you must make room, for the curtain must be let down, to prepare the auction-room.

Med. My Lord, I believe you will be best before the curtain, for we have but little room behind, and a great deal to do.   60

Sowr. Upon my word, Mr. Medley, I must ask you the same question which one of your ladies did just now; what do you intend to sell at this auction, the whole stock in trade of some milliner or mercer who has left off business?

Med. Sir, I intend to sell such things as were never sold in any auction before, nor never will again; I can assure you, Mr. Sowrwit, this scene which I look on as the best in the whole performance, will require a very deep attention; Sir, if you should take one pinch of snuff during the whole scene, you will lose a joke by it, and yet they lie pretty deep too, and may escape observation from a moderate understanding, unless very closely attended to.   71

Sowr. I hope, however, they don't lie as deep as the dumb gentleman's politics did in the first act; if so, nothing but an inspired understanding can come at 'em.

Med. Sir, this scene is writ in allegory; and tho' I have endeavoured to make it as plain as possible, yet all allegory will require a strict attention to be understood, Sir.

Promp. Sir, everything is ready.

Med. Then draw up the curtain—come, enter Mris. Screen, and Mris. Barter.   80

The AUCTION.

Scene, an auction-room, a pulpit and forms placed, and several people [Courtiers, Officers, Beaux] *walking about, some seated near the pulpit. Enter* Mris. Screen *and* Mris. Barter.

Mris. Screen. Dear Mris. Barter.

Mris. Bart. Dear Madam, you are early today?

Mris. Screen. Oh, if one does not get near the pulpit, one does nothing, and I intend to buy a great deal today; I believe I shall buy the whole auction, at least if things go cheap; you won't bid against me?

Mris. Bart. You know I never bid for anything.

Enter Banter *and* Dangle.

Bant. That's true, Mris. Barter, I'll be your evidence.

Mris. Screen. Are you come? Now I suppose we shall have fine bidding; I don't expect to buy cheaper than at a shop.

Bant. That's unkind, Mris. Screen, you know I never bid against you; it would be cruel to bid against a lady who frequents auctions, only with a design one day or other to make one great auction of her own: no, no, I will not prevent the filling your warehouse; I assure you, I bid against no haberdashers of all wares.   94

Mris. Bart. You are a mighty civil person, truly.

Bant. You need not take up the cudgels, Madam, who are of no more consequence at an auction, than a mayor at a sessions; you only come here where you have nothing to do, to shew people you have nothing to do anywhere else.

Mris. Bart. I don't come to say rude things to all the world, as you do.

80 s.d. *forms*] Benches.

Bant. No, the world may thank heaven, that did not give you wit enough to do that.   101

Mris. Screen. Let him alone, he will have his jest.

Mris. Bart. You don't think I mind him, I hope; but pray, Sir, of what great use is your friend, Mr. Dangle, here?

Bant. Oh, he is of very great use to all women of understanding.

Dang. Ay! Of what use am I, pray?

Bant. To keep 'em at home, that they may not hear the silly things you say to 'em.

Mris. Screen. I hope, Mr. Banter, you will not banish all people from places where they are of no consequence; you will allow 'em to go to an assembly, or a masquerade, without either playing, dancing or intriguing; you will let people go to an opera without any ear, to a play without any taste, and to a church without any religion?   113

Enter Mr. Hen *Auctioneer* (*bowing*).

Mris. Screen. Oh! Dear Mr. Hen, I am glad you are come, you are horrible too late today.

Hen. Madam, I am just mounting the pulpit; I hope you like the catalogue, ladies?

Mris. Screen. There are some good things here, if you are not too dilatory with your hammer.

Bant. Boy, give me a catalogue.   120

Hen. [*In the pulpit.*] I dare swear, gentlemen and ladies, this auction will give general satisfaction; it is the first of its kind which I ever had the honour to exhibit, and I believe I may challenge the world to produce some of the curiosities which this choice cabinet contains: a catalogue of curiosities which were collected by the indefatigable pains of that celebrated virtuoso, Peter Humdrum, Esq; which will be sold by auction, by Christopher Hen, on Monday the 21st day of March, beginning at Lot 1. Gentlemen and ladies, this is Lot 1. A most curious remnant of political honesty. Who puts it up, gentlemen? It will make you a very good cloak, you see 'tis both sides alike, so you may turn it as often as you will—come, five pounds for this curious remnant; I assure you, several great men have made their birthday suits out of the same piece—it will wear for ever, and never be the worse for wearing—five pounds are bid—nobody more than five pounds for this curious piece of political honesty. Five pounds, no more—[*Knocks.*] Lord Both-Sides. Lot 2. A most delicate piece of patriotism, gentlemen, who bids? Ten pounds for this piece of patriotism?   136

1 Court. I would not wear it for a thousand pounds.

126–7 Christopher Hen . . . March] Christopher Cock was a well-known auctioneer. *The Historical Register* opened on 21st March.

Hen. Sir, I assure you, several gentlemen at court have worn the same; 'tis quite a different thing within to what it is without.

1 Court. Sir, it is prohibited goods, I sha'nt run the risk of being brought into Westminster Hall for wearing it.   141

Hen. You take it for the old patriotism, whereas it is indeed like that in nothing but the cut, but, alas! Sir, there is a great difference in the stuff: but, Sir, I don't propose this for a town suit, this is only proper for the country; consider, gentlemen, what a figure this will make at an election—come, five pounds—one guinea—put patriotism by.

Bant. Ay, put it by, one day or other it may be in fashion.

Hen. Lot 3. Three grains of modesty: come, ladies, consider how scarce this valuable commodity is.

Mris Screen. Yes, and out of fashion too, Mr. Hen.   150

Hen. I ask you pardon, Madam, it is true French I assure you, and never changes colour on any account—half a crown for all this modesty—is there not one lady in the room who wants any modesty?

1 Lady. Pray, Sir, what is it, for I can't see it at this distance?

Hen. It cannot be seen at any distance, Madam, but it is a beautiful powder, which makes a fine wash for the complexion.

Mris. Screen. I thought you said it was true French, and would not change the colour of the skin?

Hen. No, it will not, Madam; but it serves mighty well to blush behind a fan with, or to wear under a lady's mask at a masquerade—what, nobody bid —well, lay modesty aside—Lot 4. One bottle of courage, formerly in the possession of Lieutenant Ezekiel Pipkin, citizen, alderman and tallow-chandler—what, is there no officer of the trained-bands here? Or it will serve an officer of the army, as well in time of peace, nay, even in war, gentlemen; it will serve all of you who sell out.   165

1 Offi. Is the bottle whole? Is there no crack in it?

Hen. None, Sir, I assure you; tho' it has been in many engagements in Tothill-Fields; nay, it has served a campaign or two in Hyde Park, since the alderman's death—it will never waste while you stay at home, but it evaporates immediately, if carried abroad.   170

1 Offi. Damn me, I don't want it; but a man can't have too much courage—three shillings for it.

Hen. Three shillings are bid for this bottle of courage.

1 Beau. Four.

Bant. What do you bid for courage for?

1 Beau. Nor for myself, but I have [a] commission to buy it for a lady.

1 Offi. Five.

167 Tothill-Fields . . . Hyde Park] There were riots in Tothill Fields (off Tothill Street, Westminster) and in Hyde Park in July and August, 1736.

Hen. Five shillings, five shillings for all this courage; nobody more than five shillings? [*Knocks.*] Your name, Sir?

1 Offi. MacDonald O'Thunder.   180

Hen. Lot 5 and Lot 6. All the wit lately belonging to Mr. Hugh Pantomime, composer of entertainments for the playhouses, and Mr. William Goosequill, composer of political papers in defence of a ministry; shall I put up these together?

Bant. Ay, it is a pity to part them, where are they?

Hen. Sir, in the next room, where any gentleman may see them, but they are too heavy to bring in; there are near three hundred volumes in folio.

Bant. Put them by, who the devil would bid for them, unless he was the manager of some house or other? The town has paid enough for their works already.   190

Hen. Lot 7. A very neat clear conscience, which has been worn by a judge and a bishop.

Mris. Screen. It is as clean as if it was new.

Hen. Yes, no dirt will stick to it, and pray observe how capacious it is; it has one particular quality, put as much as you will into it, it is never full: come, gentlemen, don't be afraid to bid for this, for whoever has it, will never be poor.

Beau. One shilling for it.

Hen. O fie, Sir, I am sure you want it, for if you had any conscience, you would put it up at more than that: come, fifty pounds for this conscience.

Bant. I'll give fifty pounds to get rid of my conscience with all my heart.   202

Hen. Well, gentlemen, I see you are resolved not to bid for it, so I'll lay it by. Come, Lot 8. A very considerable quantity of interest at court; come, a hundred pounds for this interest at court.

Omnes. For me, Mr. Hen?

Hen. A hundred pounds are bid in a hundred places, gentlemen.

Beau. Two hundred pounds.

Hen. Two hundred pounds, two hundred and fifty, three hundred pounds, three hundred and fifty, four hundred, five hundred, six hundred, a thousand; a thousand is bid, gentlemen, nobody more than a thousand pounds for this interest at court; nobody more than one thousand? [*Knocks.*] Mr. Littlewit.

Bant. Damn me, I know a shop where I can buy it for less.   213

L. Dap. Egad, you took me in, Mr. Medley, I could not help bidding for it.

Med. 'Tis a sure sign 'tis nature, my Lord, and I should not be surprised to see the whole audience stand up and bid for it too.

Hen. All the cardinal virtues, Lot 9. Come, gentlemen, put in these cardinal virtues?

Gent. Eighteen pence.

Hen. Eighteen pence is bid for these cardinal virtues; nobody more than eighteen pence? Eighteen pence for all these cardinal virtues, nobody more? All these virtues, gentlemen, are going for eighteen pence; perhaps there is not so much more virtue in the world, as here is, and all going for eighteen pence. [*Knocks.*] Your name, Sir?   224

Gent. Sir, here's a mistake; I thought you had said a Cardinal's virtues, 'sblood Sir, I thought to have bought a pennyworth; here's temperance and chastity, and a pack of stuff that I would not give three farthings for.

Hen. Well, lay 'em by. Lot 10 and Lot 11. A great deal of wit, and a little common sense.

Bant. Why do you put up these together? They have no relation to each other.   231

Hen. Well, the sense by itself, then. Lot 10. A little common sense—I assure you, gentlemen, this is a very valuable commodity; come, who puts it in?

Med. You observe, as valuable as it is, nobody bids; I take this, if I may speak in the style of a great writer, to be a most emphatical silence; you see, Mr. Sowrwit, no one speaks against this lot, and the reason nobody bids for it, is, because everyone thinks he has it.

Hen. Lay it by, I'll keep it myself. Lot 12.   [*Drum beats.*

Sowr. Hey-day! What's to be done now, Mr. Medley?   240

Med. Now, Sir, the sport begins.

Enter a Gentleman *laughing. Huzza within.*

Bant. What's the matter?

Gent. There's a sight without would kill all mankind with laughing; Pistol is run mad, and thinks himself a great man, and he's marching thro' the streets with a drum and fiddles.

Bant. Please heaven, I'll go and see this sight.   [*Exit.*

Omnes. And so will I.   [*Exeunt.*

Hen. Nay, if everyone else goes, I don't know why I should stay behind.
                                                                                        [*Exit.*

L. Dap. Mr. Sowrwit, we'll go too.

Med. If your Lordship will have but a little patience 'till the scene be changed, you shall see him on the stage.   251

Sowr. Is not this jest a little over-acted?

Med. I warrant we don't over-act him half so much as he does his parts; tho' 'tis not so much his acting capacity which I intend to exhibit, as his ministerial.

Sowr. His ministerial!

Med. Yes, Sir, you may remember I told you before my rehearsal, that there was a strict resemblance between the states political and theatrical;

there is a ministry in the latter as well as the former, and I believe as weak a ministry as any poor kingdom could ever boast of; parts are given in the latter to actors, with much the same regard to capacity, as places in the former have some times been, in former ages I mean; and tho' the public damn both, yet while they both receive their pay, they laugh at the public behind the scenes; and if one considers the plays that come from one part, and the writings from the other, one would be apt to think the same authors were retained in both: but, come, change the scene into the street, and then enter Pistol *cum suis*—hitherto, Mr. Sowrwit, as we have had only to do with inferior characters, such as beaux and tailors, and so forth, we have dealt in the prosaic; now we are going to introduce a more considerable person, our Muse will rise in her style: now, Sir, for a taste of the sublime; come, enter, Pistol.   [*Drum beats and fiddles play.*

Enter Pistol *and Mob.*

Pist. Associates, brethren, countrymen and friends,	272
Partakers with us in this glorious enterprise,	
Which for our consort we have undertaken;	
It grieves us much, yes, by the gods it does!	
That we whose great ability and parts	
Have raised us to this pinnacle of power,	
Entitling us Prime Minister Theatrical;	
That we should with an upstart of the stage	
Contend successless on our consort's side;	280
But tho', by just hereditary right	
We claim a lawless power, yet for some reasons,	
Which to ourself we keep as yet concealed,	
Thus to the public deign we to appeal;	
Behold how humbly the great Pistol kneels.	
Say then, Oh town, is it your royal will,	
That my great consort represent the part	
Of Polly Peachum in the *Beggar's Opera*? [*Mob hiss.*	
Thanks to the town, that hiss speaks their assent;	
Such was the hiss that spoke the great applause	290
Our mighty father met with, when he brought	
His *Riddle* on the stage; such was the hiss	

267 *cum suis*] With his followers.   271 s.d. Pistol] Theophilus Cibber (1703–58), extra-vagant son of Colley and an enemy of Fielding, was also an actor whose most popular role was Pistol. He succeeded his father as a co-manager of Drury Lane and managed the Hay-market Theatre briefly. In 1736 he had caused an uproar in theatrical circles by pushing his wife, Susannah Arne, for the part of Polly (the prerogative of Mrs. Clive) in *The Beggar's Opera*.   292 *Riddle*] Colley Cibber's *Love in a Riddle* (1729), a pastoral imitating *The Beggar's Opera* in some respects, had been hissed.

Welcomed his *Caesar* to the Egyptian shore;
Such was the hiss, in which great *John* should have expired:
But, wherefore do I try in vain to number
Those glorious hisses, which from age to age
Our family has borne triumphant from the stage?

Med. Get thee gone for the prettiest hero that ever was shewn on any stage.   [*Exit* Pistol.

Sowr. Short and sweet, faith, what, are we to have no more of him?

Med. Ay, ay, Sir; he's only gone to take a little breath.   301

L. Dap. If you please, Sir, in the meantime, we'll go take a little fire, for 'tis confounded cold upon the stage.

Med. I wait upon your Lordship: stop the rehearsal a few moments, we'll be back again instantly.   [*Exeunt.*

ACT III. SCENE I.

Enter Medley, Sowrwit, *and* Lord Dapper.

Med. Now, my Lord, for my modern Apollo: come, make all things ready, and draw the scene as soon as you can.

Sowr. Modern, why modern? You commonplace satirists are always endeavouring to persuade us, that the age we live in is worse than any other has been, whereas mankind have differed very little since the world began; for one age has been as bad as another.

Med. Mr. Sowrwit, I do not deny that men have been always bad enough; vice and folly are not the inventions of our age; but I will maintain, that what I intend to ridicule in the following scene, is the whole and sole production and invention of some people now living. And, faith, let me tell you, tho' perhaps the public may not be the better for it, it is an invention exceeding all the discoveries of every philosopher or mathematician, from the beginning of the world to this day.   13

Sowr. Ay, pray what is it?

Med. Why, Sir, it is a discovery lately found out, that a man of great parts, learning and virtue, is fit for no employment whatever; that an estate renders a man unfit to be trusted, that being a blockhead is a qualification for

---

293 *Caesar*] *Caesar in Egypt:* Drury Lane, 1724; published 1725. 294 great *John*] Colley Cibber's *Papal Tyranny in the Reign of King John*, an alteration of Shakespeare's *King John*, was written and rehearsed in 1736. But Cibber, rebuked by Pope and others for meddling with Shakespeare, withdrew the play, and it was not produced until 1745. Fielding attacks it in more detail in Act III.

business; that honesty is the only sort of folly for which a man ought to be utterly neglected and contemned. And—but here is the inventor himself.   20

Scene draws, and discovers Apollo *in a great chair, surrounded by attendants.*

Come, bring him forward, that the audience may see and hear him: you must know, Sir, this is a bastard of Apollo, begotten on that beautiful nymph Moria, who sold oranges to Thespis's company, or rather cart-load of comedians; and being a great favourite of his father's, the old gentleman settled upon him the entire direction of all our playhouses and poetical performances whatever.

Apol. Prompter.

Promp. Sir.

Apol. Is there anything to be done?

Promp. Yes, Sir, this play to be cast.   30

Apol. Give it me. *The Life and Death of King John*, written by Shakespeare: who can act the King?

Promp. Pistol, Sir, he loves to act it behind the scenes.

Apol. Here are a parcel of English lords.

Promp. Their parts are but of little consequence, I will take care to cast them.

Apol. Do but be sure you give them to actors who will mind their cues—Falconbridge—what sort of a character is he?

Promp. Sir, he is a warrior, my cousin here will do him very well.

1 Play. I do a warrior! I never learnt to fence.   40

Apol. No matter, you will have no occasion to fight; can you look fierce, and speak well?

1 Play. Boh!

Apol. I would not desire a better warrior in the house than your self—Robert Falconbridge—what, is this Robert?

Promp. Really, Sir, I don't well know what he is, his chief desire seems to be for land, I think; he is no very considerable character, anybody may do him well enough; or if you leave him quite out, the play will be little the worse for it.

Apol. Well, I'll leave it to you—Peter of Pomfret, a prophet—have you anybody that looks like a prophet?   51

Promp. I have one that looks like a fool.

Apol. He'll do—Philip of France.

Promp. I have cast all the French parts, except the Ambassador.

22 a bastard of Apollo] Walpole, Theophilus Cibber, Lewis Theobald, and Charles Fleetwood, the patentee of Drury Lane, have all been suggested as possible originals of this figure. Or he may simply represent any arbitrary, unqualified, self-appointed 'lord' over the drama.

Apol. Who shall do it? His part is but short. Have you never a good genteel figure, and one that can dance? For as the English are the politest people in Europe, it will be mighty proper that the Ambassador should be able at his arrival to entertain them with a jig or two.

Promp. Truly, Sir, here are abundance of dancing-masters in the house, who do little or nothing for their money.   60

Apol. Give it to one of them; see that he has a little drollery tho' in him, for Shakespeare seems to have intended him as a ridiculous character, and only to make the audience laugh.

Sowr. What's that, Sir? Do you affirm that Shakespeare intended the Ambassador Chatilion a ridiculous character?

Med. No, Sir, I don't.

Sowr. Oh, Sir, your humble servant, then I misunderstood you; I thought I had heard him say so.

Med. Yes, Sir, but I shall not stand to all he says.

Sowr. But, Sir, you should not put a wrong sentiment into the mouth of the God of Wit.   71

Med. I tell you, he is the God only of modern wit, and he has a very just right to be God of most of the modern wits that I know; of some who are liked for their wit; of some who are preferred for their wit; of some who live by their wit; of those ingenious gentlemen who damn plays, and those who write them too perhaps. Here comes one of his votaries; come, enter, enter— enter Mr. Ground-Ivy.

Enter Ground-Ivy.

Ground. What are you doing here?

Apol. I am casting the parts in the tragedy of *King John.*

Ground. Then you are casting the parts in a tragedy that won't do.

Apol. How, Sir! Was it not written by Shakespeare, and was not Shakespeare one of the greatest geniuses that ever lived?   82

Ground. No, Sir, Shakespeare was a pretty fellow, and said some things which only want a little of my licking to do well enough; *King John*, as now writ, will not do—but a word in your ear, I will make him do.

Apol. How?

Ground. By alteration, Sir. It was a maxim of mine, when I was at the head of theatrical affairs, that no play, tho' ever so good, would do without alteration—for instance, in the play before us, the bastard Falconbridge is a most effeminate character, for which reason I would cut him out, and put all his sentiments in the mouth of Constance, who is so much properer to speak them—let me tell you, Mr. Apollo, propriety of character, dignity of diction,

---

77 s.d. Ground-Ivy] Colley Cibber (1671–1757), who had altered *King John* (see Act II, Sc. i, l. 294 n.). The playbills read 'Mr. Ground Ivy, a Laureat'.

and emphasis of sentiment, are the things I chiefly consider on these occasions.

Promp. I am only afraid, as Shakespeare is so popular an author, and you, asking your pardon, so unpopular.

Ground. Damn me, I'll write to the town, and desire them to be civil, and that in so modest a manner, that an army of Cossacks shall be melted: I'll tell them that no actors are equal to me, and no authors ever were superior: and how do you think I can insinuate that in a modest manner?   100

Promp. Nay, faith, I can't tell.

Ground. Why, I'll tell them that the former only tread on my heels, and that the greatest among the latter have been damned as well as myself; and after that, what do you think of your popularity? I can tell you, Mr. Prompter, I have seen things carried in the House against the voice of the people before today.

Apol. Let them hiss, let them hiss, and grumble as much as they please, as long as we get their money.

Med. There, Sir, is the sentiment of a great man, and worthy to come from the great Apollo himself.   110

Sowr. He's worthy his sire, indeed, to think of this gentleman for altering Shakespeare.

Med. Sir, I will maintain this gentleman as proper as any man in the Kingdom for the business.

Sowr. Indeed!

Med. Ay, Sir, for as Shakespeare is already good enough for people of taste, he must be altered to the palates of those who have none; and if you will grant that, who can be properer to alter him for the worse? But if you are so zealous in old Shakespeare's cause, perhaps you may find by-and-by all this come to nothing—now for Pistol.   120

Pistol *enters, and overturns his father.*

Ground. Pox on't, the boy treads close on my heels in a literal sense.

Pist. Your pardon, Sir, why will you not obey
     Your son's advice, and give him still his way;
     For you, and all who will oppose his force,
     Must be o'erthrown in his triumphant course.

Sowr. I hope, Sir, your Pistol is not intended to burlesque Shakespeare.

Med. No, Sir, I have too great an honour for Shakespeare to think of burlesquing him, and to be sure of not burlesquing him, I will never attempt to alter him, for fear of burlesquing him by accident, as perhaps some others have done.   130

L. Dap. Pistol is the young captain.

Med. My Lord, Pistol is every insignificant fellow in town, who fancies

himself of great consequence, and is of none; he is my Lord Pistol, Captain
Pistol, Counsellor Pistol, Alderman Pistol, Beau Pistol, and—and—odso,
what was I going to say? Come, go on.

Apol. Prompter, take care that all things well go on;
    We will retire, my friend, and read *King John.*   [*Exeunt.*

Sowr. To what purpose, Sir, was Mr. Pistol introduced?

Med. To no purpose at all, Sir; 'tis all in character, Sir, and plainly shews
of what mighty consequence he is—and there ends my article from the
theatre.   141

Sowr. Hey-day! What's become of your two Pollys?

Med. Damned, Sir, damned; they were damned at my first rehearsal, for
which reason I have cut them out; and to tell you the truth, I think the town
has honoured 'em enough with talking of 'em for a whole month; tho',
faith, I believe it was owing to their having nothing else to talk of. Well, now
for my patriots—you will observe, Mr. Sowrwit, that I place my politicians
and my patriots at opposite ends of my piece; which I do, Sir, to shew the
wide difference between them; I begin with my politicians, to signify that
they will always have the preference in the world, to patriots, and I end with
patriots, to leave a good relish in the mouths of my audience.   151

Sowr. Ay? By your dance of patriots, one would think you intended to turn
patriotism into a jest.

Med. So I do—but don't you observe I conclude the whole with a dance of
patriots? Which plainly intimates, that when patriotism is turned into a jest,
there is an end of the whole play: come, enter four patriots—you observe I
have not so many patriots as politicians; you will collect from this, that they
are not so plenty.

Sowr. Where does the scene lie now, Sir?

Med. In Corsica, Sir, all in Corsica.   160

Enter four Patriots *from different doors, who meet in
the centre, and shake hands.*

Sowr. These patriots seem to equal your greatest politicians in their
silence.

Med. Sir, what they think now, cannot well be spoke, but you may
conjecture a great deal from their shaking their heads; they will speak by-and-
by—as soon as they are a little heated with wine: you cannot, however, expect
any great speaking in this scene; for tho' I do not make my patriots politicians, I don't make them fools.

142 two Pollys] The first playbills include 'Polly Smart' and 'Polly Soft', but they do not
appear in the first edition. It is clear from Medley's remark that the audience disapproved of
the scene and it was dropped.   147 patriots] The Patriots were a party opposed to Walpole.
Cf. Johnson: 'Patriotism is the last refuge of a scoundrel.'

Sowr. But, methinks, your patriots are a set of shabby fellows.

Med. They are the cheaper dressed; besides, no man can be too low for a patriot, tho' perhaps it is possible he may be too high.   170

1 Patr. Prosperity to Corsica.

2 Patr. Liberty and property.

3 Patr. Success to trade.

4 Patr. Ay, to trade—to trade—particularly to my shop.

Sowr. Why do you suffer that actor to stand laughing behind the scenes, and interrupt your rehearsal?

Med. O, Sir, he ought to be there; he's a-laughing in his sleeve at the patriots; he's a very considerable character—and has much to do by-and-by.

Sowr. Methinks the audience should know that, or perhaps they may mistake him as I did, and hiss him.   180

Med. If they should, he's a pure impudent fellow, and can stand the hisses of them all; I chose him particularly for the part—go on, patriots.

1 Patr. Gentlemen, I think this our island of Corsica is an ill state; I do not say we are actually in war, for that we are not; but, however, we are threatened with it daily, and why may not the apprehension of a war, like other evils, be worse then the evil itself? For my part, this I will say, this I will venture to say, that let what will happen, I will drink a health to peace.

Med. This gentleman is the noisy patriot, who drinks and roars for his country, and never does either good or harm in it—the next is the cautious patriot.   190

2 Patr. Sir, give me your hand; there's truth in what you say, and I will pledge you with all my soul, but remember it is all under the rose.

3 Patr. Look'ee, gentlemen, my shop is my country; I always measure the prosperity of the latter by that of the former. My country is either richer or poorer, in my opinion, as my trade rises or falls; therefore, Sir, I cannot agree with you, that a war would be disserviceable: on the contrary, I think it the only way to make my country flourish; for as I am a sword-cutler, it would make my shop flourish, so here's to war.

Med. This is the self-interested patriot, and now you shall hear the fourth and last kind, which is the indolent patriot, one who acts as I have seen a prudent man in company, fall asleep at the beginning of a fray, and never wake till the end on't.   202

4 Patr. [*Waking.*] Here's to peace or war, I do not care which.

Sowr. So this gentleman being neutral, peace has it two to one.

Med. Perhaps neither shall have it; perhaps I have found a way to reconcile both parties: but go on.

1 Patr. Can anyone, who is a friend to Corsica, wish for war, in our present circumstances?—I desire to ask you all one question, are we not a set of miserable poor dogs?

Omnes. Ay, ay.   210
3 Patr. That we are, sure enough; that nobody will deny.

Enter Quidam.

Quid. Yes, Sir, I deny it. [*All start.*] Nay, gentlemen, let me not disturb
you, I beg you will all sit down. I am come to drink a glass with you—can
Corsica be poor while there is this in it? [*Lays a purse on the table.*] Nay, be
not afraid of it, gentlemen, it is honest gold I assure you; you are a set of poor
dogs, you agree, I say you are not, for this is all yours, there, [*Pours it on the
table.*] take it among you.
1 Patr. And what are we to do for it?
Quid. Only say you are rich, that's all.
Omnes. Oh, if that be all!   [*They snatch up the money.*
Quid. Well, Sir, what is your opinion now? Tell me freely.   221
1 Patr. I will. A man may be in the wrong through ignorance, but he's a
rascal, who speaks with open eyes against his conscience—I own I thought
we were poor, but, Sir, you have convinced me that we are rich.
Omnes. We are all convinced.
Quid. Then you are all honest fellows, and here is to your healths, and
since the bottle is out, hang sorrow, cast away care, e'en take a dance, and I
will play you a tune on the fiddle.
Omnes. Agreed.
1 Patr. Strike up when you will, we are ready to attend your motions.

[*Dance here;* Quidam *dances out, and they all dance after him.*]

Med. Perhaps there may be something intended by this dance, which
you don't take.   232
Sowr. Ay, what prithee?
Med. Sir, every one of these patriots have a hole in their pockets, as Mr.
Quidam the fiddler there knows, so that he intends to make them all dance
till all the money is fallen through, which he will pick up again, and so lose
not one halfpenny by his generosity; so far from it, that he will get his wine
for nothing, and the poor people, alas! out of their own pockets, pay the
whole reckoning. This, Sir, I think is a very pretty pantomime trick, and an
ingenious burlesque on all the fourberies which the great Lun has exhibited
in all his entertainments: and so ends my play, my farce, or what you please
to call it; may I hope it has your Lordship's approbation?   242
L. Dap. Very pretty, indeed, 'tis very pretty.
Med. Then, my Lord, I hope I shall have your encouragement; for things

211 s.d. Quidam] The Prime Minister, Sir Robert Walpole (1676–1745). Early playbills
read *Quidam Anglicae*. Cf. Dedication, l. 124.   240 fourberies] Tricks, deceptions.   240 the
great Lun] The name used by John Rich when playing Harlequin in pantomime.

in this town do not always succeed according to their merit; there is a vogue, my Lord, which if you will bring me into, you will lay a lasting obligation on me: and you, Mr. Sowrwit, I hope, will serve me among the critics, that I may have no elaborate treatise writ to prove that a farce of three acts is not a regular play of five. Lastly, to you, gentlemen, whom I have not the honour to know, who have pleased to grace my rehearsal; and you, ladies, whether you be Shakespeare's ladies, or Beaumont and Fletcher's ladies, I hope you will make allowances for a rehearsal;   252

> And kindly all report us to the town;
> No borrowed, nor no stolen goods we've shown,
> If witty, or if dull, our play's our own.

251 Shakespeare's ladies] A women's group dedicated to revivals of Shakespearean drama.

A WILL AND NO WILL

Charles Macklin

1697?–1797

The stage career of the Irishman Charles Macklin spans most of the eighteenth century. He was acting in Bristol and London by 1725, and remained in the theatre until 1789. In between, he appeared with Fielding's company at the Haymarket, befriended young David Garrick, and introduced Samuel Foote to the stage. Macklin made his reputation as a 'natural' actor in *The Merchant of Venice*, his Shylock eliciting the famous distich, attributed to Pope, 'This is the Jew/That Shakespeare drew.' Between theatre engagements he derived an income from lectures, debates, and acting lessons. Macklin wrote comedies and farces at irregular intervals, usually on the occasion of someone's benefit; when his last and best mainpiece comedy, *The Man of the World*, opened in 1781, Macklin played the lead—at eighty-four.

A Will and No Will, or A Bone for the Lawyers, was written for Mrs. Macklin's benefit[1] night at Drury Lane, 23 April 1746, and was produced half a dozen more times over the next ten seasons. It is what Georgian critics called an 'adaptation' (as distinct from a translation) of Regnard's *Le Legataire Universel* (1708). Perhaps 'Englishing', if understood broadly, is the best term for what Macklin did. He compressed five acts of heroic couplets into two acts of prose, adding several racy bits of his own, and the entire prologue. He took from the French play its basic idea and cast, as well as the general outline of the action and speeches, but thoroughly anglicized the characters and composed his own dialogue; Regnard's polished, artificial speech is unrecognizable in Macklin's curt and idiomatic version. Eighteenth-century audiences placed no particular premium on originality, and dramatists were therefore not shy about borrowing from other authors. Neither, for that matter, was Shakespeare. Had Augustan printing conventions prevailed in the early seventeenth century, the First Folio would have been full of titles such as '*Othello, the Moor of Venice; Englished* from the *Italian* of CINTHIO'; or '*The Winter's Tale; out* of Mr. GREENE's *Pandosto*'.

Macklin's farce played only a few times and survived in a single MS., but the other eighteenth-century version of Regnard's play—Thomas King's

---

[1] *The London Stage* (III, 1235) says: 'Benefit Macklin.' But see the notice, p. 39, and the Prologue, l. 113.

Wit's Last Stake (1768)—became popular and was printed. The preference of Georgian theatre-goers is today difficult to understand. King sentimentalizes the conclusion, giving Bellair moral qualms about the scheme and having Isaac revoke the false will in favour of a new one that leaves all to Bellair. Moved, Bellair breaks down and confesses; a forgiving Isaac unites him with Harriet. Even Shark makes noises of reformation. Macklin's ribaldry and most of his effective stage comedy are cut by King, yet it was the latter's version which succeeded and acquired the permanency of print. Under the circumstances one may be forgiven for feeling that stage success and publication were poor guarantees of dramatic worth in the eighteenth century.

A Will illustrates Bergson's remark that the comic effect depends upon a temporary 'anaesthesia of the heart'. If the treatment of Isaac seems unfeeling, we must remind ourselves that not his age itself but his imposture of youth—the blindness that makes him yearn after Harriet—is the target of our mockery. Once he has been ridiculed into behaviour appropriate to his years the laughter should of course cease. Macklin, however, provides no such graceful resolution; he leaves Isaac and the plot dangling. It is this as much as anything which identifies his play as a farce and not a comedy.

The text is based on the Larpent MS., which Mrs. Jean B. Kern edited for the Augustan Reprint Society as No. 127-8 (1967) of their series. Acknowledgement for permission to publish this MS. is hereby made to the Huntington Library, to Mrs. Kern, and to the Augustan Reprint Society.

A WILL and NO WILL

or a

BONE for the LAWYERS

April 1746

April 15th 1746

Sir

I have given Mrs Macklin leave to act this farce for her benefit provided it meets with the approbation of my Lord Chamberlain.

Y^r
humble serv^t
J. Lacy

Dramatis Personæ

[PROLOGUE]
Rattle
Smart
Dullman
Irishman
Snarlewit

Sir Isaac Skinflint
Bellair
Doctor Leatherhead
Counsellor Cormorant
Mr. Littlewit
Monsieur du Maigre
Mr. Death
Shark
Servant

Lady Lovewealth
Harriet
Lucy

Principal parts by: Macklin, Yates, Blakes, Usher, Winstone, I. Sparks, Marr, Simpson, Mrs. Ridout, Mrs. Bennet, Mrs. Macklin.

PROLOGUE

The curtain rises, and discovers the stage disposed
in the form of a pit and crowded with actors, who make
a great noise by whistling and knocking for the farce
to begin.

Rattle. Consume them, why don't they begin?

Smart. I suppose some of them that were in the play are dressing for the farce.

Rattle. Psha! Damn the farce, they have had time enough to dress since the play has been over.

Smart. Dick Rattle, were you at the boxing match yesterday?

Rattle. No my dear, I was at the breakfasting at Ranelagh.—Curse catch me, Dick, if that is not a fine woman in the upper box there, ha!

Smart. So she is, by all that's charming—but the poor creature's married: it's all over with her.   10

Rattle. Smart, do you go to Newmarket this meeting?—Upon my soul that's a lovely woman on the right hand. But what the devil can this prologue be about? I can't imagine. It has puzzled the whole town.

Smart. Depend upon it, Jack, it is as I said.

Rattle. What's that?

Smart. Why one of Fransiques the French Harlequin's jokes; you will find that one of the players [will] come upon the stage presently, and make an apology that they are disappointed of the prologue, upon which Macklin, or some other actor, is to start up in the pit, as one of the audience, and bawl out that rather than so much good company should be disappointed he will speak a prologue himself.   21

Rattle. No, no, no, Smart, that's not it. I thought of that and have been looking carefully all over the pit, and there is not an actor in it. Now I fancy it is to be done like the wall or the man in [the] moon in *Pyramus and Thisbe*; Macklin will come in dressed like the pit, and say

> Ladies and gentlemen, I am the pit
> And a prologue I'll speak if you think fit.

Omnes. Ha! ha! ha!

Smart. By gad, Rattle, I fancy you have hit it. What do you think, Mr. Dullman?   30

Omnes. Ay, let us have Mr. Dullman's opinion of it.

17 [will] come] Words in square brackets are not in the MS.

Dull. Why really, gentlemen, I have been thinking of it ever since I first read it in the papers—and I fancy—though to be sure it was very difficult to find out—but at last, I think I have hit upon it.

Smart. Well, well, my dear Dullman, communicate!

Dull. I suppose there is some person here among us whose name is pit, and that he will get up presently and speak a prologue.

Omnes. O, O, O, O, O, shocking! Shocking! Well conjectured, Dullman.

Rattle. Harkee Jack, bam the Irishman, ask him if he knows anything of it.

Smart. Don't you laugh, then, he'll smoke us if you do; keep your countenance, and I'll engage I'll pitchkettle him. Pray Sir, do you know anything of this prologue?   42

Irish. Who, me? Not I, upon my honour. I know no more of it than he that made it.

Smart. A gentleman was saying just before the play was over, that you were to be the pit, and to speak the prologue. Is there any truth in it, Sir?

Irish. No indeed Sir, it is as false as the Gospel. I'll assure you, Sir, I never spoke a pit or prologue in my life—but once when I was at school, you must know Sir we acted one of Terence's tragedies there, so when the play was over I spoke the prologue to it.   50

Omnes. Ha! ha! ha! ha!

Smart. I remember your face very well. Pray Sir, don't you belong to the law?

Irish. Yes, at your service Sir—and so did my father and grandfather before me, and all my posterity. I myself solicit cause at the Old Bailey and Hicks's Hall, so I am come to see this *Bone for the Lawyers*, because they say it is a pun upon us gentlemen of the long robe.

Omnes. Ha! ha! ha!

Rattle. He is a poor ridiculous fellow, Jack. [*Aside.*] He is as great a Teague as Barrington himself.   60

Smart. Hush! Hush! Pray Sir, may I crave your name?

Irish. Yes you may indeed and welcome, Sir. My name is Langhlinbullruderrymackshoughlinbulldowny, at your service. And if you have any friend who is indicted for robbery or murder at any time, or has any other law suits upon his hands at the Old Bailey or Hicks's Hall, I should be proud to serve you and to be concerned in the cause likewise.

---

39 bam] Perplex, confound (abbr. of 'bamboozle').   41 pitchkettle] To utterly puzzle, to nonplus.   47 it is . . . Gospel] All underlining in the MS. is by the Lord Chamberlain's censor; it indicates that the words so marked must be omitted in the performance. 55 Hicks's Hall] The sessions house of Middlesex from 1612 to 1782.   59 Teague] A generic nickname for an Irishman.   60 Barrington] Probably William Wildman, 2nd Viscount Barrington (1717–93), an M.P. active chiefly in military affairs. In 1745 he had proposed a national militia.

Smart. Whenever I have a friend in such circumstances, you may depend upon being retained.

Irish. Sir, I'll assure you no man in England understands the practice of those courts better than myself. I know my Croaker upon all the inries, and for an evidence the devil a man in Westminster Hall can tell an evidence what to say better than I that shits here, or hark you, if you, if you should happen to want a witness upon occasion, I believe, Sir, I could serve you.

Smart. Sir, I am infinitely obliged to you. }
Irish. Sir, I am your most obsequious.   } [*Bowing.*]   74

Rattle. But pray, Sir, what kind of a prologue do you think we shall have tonight?

Irish. Why I believe it will be a kind of a prologue that will be spoken by the pit.

Rattle. Ay, that we suppose. But in what manner?   80

Irish. Why I am come here on purpose to know that, but I suppose it will be in the manner of—a—a—by my shoul I don't know how it will be.

Smart. Upon my word, Sir, I think you give a very clear account of it.

Rattle. Jack, yonder's Snarlewit the poet, an intimate friend of Macklin's; you are acquainted with him; prithee call him, ten to one but he can give us the history both of the prologue and the farce.

Smart. Hiss, Mr. Snarlewit, we have room for you here, if you will come and set by us; do you know Snarlewit, Dick?

Rattle. He is a devilish odd fellow; he is one that never speaks well of any man behind his back nor ill of him to his face, and is a most terrible critic.

Snarlewit *steps over the benches and sits down*
between Rattle *and* Smart.

Snarle. Mr. Smart your servant. How do you do, Mr. Rattle? What, you are come to hear the pit speak the prologue I suppose, ha! Macklin's fine conceit.   93

Smart. Ay, we are so. Do you know anything of it?

Snarle. Psha! Psha! A parcel of stuff! A ridiculous conceit of the block-head's in imitation of a French writer who stole it from one of the Greek comic poets.

Smart. But in what manner is it to be done? Is it in prose or in verse? Or upon the stage, or really in the pit?

Snarle. Lord, Sir, the blockhead brings the pit upon the stage; and the supposed conversation there, between the play and the farce, is to be the prologue, a French conceit calculated merely to raise curiosity, and fill the house, that's all.   103

70 Croaker] For (presumably) [the famous jurist Sir Edward Coke (1552–1634).
70 inries] Possibly 'injuries' or '*in re*'s'.

Smart. Ay, and enough too, if it answers his purpose.

Irish. But pray, Sir, with humble submission, if he brings the pit upon the stage, how shall we be able to see the farce, unless we go up into the gallery?

Omnes. Ha! ha! ha!

Rattle. Very well observed Sir.

Snarle. Why this fellow's an idiot.   110

Smart. No, no, he is only a Teague. But Mr. Snarlewit, do you think this prologue will be liked?

Snarle. Psha! Psha! Liked? Impossible! So it is for his wife's benefit, and meant as a puff to fill her house, why perhaps the town may be so indulgent as to let it pass—but it is damned trash! I advised the fool against it. But he persisted. He said he was sure it would be better liked than the modern dull way of prologue-writing which for many years has been only to give the audience an historical account of the comic [stoick] or the tragic buskin, or a dull detail of the piece they were to see with the age and circumstances of the author, and how long he was writing his play. Now says Macklin, 'My prologue Sir, if it has nothing else it has novelty on its side; and as Bayes says it will elevate and surprise and all that, and if they don't laugh at it as a good prologue, I am sure,' says he, 'they will laugh at me, for its being a bad one—so that either way they will have their joke.'   124

Omnes. Ha! ha! ha!

Smart. Ay, ay, there I think he was right. The audience will laugh, I make no doubt of it, but it will be at him.

Omnes. Right! Right!

Snarle. So I told him, but he would persist.

Smart. But Mr. Snarlewit, how will he answer to the critics his making the stage represent the pit?   131

Snarle. Psha! Psha! He is below criticism, they will never trouble themselves about that. Besides, I think he may be defended very justly in that; for if the stage has a right to represent palaces and countries, nay and heaven and hell, surely it may be allowed to exhibit the pit.

Smart. Do you know anything of the farce?

Snarle. Yes, I have read it.

Smart. It is a very odd title, *A Bone for the Lawyers.* Who is the author pray? Is it known?

Snarle. Why Macklin gives out that some gentleman, a friend of his, has made him a present of it, but I shrewdly suspect it to be his own.

Rattle. Whose! Macklin's?   142

Snarle. Ay!

114 puff] Advertisement, come-on.   118 [stoick]] One word virtually illegible in MS.
121 Bayes] The obtuse author (alias Dryden) in *The Rehearsal* (1671).

Rattle. Why can he write?

Snarle. Write! Ay, and damnably too, I assure you! Ha! ha! He writ a tragedy this winter, but so merry a tragedy sure was never seen since the first night of *Tom Thumb the Great.*

Smart. I was at it and a merry tragedy it was! And a merry audience.

Snarle. I never laughed so heartily at a play in my life. If his farce has half as much fun in it as his tragedy had I'll engage it succeeds. 150

Smart. Come, come, there was some tolerable things in his tragedy.

Snarle. Psha! Psha! Stuff! Stuff! Damned stuff! Pray Sir, what do you think of Lady Catherine Gordon's letter to her father Lord Huntley, that began 'Honoured papa, hoping you are in good health as I am at this present writing'? There was a style for tragedy.

Omnes. Ha! ha! ha!

Smart. Well, I wish his farce may succeed however.

Snarle. O so do I upon my word, Sir—I have a very great regard for Macklin—but to be sure he is a very egregious blockhead ever to think of writing; that I believe everybody will allow. 160

Omnes. Ay, ay, there's nobody will dispute that with you, Mr. Snarle-wit.

Snarle. Notwithstanding he is such a blockhead, I assure you, Mr. Smart, I have an esteem for him.

Smart. Do you know what characters or business he has in his farce?

Snarle. I think his chief character is an old fellow, one Sir Isaac Skinflint, who is eaten up with diseases; and who promises everybody legacies, but dreads making a will, for the instant he does that he thinks he shall die.

Rattle. That's a very common character. My uncle was just such a superstitious wretch. 170

Snarle. And the business of the farce is to induce this old fellow to disinherit all his relations, except a nephew who wants to be his sole heir, which according to the rules of farce, you may suppose to be brought about by a footman, who upon these occasions always has more wit than his master.

Smart. But when is the prologue to begin?

Snarle. Why as soon as the curtain is drawn up you will see the stage disposed in the form of a pit, and that you are to imagine the prologue, and when they let the curtain down, why then you must suppose it to be ended.

Smart. I wonder what the audience will say when it is over. 180

Snarle. What? Why some will stare and wonder what the actors have been about, and will be still expecting the prologue, others will chuckle at their disappointment, and cry—they knew how it would be, and some will judiciously observe—what better could be expected from a prologue, to be

145 a tragedy] *Henry VII.* 154 began] MS. 'begun'. 173 suppose] MS. 'suppose it'.

C

written, and spoken by the pit. But upon the whole, I dare say, ninety-nine in a hundred will conclude it to be a parcel of low stuff—and that its only merit was, the quaintness of the conceit raised people's curiosity, and helped to fill the house, and so ends the prologue—and now let us make a noise for the farce.

The curtain is let down.

A Will and No Will

or

A Bone for the Lawyers

ACT the 1st.

Enter Shark *and* Lucy *meeting.*

Shark. Good morrow Lucy.

Lucy. Good morrow Shark.

Shark. Give me a kiss, hussy.   [*Kisses her.*

Lucy. Psha—prithee don't tousle and mousle a body so, can't you salute without rumpling one's tucker and spoiling one's things? I hate to be tumbled.   [*Adjusting herself.*

Shark. Ay, as much as you do flattery, or a looking glass.

Lucy. Well, what's your business this morning? Have you any message?

Shark. Yes, the old one: my master's duty to his gracious uncle, Sir Isaac Skinflint, and he hopes he rested well last night—that is, to translate it out of the language of compliment, into that of sincerity, he hopes the old hunks has made his will, my master his sole heir, that he has had a very bad night, and is within a few hours of giving up the ghost, and paying a visit to his old friend Beelzebub.   14

Lucy. We were afraid he would have gone off last night; he has had two of his epileptic feasts.

Shark. Why, sure the old cannibal would not offer to make his exit, without making his will? That would ruin us all.

Lucy. Nay, it would be a considerable loss to me should he die without a will: for you know he has promised me a handsome legacy.   20

Shark. And so he has to thousands, my dear; why child I don't believe he has spent thirty shillings upon himself in food for these thirty years; all gratis, all upon the sponge. Ay, ay, let Sir Isaac Skinflint alone for mumping a dinner. There has not been a churchwarden's or an overseer's feast these twenty years, but what he has been at. And when he is not at these parish

---

5 tucker] A frill of lace worn at the bodice.   11 old hunks] A crusty, stingy old man; a miser.   16 feasts] For 'fits'.   23 mumping] (1) To chew without teeth; (2) to sponge or beg.

meals he is preying upon his friends and acquaintance, and promises them all legacies. 'Well,' says he, after he has filled his paunch—'I shall not forget you. I shall remember all my friends. I have you down in my will.' Then he claps his hand upon the servant's head as he is going out.—'I shall think of you too John, you are my old friend,' but the devil a louse he gives him, an old gouty rogue! I'll warrant the old hypocrite has promised more legacies, than the Bank of England is able to pay. Has he made any mention lately of his nephew and niece in the country, Sir Roger Bumper and his sister?   34

Lucy. He expects them in town today, or tomorrow at farthest; and I believe he intends to make them joint heirs with your master.

Shark. He may intend it, but shall not accomplish it, take my word. If he does, I'll never plot again. You say he has never seen neither the nephew nor the niece, since they were children.

Lucy. Never.   40

Shark. Then he shall see them in my proper person before he sleeps, and if I don't make him disinherit them, say I am a fool and know nothing of mankind.

Lucy. Here your master comes.

Shark. He's welcome.

Enter Bellair.

Bell. O Lucy, we are all undone.

Lucy. Bless us, what's the matter, Sir?

Bell. I am just come from my lady Lovewealth's, who, to my great surprise, has assured me that my addresses to her daughter for the future will be highly improper, for that my uncle had not only refused to make such a settlement on me as she liked, but had resolved to marry Harriet himself.

Lucy. Pray Sir, what says the young lady to all this?   52

Bell. She seems to comply with her mother's avaricious temper, but has vowed to me privately, that should matters be brought to an extremity, she will never consent.

Lucy. You, Sir, must act the same part, seem to approve of the marriage by all means, for the more you oppose, the more violent they will be. Trust the affair to Shark and me, and I'll engage we bring you together in spite of age and avarice. I'll give the young lady a hint or two, which I believe will cure the old fellow of his love fit! Shark, go you and prepare your disguises, do you [act] the nephew and the niece well, and I'll warrant everything else shall thrive.   [*Exit* Shark.

Bell. Dear girl, the moment my affairs are brought to bear, you may depend upon the five hundred pounds I promised you.—Is my uncle up yet?

61 [act]] Illegible word in MS.

Lucy. He has been up this hour—here he comes. Be sure you comply with him, let him say what he will.   66

Enter Skinflint, *dressed in a night gown, a fur night cap, his hands muffled in flannel, his feet in gouty shoes.*

Bell. A good morning to you Sir.

Skin. A good morning to you nephew. Auh! Auh!

Bell. I am sorry to hear, Sir, you have had so bad a night.

Skin. I had indeed nephew; I was afraid it was all over, such another fit would carry me off, auh, auh!   71

Bell. But you are pretty well this morning I hope, Sir.

Skin. Something better but very weak—very faint indeed nephew! O-o-o very faint.

Bell. You should take something comfortable Sir—cordials to repair the breaches your illness hath made.

Skin. Lord, nephew, it would require such a monstrous deal of money, and really these syringe carriers, and clyster bags, and doctors, give themselves such airs, that a man can't have their assistance, nor any of their drugs and slops under their weight in gold; therefore I think nephew, since we are to die we had better save our money.   81

Bell. I grant you, Sir, the fees of surgeons and physicians are exorbitant,—yet as health and life are our most valuable blessings, we might lay a little out in the support of them—I mean in cases of very great danger.

Skin. No, no, the—auh, auh!—the tenement is not worth the repairs—auh—auh—I am like an old house that is ready to drop—the first high wind down I shall go—the next fit will carry me off.

Bell. Heaven forbid Sir.

Skin. Therefore, I am resolved—auh!—to settle my affairs this very day. You know, nephew, you were talking of Harriet my Lady Lovewealth's daughter; but my Lady truly will not consent to the match, unless I make you my sole heir, which you know child cannot be; as I have another nephew and a niece, Sir Roger Bumper and his sister, whom I intend to provide for.   94

Bell. Very true, Sir.

Skin. And so—Harry—as my Lady and I could not hit it off in regard to you—she hath persuaded me to marry the girl myself; what is your judgement of it nephew? Ha!

Bell. If you like it, Sir, there can be no objection to it.

Enter a Servant.

Ser. Sir, there is Mr. Littlewit the proctor come to know your commands.

78 clyster bags] Contemptuous term for a doctor.

Skin. Desire him to walk in.   [*Exit* Servant.

Enter Littlewit.

So, Mr. Littlewit. I have sent for you upon a business which will perhaps
surprise you; it is to draw up my marriage articles.   103

Litt. What, between you and death I suppose! Ha! Your will I reckon you
mean.

Skin. Dear Mr. Littlewit, your jest is very ill-timed; I mean, Sir, my marriage articles with Harriet Lovewealth, and at the same time I intend to make
my will too. Here are directions in this paper for both; and let them be drawn
up as soon as possible, and looked over by my old friend Doctor Leatherhead;
and pray bring him with you this afternoon.   110

Litt. Sir, your directions shall be observed with punctuality and expedition.   [*Exit.*

Skin. So you approve of my marriage you say, nephew?

Bell. I think it the best thing you can do, Sir.

Skin. Why nephew, notwithstanding—I am so shattered with age—and
infirmities—I assure you I have more vigour than people imagine: what think
you, Lucy?

Lucy. Your eyes, Sir, look very sparkling and lively—but I think a-um—
your other parts are not quite so brisk.

Skin. Why ay, 'tis true, my other parts are a little—a little morbific, or so,
as the doctors say; but Harriet is very young, and she will be a charming bed-
fellow. Besides, nephew, I shall have a great satisfaction in disappointing my
crew of relations, who have been like as many undertakers for these twenty
years past, enquiring not after my health but my death; but I'll be revenged
on them, I will have the pleasure of sending for 'em all, one by one, and
assuring them I will not leave a single shilling among them.   126

Enter a Servant.

Ser. Sir, my Lady Lovewealth and her daughter are come to wait on
you.

Skin. Odso, I did not expect them so soon—stay, stay boy, don't shew
them up yet, my mistress must not find me in this pickle. Go you down,
Lucy, and shew them into the parlour, but return directly and help to dress
me.   [*Exeunt* Lucy *and* Servant.
Come nephew, help me off with this gown and cap; let me make myself as
agreeable as I can for my mistress. Gently, gently, child, have a care, have a
care of my hand. [*Pulling off the gown.*] Oh: oh: oh: oh: you have touched my
gouty finger.   136

Enter Lucy.

120 morbific] Causing disease. Sir Isaac is probably groping for 'moribund' and 'soporific'.

Come hither Lucy, do you dress me: you are most used to it. Are my flannels warm?

Lucy. Here, here, all roasted—they have been at the fire these three hours.

> Lucy *and* Bellair *dress him up like a ridiculous old*
> *man; they put a heap of flannels on him, then his*
> *clothes, and a ridiculous tie wig.*

Skin. Well how do I look now? Pretty well, ha?   140
Bell. Very well Sir, and very genteel.
Skin. Now shew the ladies up Lucy. I protest this dressing hath fatigued me, auh! Auh! Auh!   [*Coughing.*
Lucy. [*To* Bellair *as she goes out.*] I have hinted something to Harriet, which I believe will break off the match infallibly.   [*Exit.*
Skin. Nephew, notwithstanding auh!—this marriage I shall make a handsome provision for you.
Bell. Sir, your health and happiness are my chiefest blessings.

> *Enter* Lady Lovewealth, Harriet, *and* Lucy.

Lady. Sir Isaac Skinflint I am glad to see you up and dressed this morning. We had a report in our neighbourhood that you died last night.   150
Skin. Ay, Madam, envious wretches who expect legacies—and who wish me in my grave—spread it abroad—'tis true I was a little out of order last night, but I'm mighty well today. Auh! Auh! Extremely well. Auh! Auh! Lucy, give me a little of that hartshorn.
Bell. Upon my word Sir, I never saw you look better. Pray young lady, what do you think?
Har. Indeed Sir, I think the gentleman looks extremely gay and healthy.
Skin. I should be very ill indeed, Madam, if such powerful eyes as yours could not give me new life.   [*Bowing very low.*
Har. O Sir your servant.   [*Curtseying very low.*
Lady. Very gallant indeed Sir.   161
Skin. Yes Madam, you will be a Medea's kettle to me; from whom I shall receive new vigour. Your charms will be a vivifying nostrum, to the morbific parts—which infirmity and age have laid hold of. You will be a julep to my heart—and my marriage will be an infallible specific, which I shall take as my last remedy.—Give me a little of that cordial.
Har. Sir, whatever commands my Lady thinks proper to lay on me, I shall think it my duty to give them an implicit obedience.
                          [*She curtsies all the while,* Skinflint *bows.*
Lady. You see, Sir Isaac, my daughter is entirely directed by my will; so if

---

162 Medea's kettle] Medea boiled Jason's father Aeson in a cauldron, with certain herbs, in order to rejuvenate him.   164 julep] A sweet, medicated drink. MS.: 'julap'.

you are ready to fulfill the agreement, that is to settle a thousand pounds a
year on her during your own life, and your whole fortune in reversion, upon
your decease, she is ready to marry you.   172

Skin. Madam, I am as ready as she, and have given orders to my lawyer to
draw up the articles for that purpose, with the utmost expedition, and I
expect them to be brought every moment ready to sign.

Lady. Then Harriet, I will leave you here child, while I call on my lawyer
in Lincoln's Inn, who is to peruse the writings—Mrs. Lucy, pray will you let
one of your men order my coach up to the door. [*Exit* Lucy.] Sir Isaac
Skinflint your servant, Mr. Bellair yours.   [*Exit.*

Skin. Come Madam, let not these naughty flannels disgust you; I can pull
em off upon—um—ahu—certain occasions; I shall look better in a few days.

Har. Better! That's impossible Sir, you can't look better.   182

Skin. O lord Madam!   [*Bowing.*

Har. [*Takes him by the hand.*] There, there's a figure, do but view him; Sir,
I never saw a finer figure, for a shroud and coffin, in my life.

Skin. [*Starting.*] Madam!

Har. I say, Sir, you are a most enchanting figure for a shroud and coffin.

Skin. Shroud and coffin!   [*He walks about, she after him.*

Har. Well I can't help admiring your intrepidity, Sir Isaac; o' my conscience, you have more courage than half the young fellows in town. Why
what a Don Quixote are you, to venture that shattered, shabby, crazy carcass
of yours into a marriage bed, with a hale constitution of nineteen!

Skin. Why really Madam—   193

Har. Why really Sir, you'll repent it.

Skin. I believe it, I believe it, Madam.

Har. What you, who are gouty, colicky, feverish, paralytic, hydropic,
asthmatic, and a thousand diseases besides, venture to light Hymen's torch!
Why, Sir, it is perfect madness; it is making but one step from your wedding
to your grave. Pray Sir, how long do you expect to live?

Skin. Not long I am sure if I marry you.   200

Har. You are in the right on't Sir; it will not be consistent with my pleasure, or my interest, that you should live above a fortnight; um, ay, in about a
fortnight I can do it. Let me see, ay, it is but pulling away the pillow in one of
your coughing fits—or speaking properly to your apothecary—a very little
ratsbane or laudanum will do the business.

Skin. O monstrous!

Bell. Madam, this is a behaviour unbecoming the daughter of Lady Lovewealth, and what I am confident her Ladyship will highly resent.

Har. You are mistaken, Sir; my Lady has consented to his death, in a fortnight after our marriage.   210

Skin. O lud! O lud!

Har. She begged hard for a month; but I could not agree to it; so now the only dispute between us is, whether he shall be poisoned or strangled.

Skin. O horrid! O terrible! So then it was agreed between you, that I should be sent out of the world, one way or t'other.

Har. Yes Sir; what other treatment could you expect, you, who are a mere walking hospital! An infirmary! O shocking! Ha! Ha! There's a figure to go to bed with.   *[Pointing at him and bursting into a laugh.*

Skin. I shall choke with rage. Auh! Auh!

Bell. Madam, I cannot stand by and see this treatment—if you use him thus before marriage, what ought he to expect after it?   221

Har. What? Why I have told him, death! Death! Death!

Skin. Ay, you have indeed, Madam; and I thank you for it. But it shall never be in your power, either to strangle or poison me. Auh! Auh! I would as soon marry a she-dragon; nephew, I beg you will turn her out—see her out of the house pray.

Bell. Madam, let me beg you will shorten your visit.

Har. O Sir, with all my heart; I see you are a confederate with your uncle in this affair, but I shall insist upon his promise of marriage; I can prove it; and assure yourself Sir, if there be law in Westminster Hall or Doctor's Commons, you shall hear from me, and so your servant, Sir.   231
                                            [Goes off in a passion.

Skin. Dear nephew see her out of the house, she has almost worried me to death! [*Sits down.*]   [*Exit* Bellair.

                          Enter Lucy.

Skin. O Lucy give me a little julep or hartshorn, or something to raise my spirits. Had ever man so happy an escape?

Lucy. Ay Sir, you'd say it was a happy escape indeed, if you knew all; why, Sir, it is whispered everywhere that she had an intrigue last summer at Scarborough with a captain of horse.

Skin. I don't in the least doubt it; she who could give ratsbane or laudanum to her husband I believe would not hesitate at a little fornication.

                        Shark *without.*
      [*Dressed like a fox hunter, drunk, knocking very loud and holloaing.*]

Shark. Haux, haux, haux, my honies heyhe! House, where the devil are you all?   242

Skin. Bless us, who is it knocks so?   [*Within.*

Lucy. The Lord knows Sir, some madman I believe—it is Shark I suppose.
                                            [*Aside.*

                          Enter Shark.

Shark. Hey house! Family! Where are you all?

Lucy. Who do you want Sir?

Shark. What's that to you, hussy? Where's Skinflint?

Lucy. Skinflint.

Shark. Ay, Skinflint.

Lucy. There is my master Sir Isaac Skinflint, Sir, in that great chair.

Shark. [*Going up to him, looking in his face and laughing.*] A damned odd sort of a figure: a cursed queer old fellow to look at. Is your name Skinflint?   253

Skin. It is, Sir.

Shark. Then give me your hand old boy.   [*Shakes him by the flannels.*

Skin. Hold, hold, Sir, you'll kill me if you ha'n't a care.

Shark. So much the better. The sooner you die the better for me.

Skin. For you! Pray Sir who are you?

Shark. Your nephew who has rid a hundred miles, on purpose to take possession of your estate.   260

Skin. Are you my nephew?

Shark. Yes Sir.

Skin. I am sorry for it.

Shark. My name is Bumper. My father, Sir Barnaby Bumper, took to wife a lady whom as I have been told was your sister; which said sister, Sir, brought me into the world, in less than four months after her marriage.

Skin. In four months.

Shark. Yes Sir. My father was a little displeased with it at first; but upon his being informed, that such forward births were frequent in your family, he was soon reconciled to it.   270

Skin. They belied our family Sir—for our family—

Shark. Hush! Hush! Don't expose them, they were always a damned whoring family. I must confess I have frequently blushed at the quickness of my mother's conception, for it has often been thrown in my teeth; but since it has made me your heir, that will set me above disgrace.

Skin. My heir!

Shark. Ay, your heir Sir, I am come to town on purpose to take possession. We had an account in the country that you were dead.

Skin. And I suppose you are not a little mortified, to find the report is false, ha?   280

Shark. Why, I am sorry to find you alive I must confess. I was in hopes to have found you stretched out, and ready for the black gentleman to say grace over you.

Skin. Sir, your servant.

Shark. May the strawberry mare knock up the next hard chase if I have not ridden as hard to be in at your earthing, as ever I did to be in at the death of a fox.

Skin. It was most affectionately done of you nephew, and I shall remember you for it.—A villain! I'll not leave him a groat.   [*Aside*.

Shark. However, since you are alive uncle, I am glad to see you look so ill.   291

Skin. I am very much obliged to you nephew. [*Aside to* Lucy.] Was there ever such a reprobate, Lucy?

Shark. They tell me you have a damned deal of money, that you have got by extortion, and usury and cheating of widows and orphans, to whom you have been guardian and executor, ha!—but I suppose you intend every grig of it for me, ha! Old boy, I'll let it fly, I'll release the yellow sinners from their iron prisons; they shall never be confined by me.

Skin. I believe you nephew.

Shark. But harkee you uncle, my sister is come to town too, and she thinks to come in for snacks—but not a grig—d'ye hear—not a grig—I must have every louse—Cousin Bellair too, that prig, I hear is looking out sharp—but if you leave a denier to any of them without my consent you shall be buried alive in one of your own iron chests, and sent as a present to your old friend Beelzebub.   305

Skin. To be sure nephew, you are so very dutiful and affectionate, that I shall be entirely directed by you. Lucy [*Aside to* Lucy.] I am afraid this villain is come to murder me, step and call Bellair this instant. [*Exit* Lucy.] Pray nephew, how long have you been in town?

Shark. I came to town late last night—and hearing you were alive, I was resolved I would not sleep, 'till I had seen you. So I went amongst the coffee houses at Covent Garden, where I made a charming riot. I fought a duel, beat the watch, kicked the bawds, broke their punch bowls, clapped an old market woman upon her head in the middle of a kennel, bullied a justice, and made all the whores as drunk—   315

Skin. As yourself, I suppose. Upon my word nephew, you have made good use of your time since you have been in town.

Shark. Ay, ha'n't I, old Skinflint? Zounds I love a riot, don't you love a riot uncle?

Skin. O most passionately.   320

Shark. Give me your hand. [*Slaps him upon the shoulder*.] Old boy, I love you for that.

Skin. O, O, O, O, he has killed me, I am murdered.

Shark. Rot your old crazy carcass, what do you cry out for, ha?

Skin. O, O, O, I can't bear to be touched.

Shark. O, O, O, damn you why don't you die then? Harkee uncle, how long do you intend to live? Ha! I'll allow you but three days, and if you don't die in that time, dead or alive I'll have you hanged, for I am resolved not to

296 grig] Farthing.   303 denier] A very tiny coin (one-twelfth of a sou).

stir out of town 'till I see that bag of bones of yours, that old rotten carcass, pailed up between four substantial elms, and laid twenty foot deep
in the earth, and then light lie the turf and flourish long bow, loll, loll,
de doll, ha! ha! Uncle I'll take care of your safe passage to Pluto, never
fear.   333

Skin. Had ever man such a reprobate relation? O the villain!

Enter Mr. Death.

Shark. O Mr. Death, your servant.

Death. I am come Sir, according to your command; pray which is the
gentleman I am to take the measure of?

Shark. That old prig, in the chair there.

Death. Sir, your humble servant.

Skin. Sir, your servant. What are your commands with me?   340

Death. Sir, my name is Death.

Skin. Death!

Death. Yes Sir, at your service, Dismal Death of —— pretty well known in
this city.

Skin. And pray, Mr. Dismal Death, what do you want with me?

Death. Sir, I am come to take measure of you for a coffin.

Skin. What! How!

Shark. Yes you old prig, I ordered him to take measure of you, and measure he shall take this instant. Do you hear, Mr. Death? Measure him,
measure the old prig, I'll hold him fast.   350

[Shark *lays hold of him while* Mr. Death *measures him.*

Skin. Are you going to murder me? You villain! Here Lucy, nephew,
murder! Murder!

Enter Lucy *and* Bellair.

Bell. How now, what's the matter? Are you going to rob my uncle?

Death. No, no, Sir, we are only taking measure of him for a coffin.

Skin. O nephew, they have almost killed me! Here is your cousin Bumper
come to take possession of my fortune whether I will or no; and has brought a
frightful fellow to take measure of me for a coffin and shroud, and swears he
will bury me within these three days dead or alive.

Bell. Are not you ashamed, cousin Bumper, to use our uncle so in-
humanly?   360

Shark. Damn you, prig, have you a mind to resent it? If you have, lug out,
and I'll soon dispatch you.   [*Draws.*

Skin. Was there ever such a bloody-minded villain? Dear nephew, come in
with me; I'll do his business for him in a more effectual way than fighting.

330 pailed] Probably for 'paled'.   361 lug out] Draw your sword.

I'll swear the peace against him and make my will, without leaving him a
shilling.   [*Exit with* Bellair.

Shark. So far the plow speeds. I think we have done Mr. Bumper's
business for him. That obstacle is pretty well removed—we have nothing to
do now but to provide for his sister the widow, and then to contrive some
means to frighten the old fellow into a will, in favour of my master.

Lucy. Ay Shark, that is the chiefest difficulty, the masterpiece, and unless
you accomplish that you do nothing.   372

Shark. I know it my dear; here, here [*Pointing to his head.*] here, here—
the embryo is here, and will come forth perfect in less than ten minutes.
Why, Lucy, I have a genius to deceit, and wanted nothing but an opportunity
to shew it.

Lucy. I think you have a very fair one now.

Shark. I have so, and never fear girl, I'll engage I make a proper use of it.
Lord, how many great men have been lost, for want of being thrown into a
proper light? On my conscience had I been bred in a court, I believe I
should have made as great a figure as ever Oliver Cromwell did. For

> The statesman's skill, like mine, is all deceit.   382
> What's policy in him—in me's a cheat.
> Titles and wealth reward his noble art,
> Cudgels and bruises mine—sometimes a cart.
> 'Twas, is, and will be, to the end of time,
> That poverty, not fraud, creates the crime.   [*Exeunt.*

ACT the 2nd.

Enter Bellair *and* Lucy.

Bell. What coach was that stopped at the door?

Lucy. My Lady Lovewealth's, Sir. I told her Miss Harriet was gone home,
and that my master was gone out in a chair to some of his lawyers, for I
could not let her see Sir Isaac.

Bell. You were right, Lucy. Where is Shark?

Lucy. In my room dressing for the widow.

Skinflint *within.*

Skin. Lucy, why Lucy, ugh, ugh, where are you wench?

365 swear the peace against him] Declare under legal oath that he is in bodily fear from
him, so that he may be sworn to keep the peace.   382–7] The entire verse passage has
been marked for exclusion by the censor.

Bell. I'll leave you with my uncle, Lucy, while I step up and hasten Shark.
[*Exit.*

Enter Skinflint.

Skin. Here Lucy, tie up my affairs. They are loose and falling about my
heels.   10

Lucy. They are always loose I think.

Skin. Lucy, did not I send for Monsieur du Maigre the apothecary?

Lucy. Yes Sir, and he will be here presently. [*Knocking.*] Hark, this is he I
suppose.

Skin. Go see; if it is, send him up. [*Exit* Lucy.] What an insupportable
vexation riches are. All my relations are watching and hovering about me,
like so many crows about a dead carrion; even Bellair, who behaves the best
of them all, has a hawk's eye, I see, after my will, and advises me in a sly
indirect manner to the making of it. A parent is used by an heir, just as a
virgin is by a rake: before we have parted with our treasure we are adored,
we are gods and goddesses, but as soon as that is over, we become as troublesome to them as an evil conscience. I'll keep my money to save my poor soul,
for to be sure I have got a great deal of it in an unfair manner; therefore in
order to make my peace hereafter, I'll leave it to build an almshouse.

Enter Lucy.

Lucy. Sir, there's a lady in deep mourning below, who says she is your
niece.   26

Skin. If she is such a canary bird as her brother that was here today, she
may go to the devil; however shew her up. [*Exit* Lucy.] She may be the
reverse of him; we ought not to condemn a whole family for one bad person.

Enter Lucy.
[*Showing in* Shark *who is dressed in weeds.*]

Lucy. Madam, this is your uncle.

Shark. Sir I have not the honour to be known to you, but the report of
your death has brought me to town, to testify the duty and affection, of an
unworthy niece for the best of uncles.

Skin. A good well-bred kind of woman. [*Aside to* Lucy.] Ay, this is something like a relation.

Lucy. I shall hear you sing another tune presently.   [*Aside.*

Skin. Pray niece give me leave to salute you, you are welcome to London.
[*Kisses him.*] My eyes are but bad—yet I think I can discover a strong
resemblance of my sister in you.   [*Peering in his face.*

Shark. Yes Sir, I was reckoned very like my mama, before I was married.
But frequent childbearing, you know Sir, will alter a woman strangely for the
worse.   42

Skin. It will so niece. You are a widow I perceive.

Shark. Yes Sir, an unfortunate widow. [*Weeps.*] I never had a dry eye since my husband died.

Skin. Pray niece, what did your husband die of?

Shark. He broke his neck a-fox-hunting.

Skin. Good lack, good lack, that was dreadful.

Shark. Ay Sir, and tho' I was but one and twenty when he died, he left me both a widow and a mother. So early a grief you may be sure must have robbed me of my bloom, and has broke me mightily.   51

Skin. As you were a widow, niece, at one and twenty, I don't suppose your husband left you many children.

Shark. Fifteen, Sir.

Skin. Fifteen, niece!   [*Starting.*

Shark. Ay fifteen Sir, I was married at fourteen.

Skin. That was very young, niece.

Shark. It was so Sir; but young girls can't keep nowadays, so I ran away with him from the boarding school. I had two children by him every ten months for six years, and I had three by him the seventh.   60

Skin. Upon my word you are a very good breeder.

Shark. Yes Sir, I was always accounted so. Besides Sir, I have had two by him since his death.

Skin. How Madam! Since his death?

Shark. Yes Sir, and I am afraid I shall have some more for, a word in your ear Sir—I find I am coming again Sir, you may feel if you please.

Skin. O fie niece, O fie, fie—why Lucy this woman is as bad as her brother.

Lucy. Indeed Sir, I am afraid so.   [*Aside.*

Skin. But I'll try her a little further; pray niece, who has been your companion and <u>bedfellow</u> for these two years past? For I presume you have not lain alone.   71

Shark. O Lord Sir, not for the world! You must know uncle, I am greatly addicted to be afraid of spirits, ghosts, witches, and fairies, and so to prevent terrifying dreams and apparitions <u>I took a religious gentleman, a very good man, to bed with me</u>—an itinerant Methodist, one Doctor Preach Field.

Skin. <u>Doctor Preach Field, I have heard of him.</u>

Shark. <u>O he's a very good man uncle I assure you, and very full of the spirit.</u>

Skin. Lucy, have not I got a hopeful parcel of relations?   [*Aside.*

Lucy. Indeed Sir, I think this lady is not extremely modest.   [*Aside.*

Skin. Why she ought to be whipped at the cart's tail. [*Aside.*] Pray niece, have not you a brother in town?   81

---

66 you may ... please] The clause is crossed out in the MS.   80 whipped at the cart's tail] Offenders against the law were tied to the back of a cart and whipped through the streets.

Shark. Yes Sir, he and I beat the watch last night at Tom King's.

Skin. O monstrous! Beat the watch, Madam!

Shark. Yes Sir, and broke all the lamps in the parish.

Skin. Very pretty employment for a lady truly, and so Madam you came to town merely to shew your duty and affection to me.

Shark. Yes Sir, and in hopes to be your heir; we had a report in the country that you was defunct, and I was in hopes to have found it true.

Skin. I am obliged to you Madam.

Shark. There is another thing we have very current in the country. I do not know how true it is.   91

Skin. What is it, I pray?

Shark. I have been told uncle, and from very good hands, that you are little better than a thief.

Skin. Madam!

Shark. And that you got all your fortune by biting and sharping, extortion, and cheating.

Skin. Harkee Madam, get out of my house this minute, or I will order somebody to throw you out of the window.

Shark. I have heard too, that for several years past, you have been an old fornicator, and that you have led a most wicked life with this girl.

Lucy. With me Madam!   102

Shark. Yes you naughty creature, and that your fornication would have had carnal symptoms, but that he took most unnatural methods to prevent your pregnancy.

Skin. Get out of my doors this minute.

Shark. Sir, you are an uncivil gentleman to bid me get out, but I find you are as great a rogue, as the most malicious report can make you.

Skin. Get out of my house I say.

Shark. Well, I'll go Sir, but depend upon it you shall not live many days after this. I'll be the death of you, if there are no more uncles in the world.

Lucy. Slip up the back stairs to my room and I'll come and undress you. [*Aside to him as she thrusts him off.*] Get you out you wicked woman, get you out.   [*Exit* Shark.

Skin. Was ever man so hope up with such a parcel of relations! Make them my heirs! I would as soon leave my money to a privateer's crew: and I verily believe they would be as thankful and make as good a use of it—I have been so worried and teased by them all, that I am not able to support any longer— I must go in and lie down, support me Lucy, or I shall fall, I am quite faint, oh, oh!   [*Exeunt.*

Enter Bellair.

82 Tom King's] The father of Tom King (1730–1805), actor and dramatist, kept a coffee house in London.   115 hope up with] i.e. made desperate by.

Bell. So! Thus far all goes well. Shark has been as successful in his widow as [in] his fox .We have routed the family of the Bumpers. There is nothing now to apprehend from that quarter. But the main difficulty is yet behind, which is to induce him to make his will, for without that my Lady Love-wealth's avarice never will consent to make my dearest Harriet mine.

Enter Lucy.

Lucy. O Sir, we are all undone!   126
Bell. Why what's the matter?
Lucy. Your uncle, Sir, is dead.
Bell. Dead!
Lucy. Ay, dead, Sir! Shark with his tricks and rogueries has so teazed him that having with much ado got into his chamber, down he fell upon the bed, and there he lies without either motion, voice, sense, pulse or understanding.
Bell. The very means I took to succeed have infallibly ruined me.

Enter Shark.

Shark. Is he gone? Is the coast clear?   134
Bell. So villain, your schemes and plots have a fine conclusion, rascal.
Shark. A fine conclusion, rascal! I don't know what conclusion they have, but I am sure it can't be worse than this reward. Pray Sir, what has happened?
Bell. Why you have killed my uncle, villain, and ruined me forever.
Shark. What! Is the old fellow dead?   140
Bell. Yes rascal, and without a will.
Shark. This is now an instance of the judgement and gratitude of mankind; if I had succeeded, I should have been a second Machiavel, and my dear Shark I shall be ever obliged to you—but now I am a rascal and a son of a whore, a blockhead and deserve my bones broke.
Bell. Well, Sir, no upbraiding now, but tell what is to be done.
Shark. What's to be done? What should be done Sir, break open his coffers, his cabinet, his strong box, seize upon his mortgage deeds, and writings, but above all take a particular care of the bank bills, and the ready cash. I have a great veneration for them, they will tell no tales to your fellow heirs, and as the old man has bit you, why do you plunder them. Do you take possession, and I'll engage I procure a lawyer who shall prove it to be something more than eleven points of the law.   153
Bell. But then my Harriet, Shark! Without her the wealth of Mexico is useless and insipid.
Shark. Upon my soul, Sir, begging your pardon, you make as ridiculous a figure in this business, as a disappointed lover in a play; why Sir, our farce is

123 yet behind] So MS. But the sense is clearly 'ahead'.

now in the very height of the plot, and it is impossible you can have your mistress till it be ended.

Bell. Nor then neither, I am afraid.   160

Shark. Lord Sir, you are too hasty. You are like the ignorant part of an audience the first night of a new play, you will have things brought about before their time. Go and take possession of the assets, I tell you, and leave the rest to the devil and the law. Get them on our side, and I'll engage you prosper in any roguery.

Bell. Well, I'll go—but I see no glimmering of hope from it.

                                                                    [*Exit* Bellair.

Shark. Lucy, do you shut up all the windows, and lock up the door.

Lucy. That's impossible, for Mr. Littlewit and Doctor Leatherhead are below with the marriage articles.

Shark. O the devil! Then we are all ruined again, hold—ha—ay—I have a thought. Lucy, do the lawyers know of the old man's death?   171

Lucy. Not a word. They are but this minute come in.

Shark. Then keep it an entire secret—I'll clinch the whole affair this instant—get me the old man's gown—and cap—his slippers, his pillow, his flannels and all his trumpery.

Lucy. Here they are, all upon the table where he shifted.

Shark. Give 'em me, quick—quick—ask no questions—so—now my cap—my gouty slippers. My flannels for my hands, here, here, pin them on, pin them on, quick—quick, so! And now my great chair—and now I am damnable ill.—O sick, sick,—auh-auh-auh! Go and tell my master how I am transmogrified, do you hear, and bid him not be surprised let what will happen, but first send up the lawyers.   [*Exit* Lucy.

Lawyers have often made false wills, for their own interests, and I see no reason now why they mayn't make one for mine. I am sure I have as good a title to be a rogue as any of them all, for my father was an Irish solicitor, my mother, a Yorkshire gypsy. I was begotten in Wales, born in Scotland, and brought up at that famous university St. Giles's Pound, and now he who has a better right to be a rogue than me, let him put in his claim. Tho' I believe nobody will dispute it with me, it is all my own today, when I come to Westminster Hall I'll resign.   190

                Enter Bellair, Lucy, Doctor Leatherhead, *and* Mr. Littlewit.
                         Pens, ink, paper, candles, etc.

Shark. So, gentlemen, when I sent for you in the morning I was foolish enough to think of marriage, but heaven pardon me, I must now think of death, of my poor precious soul, I must desire you to get my will ready as soon

176 shifted] Undressed.   187 St. Giles's Pound] Prison for debtors in St. Giles, a locality in London (west of the City) notorious for poverty and vice.

as possible; for I fear my poor fleeting life is not worth half an hour's purchase.

Doct. The sooner it is done, the better, it may procure you ease and consolation of mind.

Shark. Dear Doctor Leatherhead, hold your tongue; the less you talk, the more it will be to the purpose, I am sure. Nephew, draw near, Lucy take those candles out of my eyes, and shut that door.   200

Lucy. Sir, my Lady Lovewealth has sent her daughter to wait on you, and my Lady will be here herself immediately.

Shark. Very well, let my wife that was to be come up—and let her know how affairs are, Lucy. [*Aside to* Lucy.]   [*Exit* Lucy.

Little. [*At the table writing.*] Um, um, Sir Isaac Skinflint of the parish of um—sound sense—um weak in body—uncertainty of human life—um—last will and testament—now Sir we are ready; I have finished the preamble.

Doct. But Sir Isaac, should not this will be made in private? We always choose to have as few witnesses by as possible.

Shark. I believe you, Doctor Leatherhead: that they may produce the more lawsuits. Ay, ay, Doctor, I know the tricks of the law, the more grist, the more toll for the miller—but you shall not fill your bags out of my sack. You harpies, you cormorants, you devourers! O you bloodsuckers, auh! Auh!   214

Doct. I find Sir Isaac is still the same man.

Little. No matter Doctor, as it is the last business we shall do for him he shall pay swingingly.

Shark. I will make my will simple and plain, and before many witnesses.

Enter Harriet.

So, Harriet, you are come to see the last of the old man—well I forgive you your raillery today—come kiss me hussy or I'll disinherit you. [*Kisses her.*] You had better kiss me as a dying uncle, hussy, than a living husband, for I shall give you to my nephew.—And now, gentlemen of the black robe, who protect our properties for us: the first thing you are to do, is to fill up the blank in the marriage articles with my nephew's name instead of mine. For he I fancy, he will be much properer to manage the young lady's concerns than me. It is over with me, what think you Harriet? Don't you think he'll do it better than me, ha? Ah the young jade how she smiles, she knows what I mean; but gentlemen before I make my will, I have one thing to observe, which is, that I am a very whimsical old rogue! You all know that I believe.   230

Doct. Why you are a little whimsical, Sir Isaac sometimes, I know.

Shark. And therefore I desire a bond may immediately be prepared, for me to give my nephew, which will put it out of my power to revoke the will I shall now make in these presents, for I am so odd a fellow, that it is a hundred to one, I shall want to go from it tomorrow.

Doct. I am afraid, Sir Isaac, such a bond will not be good in law.

Little. O yes Doctor, very good. Doctor, you will hurt the practice with your scruples; what is it to us whether it be a good bond or not, it is a new case, and will be a bone of contention to us. The gown will get by it, let who will lose.   [*Aside to the* Doctor.

Doct. I believe Sir Isaac, upon second thoughts, it will be a good bond.   242

Shark. Then draw it up. And now gentlemen as to my will—*imprimis*, let all my debts be discharged.

Doct. That I believe Sir Isaac will be soon done; for I don't suppose you owe any.

Shark. Yes, I owe for the nursing of a bastard child at Windsor.

Doct. Is it possible you ever had a bastard?

Shark. Several Doctor, but they were all dropped upon different parishes, except that one. Then there are some few dribbling debts at alehouses and taverns where I used to meet my wenches—in all about twenty pounds.

Doct. I find, Mr. Littlewit, the old gentleman has been a cock of the game in his time. Good blood.   253

Little. Really Doctor Leatherhead I think so.

Shark. Item, I do constitute my nephew Bellair whole and sole executor of this my last will and testament.

Bell. O my dear uncle, shall I lose you?   [*Cries.*

Shark. Good-natured boy, how he weeps. Disinheriting and cutting off all other persons whatsoever—saving those hereafter mentioned.

Lucy. O my dear generous master.   [*Cries.*

Shark. Poor girl, she weeps too; I suppose for the same reason, to put me in mind of her. Never fear Lucy, I'll not forget you, you have been a good girl and managed my concerns with great skill and decency.   263

Doct. Proceed, Sir.

Shark. Unto Harriet Lovewealth my niece that shall be, I do give—(Lucy you know where they are) a set of diamond bracelets which were mortgaged to me, and forfeited by the Welsh lady, that used to game so much.

Lucy. I have them in this casket Sir.

Shark. Give them to me—there—I give them Harriet, but first kiss me hussy—I will have a kiss for them.   [*Kisses her and gives her the bracelet.*

Bell. Impudent rascal!   272

Shark. Item, to Lucy who for many years has served me faithfully—and who used to flatter me in all my little foibles.

Lucy. Sure never was so generous and grateful a master.   [*Cries.*

Shark. To her I bequeath, when she marries, one thousand pounds; provided it be with that honest lad Shark, not a farthing else.

Bell. How Sir, a thousand pounds! It is too much.

Shark. Not at all, nephew.

Bell. Here's a dog. [*Aside.*] Consider Sir, she's a low-bred poor person.

Shark. Poor is she? Why then Mr. Littlewit, if the girl is poor put her down another hundred, but with a proviso still that she marries Shark.

Bell. I presume Sir, you have done now.   283

Shark. Done! The gods of gratitude and generosity forbid, no I must remember poor Shark, I must not forget him—Item, to that honest fellow Shark, auh, auh!

Bell. O the rascal, he'll give half the estate to himself and Lucy.

Shark. To Shark I say, for his faithful services.

Bell. Why Sir he is the most idle, drunken—

Shark. Hold your tongue nephew, you are deceived in the young man— you don't know him so well as I, I have known him many years; he is a sober honest fellow, and has a great regard for you, and for that very reason, I leave him two hundred pounds per annum.   293

Bell. Two hundred pounds, Sir!

Shark. Pray be silent nephew, I know his virtues and good qualities, therefore, Mr. Littlewit, I think you may as well make it two hundred and fifty.

Bell. Sir! Per annum, Sir!

Shark. Ay per annum, for ten annums if I please Sir! Why sure I can do what I will with my own.   300

Bell. I beg your pardon Sir, it is a great deal too much I think.

Shark. I think not, and I believe at this juncture my thoughts are more to the purpose than yours.

Bell. But consider Sir, what can he do with so much money; such a low poor fellow that has no friends.

Shark. No friends?

Bell. No Sir, a low friendless fellow.

Shark. Nay if he is poor—set him down another hundred, Mr. Littlewit. He shall not want a friend while I am alive; for he is an honest lad, and loves a bottle and a wench as well as myself.   310

Bell. Was there ever such a tricking exorbitant rascal? [*Aside.*] Sir, I beg you'll alter that article, that relates to Shark.

Shark. Sir, I beg you'll hold your tongue. Say another word and I'll give him a thousand pounds per annum.

Bell. Sir, I humbly beg pardon.   [*Bowing very low.*

Shark. Well, beg pardon and be satisfied. I think you have reason—here I shall have you master of six or seven thousand pounds per annum (as you call it), and almost a plumb and a half in ready cole, and you are not satisfied. Say one word more, and I'll tear my will, or leave every shilling to the inhabitants of Bedlam or to the man that finds out the longitude.   320

Bell. I have done, Sir.

Shark. Pray then have done, Sir, and don't fret me.

Bell. An impudent rogue, but I must not contend with him now. [*Aside.*

Shark. Lord, it is as much trouble to give away an estate as to get it.

Doct. Mr. Bellair you should not interrupt the testator; at such a time his mind should not be disturbed.

Shark. You are in the right Doctor Leatherhead. Let me see, have I no friend that I care to oblige with two or three thousand—I am in such a generous temper that I don't care to leave off yet. I have a great mind to give Shark a handful over. But—   330

Bell. Sir.

Shark. No, I believe I have done.

Doct. Will you please to sign then?

Shark. That I would with all my heart, but that the gout and palsy prevent me.

Doct. Then we must observe, Mr. Littlewit, that the said testator does declare his inability to write.

Shark. Is the bond to my nephew ready?

Little. Yes Sir.

[*Shark.*] But is it strong, and so well drawn, that Old Nick himself should he turn pettifogger could not reverse it?   341

Doct. It is Sir.

Shark. Very well.

Doct. There, if you please to make your mark by touching the pen. [*Shark touches the pen.*] So, and put the watch over his hand, and let him take off the seal—so very well, Sir, you publish and declare this to be your last will and testament, and desire Doctor Leatherhead and Mr. Littlewit to be witnesses thereunto.

Shark. I do.

                    [*All the ceremony of signing, sealing, and delivering is performed.*
Doct. Very well, Sir Isaac, I will take care they shall be properly registered.

Shark. I beg good folks that you will step into the next room for a few moments, while I compose myself after this intolerable fatigue. Nephew pray shew them in, and do the honours of my house in the genteelest manner.

Bell. I shall Sir,—Doctor Leatherhead, Mr. Littlewit—will you walk in gentlemen?   355

318 a plumb and a half in ready cole] Cole is cash. A plumb is £100,000 or, more loosely, a large fortune.   340 [*Shark*]] MS.: *Skin.*   345 watch] For 'watch-seal', an ornamental trinket holding the seal and attached to the watch chain.

Doct. Sir your servant, Sir.

Little. Yours, we wish you better.

Shark. Your servant, your servant gentlemen, auh, auh—quick, quick. [*Coughs.*]   [*Exeunt all but* Lucy *and* Shark.

Lucy, off with my roguery, and let me appear in my native honesty. I have had gibbets and halters in my mind, a hundred times, passing and repassing since I begun this business. I am horribly afraid that the devil and Sir Isaac, for I suppose they are met by this time, will contrive some means to counterplot us. Tho' I think I shall be a match for them, if we can keep the law on our side; let me but secure that and I defy the devil and all his works. There, there they are, the precious robes of deceit. [*Throws down the old man's gown and cap.*] I think there has been transacted as ingenious a scene of iniquity, in that gown, within the short space of half an hour, as in any gown that has been traipsed into Westminster Hall, since the ingenious Mr. Wreathcock was transported—now my dear Lucy, after all this fatigue and bustle, [*Throws down the old man's dress.*] I think it would not be amiss for you and I to retire and solace ourselves, in the lawful state of procreation.   371

Lucy. Time enough fool, consider matrimony is a long journey.

Shark. True Lucy, therefore the sooner we set out the better; for love, my dear, like time, must be taken by the forelock.

Lucy. Come, come, this is no time for prating and fooling. Do you join the company to avoid suspicion, and tomorrow morning, put me in mind of it, if I am in humour, I may perhaps walk towards Doctors' Commons, and venture at a great leap in the dark with you, for so I think marriage may be justly called.

Shark. Why ay, this is speaking like one that has a mind to deal. Here's my hand, it shall stand on my side.   381

Lucy. And here's my hand. If I can help it, it shall not fail on mine.

Shark. Touch—buss—I like the sample, and am resolved to purchase the whole commodity.   [*Exit* Shark.

Monsieur du Maigre *within.*

Maigre. Mistress Lucy! Mistress Lucy! Why you no come, when your maitre Janie be so very much bad—where be you?

Lucy. Who have we here? Our apothecary Monsieur du Maigre! Pray heaven the old man is not come to life again.

Enter Monsieur du Maigre.

Maigre. O maistress Lucy for shame! Pardie why you no come to your maitre? He be dead this one half quartre de hour, and you no come. By gar he want a his gown and his cap.   391

Lucy. What, is he alive?

Maigre. Yes; he was dead, but I bring him to life, I bleed a him, and so he comes from the dead man to de life. But come come, allon[s], vite, vite, he want a de gown.   [*Takes up the gown and cap.*

Lucy. So, we have been making a will to a fine purpose.

Maigre. Allons, vite, vite, Maistress Lucy, he be very bad indeed—and he want a you ver much, allons.   [*Exeunt.*

Enter Bellair *and* Shark.

Shark. Well Sir, now who is the fool? The blockhead? Did not I tell you, we should succeed?   400

Bell. Yes, but scoundrel how did you dare to make such a will?

Shark. In what respect, Sir?

Bell. In what, rascal! To Lucy and yourself! How dare you leave so much money between you?

Shark. For the best reason in the world Sir, because I knew nobody dared to contradict me. And had I thought you would have been angry at it—I assure you Sir—I should have left as much more. Why Sir, if you will consider the affair impartially, you will find I had a right to be co-heir with you.

Bell. How so, Sir?   410

Shark. By the laws of roguery, Sir—in which it is a fundamental maxim, that in cheats of this kind all people are upon a par, and have a right to an equal snack.

Bell. Impudent rascal!

Shark. But if you think Sir, that I have behaved in this affair selfishly or unbecoming a rogue of honour, I will send in for Doctor Leatherhead and Mr. Littlewit, for they are still in the next room, and cancel the will directly.

Bell. No rascal, you know my love to Harriet will not let me consent to that.

Shark. This is just the way of the great world—the poor rogues are the men of parts and do all the business—and the rich ones not only arrogate the merit to themselves, but are for running away with all the plunder.

Enter Lucy.

Lucy. O Sir!   422

Bell. What's the matter?

Lucy. Oh! Oh! Oh! I can't speak—but your uncle's alive—that's all.
                                                       [*Sits down in a great chair.*

Shark. And that's enough to hang me, I'm sure.

Bell. Alive!

Lucy. Ay, alive Sir.

Shark. This comes of your begrudging me my snack of the spoil, Sir.

Bell. Why I thought you saw him senseless and dead.

Lucy. I thought so too; but it seems while we were about the will Monsieur du Maigre the apothecary came in and bled him in an instant, which has unfortunately—recovered him. He is within with him now, and one Counsellor Cormorant who is come upon some law business to him—O here they all come.   434

Bell. What a malicious turn of fortune this is.

Shark. Why, Sir, if you will not be ungrateful, now I believe I can secure a retreat, and such a one as the greatest general in Europe in our situation would not be ashamed of.

Bell. Dear Shark, I will do anything thou wilt.

Shark. Ay, now it is dear Shark, but know Sir, you have to deal with an Englishman, and a man of honour who scorns to put an enemy to death when he begs for quarter—tho' you have been an ungenerous ally, as ever vowed fidelity to the crown of England.—But no matter, I'll serve you still and completely.   444

Bell. But how, dear Shark?

Shark. I won't tell you—and I defy you to guess now—or anybody else that's more.—I must step into the next room for a moment, and whisper the lawyers, and in the meantime do you persist in your uncle's having made a will. That's all—don't you be like an ignorant thief before a noisy magistrate, confess and hang yourself. And you Madam, do you embronze your countenance, and keep up your character to the last.   [*Exeunt.*

Enter Skinflint *supported by* Counsellor Cormorant *and*
Monsieur du Maigre, Lucy *settling his great chair.*

Skin. Auh! Auh! Gently, gently, set me down gently pray, oh, oh, oh. [*Sits down.*] O nephew, how could you let me lie for dead so long, and never come near me?   454

Bell. Really Sir, I never heard a word that you were in any danger of dying.

Skin. And Lucy, how could you be so cruel to neglect me so long?

Lucy. Me! Lord Sir, I never knew anything of it 'till Monsieur du Maigre informed me.

Maigre. No, pardie, she not have any knowledge 'till dat me make her de intelligence.   461

Lucy. I thought you were in a sound sleep Sir, and was extremely glad of it.

Bell. And so was I, I do assure you Sir.

Skin. I am obliged to you nephew, but I had like to have slept my last.

Maigre. It is very true indeed upon my word. But dat Monsieur la avocat—here—Monsieur la what is your name s'il vous plait—I always forget.

450 embronze your countenance] Brazen it out, keep a straight face.   466 s'il vous plait]
MS.: 'si vous plais'.

Cor. Cormorant, Sir.

Maigre. Mais oui, Monsieur la Cormorant—but dat he and I come in together, just after one another, I believe I come in one, two minute before you Monsieur la Cormorant—I say but dat me come in the nick upon a my word Sir Isaac you be defunct—and then I lose my annuity upon your life, and by gar dat be very bad for Monsieur du Maigre.   472

Skin. I am obliged to you Monsieur—are the lawyers come Lucy? Mr. Littlewit and Doctor Leatherhead.

Lucy. Yes Sir, they have been here a considerable time.

Skin. Desire them to walk in.

Lucy. So now the murder's coming out.   [*Exit* Lucy.

Skin. Nephew, I am at last resolved to make my will; I shall make a proper provision for you in it. But as our soul is the immortal part of us, and most liable to be hurt, I must take care of that the first thing I do. Therefore I am resolved to appropriate so much of my fortune as will be sufficient for that purpose, to the building of an alms house.   482

Enter Doctor Leatherhead, Mr. Littlewit, Lady Lovewealth,
Shark *and* Lucy.

Skin. So gentlemen! I have altered my mind, Mr. Littlewit, since I saw you last.

Little. Concerning what, Sir?

Skin. My will. Sir.

Little. It is now too late Sir, you have put it out of your power.

Skin. Out of my power?

Doct. Ay, and out of the power of Westminster Hall! Sir Isaac, you know I gave you my opinion upon it before you made it.   490

Skin. What, is the man mad?

Doct. No Sir, I am not mad; and I would advise you not to be foolish and whimsical, as you owned about half an hour since you were subject to.

Skin. Why the men are drunk or mad, I think.

Maigre. Pardie somebody be drunk or mad among you, for by gar me no understand your vards.

Skin. Why gentlemen, I sent for you to make my will.

Doct. You did so Sir, and you have made it, and it is registered. And there is the copy. Ask your nephew, and these ladies and your maid Lucy, and the footman here.   500

Shark. No pray Sir, don't bring me into it. I was not here.

Doct. You are right, friend. I believe you were not here, but ask all the rest.

Skin. Nephew, do you know anything of all this?

Bell. Upon my word Sir, what the doctor says is true.

Skin. How! True Lucy?

Lucy. Indeed Sir, you did make a will before you had your fit, but you have forgot it I suppose.

Skin. Why this is all a contrivance, a conspiracy, a—pray when did I make this will?   510

Doct. Why Sir, it is not ten minutes since you signed it, and all these are witnesses.   [*Pointing on their own side of the room.*

Shark. No pray Sir, leave me out, I will be sworn in any court in Westminster, Sir Isaac, that I know nothing of the matter.

Maigre. By gar this Doctor Leatherhead be one ver great fripon—harkee Sir, you say he make de signature to the will in these ten a minute.

Doct. Yes Sir.

Maigre. By gar dat cannot be, fo' Monsieur la Cormorant and my self be vid him above thirteen, and he make no will in that time, Jarnie blue.

Cor. It is very true gentlemen; that we can attest.   520

Skin. Pray Doctor, let me see this will; read it if you please.

Doct. Sir Isaac Skinflint being seated in his great chair—um underwritten —sound senses tho' infirm in body.

Skin. No matter for the preamble.

Doct. Um, um, um, committed to writing his underwritten will, in manner and form following. *Imprimis*, I will that all my debts be paid.

Skin. Debts? I do not owe one shilling in the world.

Doct. You forget Sir Isaac, you owe for the nursing of a bastard child at Windsor, and several little dribbling debts where you used to meet your wenches.   530

Skin. How, a bastard! Why I never had a bastard in my life—but once— and that was forty years ago, with a great red hair wench, a maid that my father had—but it was when I was a lad and did not know what I was about.

Doct. Item, I do constitute my nephew Bellair whole and sole executor, disinheriting and cutting off all other persons.

Skin. This is all a scene of villainy.

Doct. Saving those hereafter mentioned—unto Harriet Lovewealth my niece that shall be, I do bequeath the set of diamond bracelets—mortgaged by the—

Skin. This is all a robbery.   540

Cor. Let 'em go on Sir Isaac, you have your remedy.

Skin. This is all a robbery.

Doct. To my maid Lucy, one thousand pounds.

Skin. O monstrous, I never intended to give her a farthing.

Doct. Item, to that honest fellow Slipstring Shark.

515 fripon] Rogue.   519 Jarnie blue] Corruption of a French oath, '*jarni Dieu*' ('*je renie Dieu*'), equivalent to 'zounds' or ''sdeath'.

Shark. That is me, Sir Isaac, and I humbly thank your honour.

Doct. I bequeath him three hundred pounds per annum during his natural life, to be paid out of what part of my estate he shall think proper.

Shark. O blessings on your generous heart! It was always fond of rewarding merit.   550

Skin. Read no more—I'll have you every one indicted for forgery—and conspiracy and—first take notice, Counsellor Cormorant and Monsieur du Maigre, that I deny that will to be any act of mine—and that I cancel it to all intents and purposes.

Doct. That you can't do Sir—for by way of marriage articles between Bellair and Harriet Lovewealth you have signed a deed conformable to this will.

Skin. Why this is such a piece of villainy as the records of Westminster Hall cannot match.

Cor. Do not be uneasy Sir Isaac, you have one, and one certain way of oversetting all their villainy; and that is by confessing that you made this will, and proving that you were out of your senses when you did it, which may easily be done by proper witnesses. [*Aside.*]   563

Skin. I'll confess that or anything—to get my money again, and to hang them—Doctor Leatherhead, I begin now to remember something of the making of this will.—But I can prove I was light-headed, and out of my senses when I did it.

Doct. Sir Isaac it is no affair of mine—it is your nephew's concern. If he is willing to let such chicane pass upon him he may, but if he has a mind to insist upon the will, I'll undertake to prove you were in your senses as perfectly as ever you were in your life.   571

Skin. And will you insist, nephew?

Bell. It is not in my power to be off it Sir, for in consequence that you were sincere when you made this will, my Lady Lovewealth here has given me her daughter, and her own chaplain has just now put the finishing hand to the business, in the next room, before all these witnesses.

Skin. So you won't resign.

Bell. I can't, Sir.

Skin. Come along Mr. Cormorant, I'll hamper them all—I'll prove myself out of my senses before I sleep.   [*Exit* Skinflint *and* Cormorant.

Maigre. By gar dis be all ver great, much surprise upon me, van, pardie, pardie make the man make a de vill veder he will or no, and de man say he will prove dat he be lunatic and lightheaded—by gar, me never heard de like in France, pardie, etc., etc.   [*Exit.*

Shark. Well, I believe this affair is over for tonight; and upon my word, I am heartily glad of it, for I have been in very sweating circumstances ever since it began, but especially since Sir Isaac came to life. I was afraid that single incident would have damned our whole intrigue, but thanks to the gentlemen of the gown, I now begin to have some hopes we shall succeed. I have done my master's business completely, and as executors go, I do not think that I have been too partial to myself—I believe there are several honest gentlemen who walk the 'Change, and go to church constantly, would have thought they acted very generously if they had given Bellair even an equal dividend—but I beg pardon—you are to judge, not I, and unless you approve the deed I shall renounce my share of the legacy.

> For should our will in Westminster be tried,   596
> The right, I fear, would fall on t'other side.
> Here you are absolute: confirm my cause.
> If you approve—a fig for courts and laws.

FINIS

MISS IN HER TEENS

David Garrick

1717–1779

David Garrick, the 'English Roscius', was Samuel Johnson's star pupil in the grammar school at Lichfield, but even before master and pupil walked up to London together in 1737, Garrick had acquired a love of the stage from strolling players. Though he dabbled in law school and the wine trade in the city, he moved steadily towards a theatrical career. In 1740 his first play, *Lethe*, was produced, and soon after he began to appear on the stage incognito. Rejected at first by the major theatres, he acted at Goodman's Fields (drawing huge crowds and impressing even old Alexander Pope) and in Ireland; his revolutionary naturalistic style, fostered and encouraged by Charles Macklin, moved the old-school actor James Quin to remark: 'We are all wrong if this is right.' He acted in London and Dublin with growing success until, in 1747, he could purchase half the patent of Drury Lane Theatre, which he managed up to his retirement in 1776, without ceasing to write and act. His ultimate prestige is suggested by the attendance at his funeral of Sheridan, Fox, Burke, and Johnson.

Garrick was less important as a dramatist than as an actor or manager. Most of his thirty-odd plays were hasty trifles or alterations, but he stood out as the greatest actor in an age of brilliant acting. 'His face was a language,' said a deaf admirer. And as manager for three decades of England's most prestigious theatre he became the unofficial arbiter of national dramatic fare; the Laureate, William Whitehead, wrote to him: 'A nation's taste depends on you.' For the most part Garrick used his influence to support English classics and contemporary authors against French plays and vaudeville spectaculars, although he was forced by his public to grave concessions on these points.

An exception to the general negligibility of Garrick's dramatic writing is his adaptation of D'Ancourt's *La Parisienne*, *Miss in Her Teens*, which inaugurated the genre of the English short comedy (or *petite pièce*, or *petite comédie*—the type being well known in France). Garrick had written a sentimentalized but essentially comic afterpiece, *The Lying Valet*, in 1741, and its popularity was not lost on him. The formula sketched there and elaborated in *Miss in Her Teens*—a truncated comedy plus satiric farce—recurs dozens of times in the eighteenth century after 1747. The manifesto-like prologue reveals that Garrick was fully conscious of his pioneering role. The play was an immediate and lasting success. Opening at Covent Garden Theatre on 17 January 1747, it had 41 performances at five London theatres during its first season, and more than 250 performances during Garrick's stage career.

Historical interest apart, the play is slight but pleasant. Most of the characters are types who were already drawing laughs on the Roman stage, and those of Fribble (one of Garrick's most popular roles) and Flash were praised throughout the century as 'eminently comic'. The exposure and defeat of these two timeless butts, and of that equally ancient obstacle to young love, the *senex amans* Sir Simon, occupy almost the entire second half of the play. By the beginning of Act II most of the important plot-action has been resolved; thenceforth playwright and audience concentrate on the ridicule of impostors (this early lowering of comic tension is typical of Garrick's work). If 'dark comedy' is the prolongation of serious or tragic possibilities until very near the end, then there could be no 'lighter' comedy than *Miss in Her Teens*.

The text is based on the first edition, 1747.

MISS *in her* TEENS:

OR, THE

MEDLEY of LOVERS.

A

FARCE.

IN TWO ACTS.

As it is Perform'd at the

THEATRE-ROYAL in *Covent-Garden.*

LONDON:

Printed for J. and R. TONSON and S. DRAPER
in the *Strand.* 1747.

[Price One Shilling.]

D

ADVERTISEMENT.

The Author takes this Opportunity to return the Publick his Thanks for their so favourable Reception of the following Trifle; the Hint of which is taken from the *French*. Whether the Plot and Characters are alter'd for the better or worse, may be seen by comparing it with *La Parisienne* of *D'Ancourt*.

PROLOGUE.

WRITTEN by a FRIEND.

Too long has Farce, neglecting Nature's Laws,
Debas'd the Stage, and wrong'd the Comic Cause;
To raise a Laugh has been her sole Pretence,
Tho' dearly purchas'd at the Price of Sense;
This Child of Folly gain'd Increase with Time;
Fit for the Place, succeeded Pantomime*;*
Reviv'd her Honours, join'd her motley Band,
And Song, and low Conceit, o'erran the Land.

  More gen'rous Views inform our Author's Breast,
From real Life his Characters are drest;   10
He seeks to trace the Passions of Mankind,
And while he spares the Person, paints the Mind.
In pleasing Contrast he attempts to shew
The vap'ring Bully, and the frib'ling Beau,
Cowards alike, that full of Martial Airs,
And this as tender as the Silk he wears.

  Proud to divert, not anxious for Renown,
Oft has the Bard essay'd to please the Town,
Your full Applause out-paid his little Art,
He boasts no Merit, but a grateful Heart;   20
Pronounce your Doom, he'll patiently submit,
Ye sovereign Judges of all Works of Wit!
To you the Ore is brought, a lifeless Mass,
You give the Stamp, and then the Coin may pass.

  Now whether Judgment prompt you to forgive,
Whether you bid this trifling Offspring live,
Or with a Frown should send the sickly Thing,
To sleep whole Ages under Dulness' Wing;
To your known Candour we will always trust,
You never were, nor can you be unjust.   30

Dramatis Personæ

MEN

SIR Simon Loveit   Mr. Hippisly
Captain Loveit   Mr. Havard
Fribble   Mr. Garrick
Flash   Mr. Woodward
Puff   Mr. Chapman
Jasper   Mr. Arthur

WOMEN

Miss Biddy   Miss Hippisly
Aunt   Mrs. Martin
Tag   Mrs. Pritchard

Miss in Her Teens

ACT I. SCENE I.

SCENE, *A street.*

Enter Captain Loveit *and* Puff.

Capt. This was the place we were directed to; and now, Puff, if I can get no intelligence of her, what will become of me?

Puff. And me too, Sir.—You must consider I am a married man, and can't bear fatigue as I have done.—But pray, Sir, why did you leave the Army so abruptly, and not give me time to fill my knapsack with common necessaries? Half a dozen shirts, and your regimentals, are my whole cargo.

Capt. I was wild to get away, and as soon as I obtained my leave of absence, I thought every moment an age till I returned to the place where I first saw this young, charming, innocent, bewitching creature—

Puff. With fifteen thousand pounds for her fortune—strong motives, I must confess.—And now, Sir, as you are pleased to say you must depend upon my care and abilities in this affair, I think I have a just right to be acquainted with the particulars of your passion, that I may be the better enabled to serve you. 14

Capt. You shall have 'em.—When I left the University, which is now seven months since, my father, who loves his money better than his son, and would not settle a farthing upon me—

Puff. Mine did so by me, Sir.

Capt. Purchased me a pair of colours at my own request; but before I joined the regiment, which was going abroad, I took a ramble into the country with a fellow-collegian, to see a relation of his who lived in Berkshire—

Puff.—A party of pleasure, I suppose. 22

Capt. During a short stay there, I came acquainted with this young creature; she was just come from the boarding-school, and though she had all the simplicity of her age and the country, yet it was mixed with such sensible vivacity, that I took fire at once—

Puff. I was tinder myself at that age. But pray, Sir, did you take fire before you knew of her fortune?

Capt. Before, upon my honour.

Puff. Folly and constitution—but on, Sir. 30

Capt. I was introduced to the family by the name of *Rhodophil* (for so my companion and I had settled it); at the end of three weeks I was obliged to attend the call of honour in Flanders.

Puff. Your parting, to be sure, was heart-breaking.

Capt. I feel it at this instant.—We vowed eternal constancy, and I promised to take the first opportunity of returning to her: I did so, but we found the house shut up, and all the information, you know, that we could get from the neighbouring cottage was, that Miss and her aunt were removed to town, and lived somewhere near this part of it.

Puff. And now we are got to the place of action, propose your plan of operation.   41

Capt. My father lives but in the next street, so I must decamp immediately for fear of discoveries; you are not known to be my servant, so make what inquiries you can in the neighbourhood, and I shall wait at the inn for your intelligence.

Puff. I'll patrol hereabouts, and examine all that pass; but I've forgot the word, Sir—Miss Biddy—

Capt. Bellair—

Puff. A young lady of wit, beauty, and fifteen thousand pounds fortune—but, Sir—   50

Capt. What do you say, Puff?

Puff. If Your Honour pleases to consider that I had a wife in town whom I left somewhat abruptly half a year ago, you'll think it, I believe, but decent, to make some enquiry after her first; to be sure it would be some small consolation to me to know whether the poor woman is living, or has made away with herself, or—

Capt. Pr'ythee don't distract me; a moment's delay is of the utmost consequence; I must insist upon an immediate compliance with my commands.

                                       [*Exit* Captain.

Puff. The Devil's in these fiery young fellows! They think of nobody's wants but their own. He does not consider that I am flesh and blood as well as himself. However, I may kill two birds at once; for I shan't be surprised if I meet my lady walking the streets—but who have we here? Sure I should know that face?   63

Enter Jasper *from a house.*

Puff. Who's that? My old acquaintance, Jasper?

Jasper. What, Puff! Are you here?

Puff. My dear friend! [*Kisses him.*] Well, and how Jasper! Still easy and happy! *Toujours le même!*—What intrigues now? What girls have you ruined, and what cuckolds made, since you and I used to beat up together, eh?

Jasper. Faith, business has been very brisk during the war; men are scarce, you know; not as I can say I ever wanted amusement in the worst of times.— But harkye, Puff—   72

Puff. Not a word aloud, I am incognito.

Jasper. Why faith, I should not have known you, if you had not spoke first; you seem to be a little *dishabille* too, as well as incognito. Who do you honour with your service now? Are you from the wars?

Puff. Piping hot, I assure you; fire and smoke will tarnish, Jasper; a man that will go into such service as I have been in, will find his clothes the worse for wear, take my word for it: but how is it with you? [*Salutes him.*] What, you still serve, I see? You live at that house, I suppose?   81

Jasper. I don't absolutely live, but I am most of my time there; I have within these two months entered into the service of an old gentleman, who hired a reputable servant, and dressed him as you see, because he has taken it into his head to fall in love.

Puff. False appetite and second childhood! But pr'ythee, what's the object of his passion?

Jasper. No less than a virgin of sixteen, I assure you.

Puff. Oh, the toothless old dotard!

Jasper. And he mumbles and plays with her till his mouth waters; then he chuckles till he cries, and calls it his *Bid*, and his *Bidsy*, and is so foolishly fond—   92

Puff. Bidsy! What's that?—

Jasper.—Her name is *Biddy*.

Puff. Biddy! What, Miss *Biddy Bellair*?

Jasper.—The same.—

Puff. I have no luck, to be sure. [*Aside.*]—Oh! I have heard of her; she's of a pretty good family, and has some fortune, I know. But are things settled? Is the marriage fixed?

Jasper. Not absolutely; the girl, I believe, detests him; but her aunt, a very good prudent old lady, has given her consent, if he can gain her niece's; how it will end I can't tell—but I am hot upon't myself.   102

Puff.—The devil! Not marriage, I hope.

Jasper. That is not yet determined.

Puff. Who is the lady, pray?

Jasper. A maid in the same family, a woman of honour, I assure you. She has one husband already, a scoundrel sort of a fellow that has run away from her, and listed for a soldier; so towards the end of the campaign she hopes to

---

70 the war] Of the Austrian Succession, which England entered in 1743; it terminated in the Treaty of Aix-la-Chapelle (1748). 75 *dishabille*] Negligently dressed, unkempt. Probably pronounced 'dish-uh-bill'.

have a certificate he's knocked o' th' head. If not, I suppose, we shall settle
matters another way.   110

Puff. Well, speed the plough.—But harkye, consummate without the certificate if you can—keep your neck out of the collar—do—I have wore it
these two years, and damnably galled I am.—

Jasper. I'll take your advice; but I must run away to my master, who will be
impatient for an answer to his message which I have just delivered to the
young lady; so, dear Mr. Puff, I am your most obedient humble servant.

Puff. And I must to our agent's for my arrears. If you have an hour to spare,
you'll hear of me at George's or the Tilt-Yard.—*Au revoir*, as we say abroad.
[*Exit* Jasper.] Thus we are as civil and as false as our betters; Jasper and I
were always the *Beau Monde* exactly; we ever hated one another heartily, yet
always kiss, and shake hands.—But now to my master, with a head full of
news, and a heart full of joy!   [*Going, starts.*
      Angels, and Ministers of Grace, defend me!
It can't be! By heavens, it is, that fretful porcupine, my wife! I can't stand it;
what shall I do? I'll try to avoid her.   125

                            Enter Tag.

Tag. It must be him! I'll swear to the rogue at a mile's distance; he either has
not seen me, or won't know me; if I can keep my temper I'll try him farther.

Puff. I sweat—I tremble—She comes upon me!

Tag. Pray, good sir, if I may be so bold—

Puff. I have nothing for you, good woman, don't trouble me.

Tag. If Your Honour pleases to look this way—   131

Puff. The kingdom is over-run with beggars; I suppose the last I gave to
has sent this, but I have no more loose silver about me, so pr'ythee, woman,
don't disturb me.

Tag. I can hold no longer; oh you villain, you! Where have you been,
scoundrel? Do you know me now, varlet?   [*Seizes him.*

Puff. Here Watch, Watch,—Zounds, I shall have my pockets picked.

Tag. Own me this minute, hang-dog, and confess everything, or by the
rage of an injured woman, I'll raise the neighbourhood, throttle you, and
send you to Newgate.   140

Puff. Amazement! What, my own dear Tag! Come to my arms, and let me
press you to my heart, that pants for thee, and only thee, my true and lawful
wife.—Now my stars have over-paid me for the fatigue and dangers of the
field; I have wandered about like Achilles in search of faithful Penelope, and
the gods have brought me to this happy spot.

---

    118 the Tilt-Yard] A tilting-ground at the old Royal Palace at Whitehall.   123 *Angels...
defend me!*] An incantation to ward off evil spirits. Cf. *Hamlet*, I. iv. 39.   144 Achilles]
Confused for Ulysses.

Tag. The fellow's cracked for certain. Leave your bombastic stuff, and tell me, rascal, why you left me, and where you have been these six months, heh?

Puff. We'll reserve my adventures for our happy winter evenings—And shall only tell you now, that my heart beat so strong in my country's cause, and being instigated either by honour or the devil (I can't tell which), I set out for Flanders, to gather laurels, and lay 'em at thy feet.   151

Tag. You left me to starve, villain, and beg my bread, you did so.

Puff. I left you too hastily I must confess, and often has my conscience stung me for it.—I am got into an officer's service, have been in several actions, gained some credit by my behaviour, and am now returned with my master, to indulge the gentler passions.

Tag. Don't think to fob me off with this nonsensical talk; what have you brought me home beside?

Puff. Honour, and immoderate love.

Tag. I could tear your eyes out.   160

Puff. Temperance, or I walk off.

Tag. Temperance, traitor, temperance! What can you say for yourself? Leave me to the wide world—

Puff. Well, I have been in the wide world too, han't I? What would the women have?

Tag. Reduce me to the necessity of going to service.   [*Cries.*

Puff. Why, I'm in service too, your lord and master, an't I, you saucy jade, you?—Come, where dost live, hereabouts? Hast got good vails? Dost go to market? Come, give me a kiss, darling, and tell me where I shall pay my duty to thee.   170

Tag. Why, there I live, at that house.

[*Pointing to the house* Jasper *came out of.*

Puff. What, there! That house?

Tag. Yes, there, that house.

Puff. Huzza! We're made for ever, you slut, you! Huzza! Everything conspires this day to make me happy—Prepare for an inundation of joy! My master is in love with your Miss Biddy over head and ears, and she with him: I know she is courted by some old fumbler, and her aunt is not against the match; but now we are come the town will be relieved, and the governor brought over; in plain English, our fortune is made; my master must marry the lady, and the old gentleman may go to the devil.   180

Tag. Heyday! What is all this?

Puff. Say no more, the dice are thrown, doublets for us; away to your young mistress, tell her Rhodophil will be with her immediately; then if her blood does not mount to her face like quicksilver in a weather-glass, and point to extreme hot, believe the whole a lie, and your husband no politician.

168 vails] Servants' perquisites, 'tips'.   184 weather-glass] A thermometer or barometer.

Tag. This is news, indeed! I have had the place but a little while, and have not quite got into the secrets of the family; but part of your story is true, and if you'll bring your master, and Miss is willing, I warrant we'll be too hard for the old folks.

Puff. I'll about it straight;—but hold, Tag, I had forgot.—Pray how does Mr. Jasper do?   191

Tag. Mr. Jasper!—What do you mean? I—I—I—

Puff. What, out of countenance, child! Oh fie! Speak plain, my dear.—And the certificate, when comes that, heh, love?

Tag. He has sold himself and turned conjurer, or he could never have known it.   [*Aside.*

Puff. Are not you a jade?—Are not you a Jezebel?—Aren't you a—

Tag. O ho, temperance! Or I walk off—

Puff. I know I am not finished yet, and so I am easy; but more thanks to my fortune than your virtue, Madam.   200

Aunt. [*Within.*] Tag, Tag, where are you, Tag?

Tag. Coming, Madam.—My old lady calls; away, to your master, and I'll prepare his reception within.

Puff. Shall I bring the certificate with me?   [*Exit.*

Tag. Go, you graceless rogue, you richly deserve it.   [*Exit.*

[SCENE II.] SCENE *changes to a chamber.*

Enter Aunt *and* Tag.

Aunt. Who was that man you were talking to, Tag?

Tag. A cousin of mine, Madam, that brought me some news from my aunt in the country.

Aunt. Where's my niece? Why are you not with her?

Tag. She bid me leave her alone—she's so melancholy, Madam, I don't know what's come to her of late.—

Aunt. The thoughtfulness that is natural upon the approach of matrimony, generally occasions a decent concern.

Tag. And do you think, Madam, a husband of threescore and five—

Aunt. Hold, Tag, he protests to me he is but five and fifty.   10

Tag. He is a rogue, Madam, and an old rogue, and a fumbling old rogue, which is the worst of rogues.—

Aunt. Alas! Youth or age, 'tis all one to her; she is all simplicity without experience: I would not force her inclinations, but she's so innocent she won't know the difference—

Tag. Innocent! Ne'er trust to that, Madam; I was innocent myself once, but *live and learn* is an old saying, and a true one:—I believe, Madam, nobody is more innocent than yourself, and a good maid you are to be sure; but though you really don't *know* the difference, yet you can *fancy it* I warrant you. 20

Aunt. I should prefer a large jointure to a small one, and that's all; but 'tis impossible that Biddy should have desires, she's but newly come out of the country, and just turned of sixteen.

Tag. That's a ticklish age, Madam! I have observed she does not eat, nor she does not sleep; she sighs, and she cries, and she loves moon-light; these, I take it, are very strong symptoms.

Aunt. They are very unaccountable, I must confess; but you talk from a depraved mind, Tag, hers is simple and untainted.

Tag. She'll make him a cuckold though for all that, if you force her to marry him. 30

Aunt. You shock me, Tag, with your coarse expressions; I tell you, her chastity will be her guard, let her husband be what he will.

Tag. Chastity! Never trust to that, Madam; get her a husband that's fit for her, and I'll be bound for her virtue; but with such a one as Sir Simon, I'm a rogue if I'd answer for my own.

Aunt. Well, Tag, the child shall never have reason to repent of my severity; I was going before to my lawyers to speak about the articles of marriage, I will now put a stop to 'em for some time, till we can make further discoveries.

Tag. Heaven will bless you for your goodness; look where the poor bird comes, quite moped and melancholy; I'll set my pump at work, and draw something from her before your return, I warrant you. [*Exit* Aunt.] There goes a miracle; she has neither pride, envy, or ill-nature, and yet is near sixty, and a virgin. 44

Enter Biddy.

Biddy. How unfortunate a poor girl am I, I dare not tell my secrets to anybody, an if I don't I'm undone—Heigho! [*Sighs.*] Pray, Tag, is my aunt gone to her lawyer about me? Heigho!

Tag. What's that sigh for, my dear young mistress?

Biddy. I did not sigh, not I— [*Sighs.*

Tag. Nay, never gulp 'em down, they are the worst things you can swallow. There's something in that little heart of yours, that swells it and puffs it, and will burst it at last, if you don't give it vent. 52

Biddy. What would you have me tell you? [*Sighs.*

Tag. Come, come, you are afraid I'll betray you, but you had as good speak. I may do you some service you little think of.

Biddy. It is not in your power, Tag, to give me what I want. [*Sighs.*

Tag. Not directly, perhaps; but I may be the means of helping you to it; as

for example—if you should not like to marry the old man your aunt designs
for you, one might find a way to break—

Biddy. His neck, Tag?   60

Tag. Or the match; either will do, child.

Biddy. I don't care which indeed, so I was clear of him—I don't think I'm
fit to be married.

Tag. To him you mean—You have no objection to marriage, but the man,
and I applaud you for it: but come, courage, Miss, never keep it in; out with
it all—

Biddy. If you'll ask me any questions, I'll answer 'em, but I can't tell you
any thing of myself, I shall blush if I do.

Tag. Well then—In the first place, pray tell me, Miss Biddy Bellair, if you
don't like somebody better than old Sir Simon Loveit?   70

Biddy. Heigho!

Tag. What's 'Heigho', Miss?

Biddy. When I say 'Heigho!' it means 'yes'.

Tag. Very well; and this somebody is a young, handsome fellow?

Biddy. Heigho!

Tag. And if you were once his, you'd be as merry as the best of us?

Biddy. Heigho!

Tag. So far so good; and since I have got you to wet your feet, souse over
head at once, and the pain will be over.

Biddy. There—then. [*A long sigh.*] Now help me out, Tag, as fast as you
can.   81

Tag. When did you hear from your gallant?

Biddy. Never since he went to the Army.

Tag. How so?

Biddy. I was afraid the letters would fall into my aunt's hands, so I would
not let him write to me; but I had a better reason then.

Tag. Pray let's hear that too.

Biddy. Why, I thought if I should write to him and promise him to love
nobody else, and should afterwards change my mind, he might think I was
inconstant, and call me a coquette.   90

Tag. What a simple innocent it is! [*Aside.*] And have you changed your
mind, Miss?

Biddy. No indeed, Tag, I love him the best of any of 'em.

Tag. Of any of 'em! Why, have you any more?

Biddy. Pray don't ask me.

Tag. Nay, Miss, if you only trust me by halves, you can't expect—

Biddy. I will trust you with everything.—When I parted with him, I grew
melancholy; so in order to divert me, I have let two others court me till he
returns again.

Tag. Is that all, my dear? Mighty simple, indeed.   [*Aside.*

Biddy. One of 'em is a fine blustering man, and is called Captain Flash; he is always talking of fighting, and wars; he thinks he's sure of me, but I shall balk him; we shall see him this afternoon, for he pressed strongly to come, and I have given him leave, while my aunt's taking her afternoon's nap.

Tag. And who is the other, pray?   105

Biddy. Quite another sort of a man, he speaks like a lady for all the world, and never swears as Mr. Flash does, but wears nice white gloves, and tells me what ribbons become my complexion, where to stick my patches, who is the best milliner, where they sell the best tea, and which is the best wash for the face, and the best paste for the hands; he is always playing with my fan, and shewing his teeth, and whenever I speak he pats me—so—and cries, 'The devil take me, Miss Biddy, but you'll be my perdition.'—Ha, ha, ha!

Tag. Oh the pretty creature! And what do you call him pray?   113

Biddy. His name's Fribble; you shall see him too, for by mistake I appointed 'em at the same time; but you must help me out with 'em.

Tag. And suppose your favourite should come too—

Biddy. I should not care what became of the others.

Tag. What's his name?

Biddy. It begins with an *R*—*h*—*o*—

Tag. I'll be hanged if it is not Rhodophil.   120

Biddy. I am frightened at you! You are a witch, Tag!

Tag. I am so, and I can tell your fortune too. Look me in the face. The gentleman you love most in the world will be at our house this afternoon; he arrived from the Army this morning, and dies till he sees you.

Biddy. Is he come, Tag? Don't joke with me—

Tag. Not to keep you longer in suspense, you must know the servant of your Strephon, by some unaccountable fate or other, is my lord and master; he has just been with me, and told me of his master's arrival and im-patience—

Biddy. Oh my dear, dear Tag, you have put me out of my wits—I am all over in a flutter—I shall leap out of my skin—I don't know what to do with myself.—Is he come, Tag?—I am ready to faint—I'd give the world I had put on my pink and silver robings today.   133

Tag. I assure you, Miss, you look charmingly!

Biddy. Do I indeed though? I'll put a little patch under my left eye, and powder my hair immediately.

Tag. We'll go to dinner first, and then I'll assist you.

Biddy. Dinner! I can't eat a morsel—I don't know what's the matter with me—my ears tingle, my heart beats, my face flushes, and I tremble every joint of me—I must run in and look myself in the glass this moment.

127 Strephon] The conventional rustic lover of pastoral romance.

Tag. Yes, she has it, and deeply too; this is no hypocrisy—　　141
　　　Not art, but nature now performs her part,
　　　And every word's the language of the heart.

End of the First Act.

ACT II. SCENE I.

SCENE *continues.*

Enter Captain Loveit, Biddy, Tag, *and* Puff.

Capt. To find you still constant, and to arrive at such a critical juncture, is the height of fortune and happiness.

Biddy. Nothing shall force me from you; and if I am secure of your affections—

Puff. I'll be bound for him, Madam, and give any security you can ask.

Tag. Everything goes on to our wish, Sir; I just now had a second conference with my old lady, and she was so convinced by my arguments, that she returned instantly to the lawyer to forbid the drawing out of any writings at all, and she is determined never to thwart Miss's inclinations, and left it to us to give the old gentleman his discharge at the next visit.　　10

Capt. Shall I undertake the old dragon?

Tag. If we have occasion for help, we shall call for you.

Biddy. I expect him every moment, therefore I'll tell you what, Rhodophil, you and your man shall be locked up in my bed-chamber till we have settled matters with the old gentleman.

Capt. Do what you please with me.

Biddy. You must not be impatient though.

Capt. I can undergo anything with such a reward in view, one kiss and I'll be quite resigned—and now shew me the way.　　　　　　　[*Exeunt.*

Tag. Come, Sirrah, when I have got you under lock and key, I shall bring you to reason.　　21

Puff. Are your wedding-clothes ready, my dove? The certificate's come.

Tag. Go follow your Captain, Sirrah—march—you may thank heaven I had patience to stay so long.　　　　　　　[*Exeunt* Tag *and* Puff.

Enter Biddy.

Biddy. I was very much alarmed for fear my two gallants should come in upon us unawares; we should have had sad work if they had: I find I love

Rhodophil vastly, for though my other sparks flatter me more, I can't abide the thoughts of 'em now—I have business upon my hands enough to turn my little head, but egad my heart's good, and a fig for dangers—let me see, what shall I do with my two gallants? I must, at least, part with 'em decently; suppose I set 'em together by the ears?—The luckiest thought in the world! For if they won't quarrel (as I believe they won't) I can break with 'em for cowards, and very justly dismiss 'em my service; and if they will fight, and one of 'em should be killed, the other will certainly be hanged, or run away, and so I shall very handsomely get rid of both.—I am glad I have settled it so purely.   37

Enter Tag.

Well, Tag, are they safe?

Tag. I think so, the door's double-locked, and I have the key in my pocket.

Biddy. That's pure; but have you given 'em anything to divert 'em?

Tag. I have given the Captain one of your old gloves to mumble, but my Strephon is diverting himself with the more substantial comforts of a cold venison pasty.   43

Biddy. What shall we do with the next that comes?

Tag. If Mr. Fribble comes first, I'll clap him up into my lady's store-room; I suppose he is a great maker of marmalade himself, and will have an opportunity of making some critical remarks upon our pastry and sweetmeats.

Biddy. When one of 'em comes, do you go and watch for the other, and as soon as you see him, run in to us, and pretend it is my aunt, and so we shall have an excuse to lock him up until we want him.   50

Tag. You may depend upon me; here is one of 'em.—

Enter Fribble.

Biddy. Mr. Fribble, your servant—

Frib. Miss Biddy, your slave—I hope I have not come upon you abruptly; I should have waited upon you sooner, but an accident happened that discomposed me so, that I was obliged to go home again to take drops.

Biddy. Indeed you don't look well, Sir.—Go, Tag, and do as I bid you.

Tag. I will, Madam.   [*Exit.*

Biddy. I have set my maid to watch my aunt, that we may'nt be surprised by her.

Frib. Your prudence is equal to your beauty, Miss, and I hope your permitting me to kiss your hands, will be no impeachment of your understanding.   62

Biddy. I hate the sight of him. [*Aside.*] I was afraid I should not have had the pleasure of seeing you, pray let me know what accident you met with, and what's the matter with your hand? I shan't be easy till I know.

Frib. Well, I vow, Miss Biddy, you're a good *creater*,—I'll endeavour to
muster up what little spirits I have, and tell you the whole affair—hem!—
But first you must give me leave to make you a present of a small pot of my
lip-salve; my servant made it this morning—the ingredients are innocent, I
assure you; nothing but the best virgin's-wax, conserve of roses, and lily of
the valley water.   71

Biddy. I thank you, Sir, but my lips are generally red, and when they an't,
I bite 'em.

Frib. I bite my own, sometimes, to pout 'em a little, but this will give 'em a
softness, colour, and an agreeable *moister*.—Thus let me make an humble
offering at that shrine, where I have already sacrificed my heart.

                                              [*Kneels and gives the pot.*
Biddy. Upon my word that's very prettily expressed, you are positively the
best company in the world—I wish he was out of the house.   [*Aside.*

Frib. But to return to my accident, and the reason why my hand is in this
condition—I beg you'll excuse the appearance of it, and be satisfied that
nothing but mere necessity could have forced me to appear thus muffled
before you.   82

Biddy. I am very willing to excuse any misfortune that happens to you,
Sir.   [*Curtsies.*

Frib. You are vastly good, indeed,—thus it was,—hem!—You must know,
Miss, there is not an animal in the creation I have so great an aversion to, as
those hackney-coach fellows.—As I was coming out of my lodgings,—says
one of 'em to me, 'Would Your Honour have a coach?'—'No, man,' said I,
'not now,' (with all the civility imaginable)—'I'll carry you and your doll
too,' (says he) 'Miss Margery, for the same price.'—Upon which, the masculine beasts about us fell a-laughing; then I turned round in a great passion.
'Curse me,' (says I) 'fellow, but I'll trounce thee.'—And, as I was holding
out my hand in a threatening *poster*,—thus;—he makes a cut at me with his
whip, and striking me over the nail of my little finger, it gave me such
exquisite *torter* that I fainted away; and while I was in this condition, the
mob picked my pocket of my purse, my scissors, my Mocoa smelling-bottle,
and my huswife.   97

Biddy. I shall laugh in his face. [*Aside.*] I am afraid you are in great pain;
pray sit down, Mr. Fribble, but I hope your hand is in no danger.

                                                             [*They sit.*
Frib. Not in the least, Ma'am; pray don't be apprehensive.—A milk-
poultice, and a gentle sweat tonight, with a little manna in the morning, I am
confident, will relieve me entirely.

    96–7 Mocoa smelling-bottle . . . huswife] A strong scent from near Mocha in Yemen, and
a pocket-case for sewing materials. 101 manna] A juice exuded from the flowering
(manna-) ash, used medicinally as a mild laxative.

Biddy. But pray, Mr. Fribble, do you make use of a huswife?

Frib. I can't do without it, Ma'am; there is a club of us, all young bachelors, the sweetest society in the world; and we meet three times a week at each other's lodgings, where we drink tea, hear the chat of the day, invent fashions for the ladies, make models of 'em, and cut out patterns in paper. We were the first inventors of knotting, and this fringe is the original produce and joint labour of our little community.

Biddy. And who are your pretty set, pray?   110

Frib. There's Phil Whiffle, Jacky Wagtail, my Lord Trip, Billy Dimple, Sir Dilberry Diddle, and your humble—

Biddy. What a sweet collection of happy creatures!

Frib. Indeed and so we are, Miss.—But a prodigious fracas disconcerted us a little on our visiting-day at Billy Dimple's—three drunken naughty women of the town burst into our club-room, broke six looking-glasses, scalded us with the slop-basin, and *scrat* poor Phil Whiffle's cheek in such a manner, that he has kept his bed these three weeks.

Biddy. Indeed, Mr. Fribble, I think all our sex have great reason to be angry; for if you are so happy now you are bachelors, the ladies may wish and sigh to very little purpose.   121

Frib. You are mistaken, I assure you; I am prodigiously rallied about my passion for you, I can tell you that, and am looked upon as lost to our society already; he, he, he!

Biddy. Pray, Mr. Fribble, now you have gone so far, don't think me impudent if I long to know how you intend to use the lady who shall be honoured with your affections?

Frib. Not as most other wives are used, I assure you; all the domestic business will be taken off her hands; I shall make the tea, comb the dogs, and dress the children myself, if I should be blessed with any; so that though I'm a commoner, Mrs. Fribble will lead the life of a woman of quality; for she will have nothing to do, but lie in bed, play at cards, and scold the servants.

Biddy. What a happy creature she must be!   133

Frib. Do you really think so? Then pray let me have a little *serous* talk with you.—Though my passion is not of a long standing, I hope the sincerity of my intentions—

Biddy. Ha, ha, ha!

Frib. Go, you wild thing. [*Pats her.*] The devil take me but there is no talking to you.—How can you use me in this barbarous manner! If I had the constitution of an alderman it would sink under my sufferings—*hooman nater* can't support it—   141

Biddy. Why, what would you do with me, Mr. Fribble?

Frib. Well, I vow I'll beat you if you talk so—don't look at me in that manner—flesh and blood can't bear it—I could—but I won't grow indecent—

Biddy. But pray, Sir, where are the verses you were to write upon me? I find if a young lady depends too much upon such fine gentlemen as you, she'll certainly be disappointed.

Frib. I vow, the flutter I was put into this afternoon has quite turned my senses—there they are though—and I believe you'll like 'em.—

Biddy. There can be no doubt of it.   150

Frib. I protest, Miss, I don't like that curtsey—look at me, and always rise in this manner. [*Shews her.*] But, my dear *creater*, who put on your cap today? They have made a fright of you, and it's as yellow as old Lady Crowfoot's neck.—When we are settled, I'll dress your head myself.

Biddy. Pray read the verses to me, Mr. Fribble.

Frib. I obey—hem!—'William Fribble, Esq; to Miss Biddy Bellair'—greeting.

> No ice so hard, so cold as I,
> 'Till warmed and softened by your eye;
> And now my heart dissolves away   160
> In dreams by night and sighs by day;
> No brutal passion fires my breast,
> Which loathes the object when possessed;
> But one of harmless, gentle kind,
> Whose joys are centred—in the mind:
> Then take with me, love's better part,
> His downy wing, but not his dart.

How do you like 'em?

Biddy. Ha, ha, ha! I swear they are very pretty—but I don't quite understand 'em.   170

Frib. These light pieces are never so well understood in reading as singing; I have set 'em myself, and will endeavour to give 'em you—*la, la*—I have an abominable cold, and can't sing a note; however the tune's nothing, the manner's all.

No ice so hard, etc.   [Sings.

Enter Tag, running.

Tag. Your aunt! Your aunt! Your aunt, Madam!

Frib. What's the matter?

Biddy. Hide, hide Mr. Fribble, Tag, or we are ruined.

Frib. Oh! For heaven's sake, put me anywhere, so I don't dirty my clothes.

Biddy. Put him into the store-room, Tag, this moment.   180

Frib. Is it a damp place, Mrs. Tag? The floor is boarded, I hope?

Tag. Indeed it is not, Sir.

Frib. What shall I do? I shall certainly catch my death! Where's my cambric handkerchief, and my salts? I shall certainly have my hysterics!

[*Runs in* [*with* Tag].

Biddy. In, in, in—So now let the other come as soon as he will; I should not care if I had twenty of 'em, so they would but come one after another.

Enter Tag.

Was my aunt coming?

Tag. No, 'twas Mr. Flash, I suppose, by the length of his stride, and the cock of his hat. He'll be here this minute.—What shall we do with him?

Biddy. I'll manage him, I warrant you, and try his courage; be sure you are ready to second me—we shall have pure sport.   191

Tag. Hush! Here he comes.

Enter Flash, *singing*.

Flash. Well my blossom, here am I! What hopes for a poor dog, eh? How! The maid here! Then I've lost the town, dammee! Not a shilling to bribe the governor; she'll spring a mine, and I shall be blown to the devil.   [*Aside*.

Biddy. Don't be ashamed, Mr. Flash; I have told Tag the whole affair, and she's my friend I can assure you.

Flash. Is she? Then she won't be mine I am certain. [*Aside*.] Well Mrs. Tag, you know, I suppose, what's to be done: this young lady and I have contracted ourselves, and so, if you please to stand bride-maid, why we'll fix the wedding-day directly.   201

Tag. The wedding-day, Sir?

Flash. The wedding-day, Sir? Ay, Sir, the wedding-day, Sir, what have you to say to that, Sir?

Biddy. My dear Captain Flash, don't make such a noise, you'll wake my aunt.

Flash. And suppose I did, child, what then?

Biddy. She'd be frightened out of her wits.

Flash. At me, Miss, frightened at me? *Tout au contraire*, I assure you, you mistake the thing, child; I have some reason to believe I am not quite so shocking.   [*Affectedly*.

Tag. Indeed, Sir, you flatter yourself—But pray, Sir, what are your pretensions?   213

Flash. The lady's promises, my own passion, and the best mounted blade in the three Kingdoms. If any man can produce a better title, let him take her; if not, the devil mince me, if I give up an atom of her.

Biddy. He's in a fine passion, if he would but hold it.

Tag. Pray, Sir, hear reason a little.

Flash. I never do, Madam; it is not my method of proceeding; here's my logic! [*Draws his sword.*] Sa, sa,—my best argument is cart over arm, Madam, ha, ha, [*Lunges.*] and if he answers that, Madam, through my small guts, my breath, blood, and mistress are all at his service—nothing more, Madam.

Biddy. This'll do, this'll do.   223

Tag. But Sir, Sir, Sir?

Flash. But Madam, Madam, Madam: I profess blood, Madam, I was bred up to it from a child; I study the book of fate, and the camp is my university; I have attended the lectures of Prince Charles upon the Rhine, and Bathiani upon the Po, and have extracted knowledge from the mouth of a cannon. I'm not to be frightened with squibs, Madam, no, no.

Biddy. Pray, dear Sir, don't mind her, but let me prevail with you to go away this time—your passion is very fine to be sure, and when my aunt and Tag are out of the way, I'll let you know when I'd have you come again.

Flash. When you'd have me come again, child? And suppose I never would come again, what do you think of that now, ha? You pretend to be afraid of your aunt; your aunt knows what's what too well to refuse a good match when it's offered.—Lookee, Miss, I'm a man of honour, glory's my aim, I have told you the road I am in, and do you see here, child, [*Shewing his sword.*] no tricks upon travellers.   238

Biddy. But pray, Sir, hear me.

Flash. No, no, no, I know the world, Madam, I am as well known at Covent Garden as the Dial, Madam: I'll break a lamp, bully a constable, bam a justice, or bilk a box-keeper with any man in the Liberties of Westminster; what do you think of me now, Madam?

Biddy. Pray don't be so furious, Sir.

Flash. Come, come, come, few words are best, somebody's happier than somebody, and I'm a poor silly fellow; ha, ha,—that's all.—Look you, child, to be short (for I'm a man of reflection), I have but a *bagatelle* to say to you: I am in love with you up to hell and desperation, may the sky crush me if I am not.—But since there is another more fortunate than I, adieu, Biddy! Prosperity to the happy rival, patience to poor Flash; but the first time we meet,—gunpowder be my perdition, but I'll have the honour to cut a throat with him.   [*Going.*

Biddy. [*Stopping him.*] You may meet with him now if you please.

Flash. Now, may I!—Where is he? I'll sacrifice the villain.   [*Aloud.*

Tag. Hush! He's but in the next room.   255

---

220 cart over arm] A duelling manoeuvre. 'Cart' is for '*carte*' or '*quarte*', the fourth thrust in formal fencing.   227–8 Prince Charles . . . the Po] Karl Alexander, Prince Charles of Lorraine (1712–80), was celebrated for his brilliant crossing of the Rhine with the Austrian Army in 1744, during the War of the Austrian Succession. 'Bathiani' is Prince Karl von Batthyanyi (1697–1772), a Hungarian field-marshal prominent in the same war.   241 bam] Trick, impose on (abbr. of 'bamboozle').

Flash. Is he? Ram me [*Low*.] into a mortar-piece, but I'll have vengeance; my blood boils to be at him.—Don't be frightened, Miss?

Biddy. No, Sir, I never was better pleased, I assure you.

Flash. I shall soon do his business.

Biddy. As soon as you please, take your own time.   260

Tag. I'll fetch the gentleman to you immediately.   [*Going*.

Flash. [*Stopping her*.] Stay, stay a little; what a passion I am in!—Are you sure he is in the next room?—I shall certainly tear him to pieces—I would fain murder him like a gentleman too.—Besides, this family shan't be brought into trouble upon my account.—I have it—I'll watch for him in the street, and mix his blood with the puddle of the next kennel.   [*Going*.

Biddy. [*Stopping him*.] No, pray Mr. Flash, let me see the battle, I shall be glad to see you fight for me, you shan't go, indeed.

Tag. [*Holding him*.] Oh, pray let me see you fight; there were two gentlemen *fit* yesterday, and my mistress was never so diverted in her life—I'll fetch him out.   [*Exit*.

Biddy. Do, stick him, stick him, Captain Flash; I shall love you the better for it.   273

Flash. D—n your love, I wish I was out of the house.   [*Aside*.

Biddy. Here he is.—Now speak some of your hard words, and run him through—

Flash. Don't be in fits now—   [*Aside to* Biddy.

Biddy. Never fear me.

Enter Tag *and* Fribble.

Tag. [*To* Fribble.] Take it on my word, Sir, he is a bully, and nothing else.

Frib. [*Frightened*.] I know you are my good friend, but perhaps you don't know his disposition.   281

Tag. I am confident he is a coward.

Frib. Is he? Nay, then I'm his man.

Flash. I like his looks, but I'll not venture too far at first.

Tag. Speak to him, Sir.

Frib. I will—I understand, Sir—hem—that you—by Mrs. Tag here,—Sir,—who has informed me—hem—that you have sent her, to inform me—Sir,—that you would be glad to speak with me.—Demmee—   [*Turns off*.

Flash. I can speak to you, Sir—or to anybody, Sir—or I can let it alone and hold my tongue,—if I see occasion, Sir, dammee—   [*Turns off*.

Biddy. Well said, Mr. Flash, be in a passion.   291

Tag. [*To* Fribble.] Don't mind his looks, he changes colour already; to him, to him.   [*Pushes him*.

Frib. Don't hurry me, Mrs. Tag, for heaven's sake! I shall be out of breath before I begin if you do,—Sir,—[*To* Flash.] if you can't speak to a gentleman in another manner, Sir,—why then I'll venture to say, you had better hold your tongue—oons.

Flash. Sir, you and I are of different opinions.

Frib. You and your opinion may go to the devil,—take that.

[*Turns off to* Tag.

Tag. Well said, Sir, the day's your own.   300

Biddy. What's the matter, Mr. Flash? Is all your fury gone? Do you give me up?

Frib. I have done his business.

Flash. Give you up, Madam! No, Madam; when I am determined in my resolutions I am always calm; 'tis our way, Madam; and now I shall proceed to business.—Sir, I beg to say a word to you in private.

Frib. Keep your distance, fellow, and I'll answer you.—That lady has confessed a passion for me, and as she has delivered up her heart into my keeping, nothing but my '*art's* blood shall purchase it. Demnation!

Tag. Bravo! Bravo!   310

Flash. If those are the conditions, I'll give you earnest for it directly. [*Draws.*] Now, villain, renounce all right and title this minute, or the torrent of my rage will overflow my reason, and I shall annihilate the nothingness of your soul and body in an instant.

Frib. I wish there was a constable at hand to take us both up; we shall certainly do one another a prejudice.

Tag. No, you won't indeed, Sir; pray bear up to him; if you would but draw your sword, and be in a passion, he would run away directly.

Frib. Will he? [*Draws his sword.*] Then I can no longer contain myself— hell and furies! Come on, thou savage brute.   320

Tag. Go on, Sir.   [*Here they stand in fighting postures, while*
                                        Biddy *and* Tag *push 'em forward.*

Flash. Come on.

Biddy. Go on.

Frib. Come on, rascal.

Tag. Go on, Sir.

                          Enter Captain Loveit *and* Puff.

Capt. What's the matter, my dear?

Biddy. If you won't fight, here's one that will. Oh Rhodophil, these two sparks are your rivals, and have pestered me these two months with their addresses; they forced themselves into the house, and have been quarrelling about me, and disturbing the family; if they won't fight, pray kick 'em out of the house.   331

Capt. What's the matter, gentlemen?

                                        [*They both keep their fencing posture.*

Flash. Don't part us, Sir.

Frib. No, pray Sir don't part us, we shall do you a mischief.

Capt. Puff, look to the other gentleman, and call a surgeon.

Biddy and *Tag.* Ha, ha, ha!

Puff. Bless me! How can you stand under your wounds, Sir?

Frib. Am I hurt, Sir?

Puff. Hurt, Sir! Why you have—let me see—pray stand in the light—one, two, three through the heart; and let me see—hum—eight through the small guts! Come, Sir, make it up a round dozen, and then we'll part you.

All. Ha, ha, ha!   342

Capt. Come here, Puff.   [*Whispers, and looks at* Flash.

Puff. 'Tis the very same, Sir.

Capt. [*To* Flash.] Pray, Sir, have not I had the pleasure of seeing your face abroad?

Flash. I have served abroad.

Capt. Had not you the misfortune, Sir, to be missing at the last engagement in Flanders?

Flash. I was found amongst the dead in the field of battle.   350

Puff. He was the first that fell, Sir; the wind of a cannon-ball struck him flat upon his face; he had just strength enough to creep into a ditch, and there he was found after the battle in a most deplorable condition.

Capt. Pray, Sir, what advancement did you get by the service of that day?

Flash. My wounds rendered me unfit for service, and I sold out.

Puff. Stole out, you mean. We hunted him, by scent, to the waterside, thence he took shipping for England, and, taking the advantage of my master's absence, has attacked his citadel, which we are luckily come to relieve, and drive His Honour into the ditch again.

All. Ha, ha, ha!   360

Frib. He, he, he!

Capt. And now, Sir, how have you dared to shew your face again in open day, or wear even the outside of a profession you have so much scandalized by your behaviour? I honour the name of soldier, and as a party concerned am bound not to see it disgraced; as you have forfeited your title to honour, deliver up your sword this instant.

Flash. Nay, good Captain—

Capt. No words, Sir.   [*Takes his sword.*

Frib. He's a sad scoundrel; I wish I had kicked him.

Capt. The next thing I command—leave this house, change the colour of your clothes and fierceness of your looks, appear from top to toe the wretch, the very wretch thou art; or if you put on looks that belie the native baseness of thy heart, be it where it will, this shall be the reward of thy impudence and disobedience.   [*Kicks him, and he runs off.*

Biddy. Oh, my dear Rhodophil!   375

Frib. What an infamous rascal it is! I thank you, Sir, for this favour; but I must after, and cane him.   [*Going, is stopped by the* Captain.

Capt. One word with you too, Sir.

Frib. With me, Sir?

Capt. You need not tremble, I shan't use you roughly.   380

Frib. I am certain of that, Sir; but I am sadly troubled with weak nerves.

Capt. Thou art of a species too despicable for correction; therefore be gone, and if I see you here again, your insignificancy shan't protect you.

Frib. I am obliged to you for your kindness; but if ever I have anything to do with intrigues again!—   [*Aside* [*and exit*].

All. Ha, ha, ha!

Puff. Shall I ease you of your trophy, Sir?

Capt. Take it, Puff, as some small recompence for thy fidelity, thou canst better use it than its owner.

Puff. I wish Your Honour had a patent to take such trifles from every pretty gentleman that could spare 'em; I would set up the largest cutler's shop in the kingdom.   392

Capt. Well said, Puff.

Biddy. But pray, Mr. Fox, how did you get out of your hole? I thought you was locked in?

Capt. I shot the bolt back when I heard a noise; and thinking you were in danger, broke my confinement without any other consideration than your safety.   [*Kisses her hand.*

Sir Simon. [*Without.*] Biddy, Biddy. Why, Tag.

Biddy. There's the old gentleman; run in, run in.   400

[*Exeunt* Captain *and* Puff. Tag *opens the door.*

Enter Sir Simon *and* Jasper.

Sir Sim. Where have you been, Biddy? Jasper and I have knocked and called as loud and as long as we were able: what were you doing, child?

Biddy. I was reading part of a play to Tag, and we came as soon as we heard you.

Sir Sim. What play, moppet?

Biddy. *The Old Bachelor*, and we were just got to old Nykyn as you knocked at the door.

Sir Sim. Fie, fie, child; I never heard you talk at this rate before; I'm afraid you, Tag, put these things into her head.   410

Tag. I, Sir? I vow, Sir Simon, she knows more than you can conceive; she

---

407 Nykyn] Laetitia's pet name for her husband Fondlewife, the uxorious, cuckolded banker in Congreve's comedy (1693).

surprises me, I assure you, though I have been married these two years, and lived with bachelors most part of my life.

Sir Sim. Do you hear, Jasper? I'm all over in a sweat.—Pray, Miss, have not you had company this afternoon? I saw a young fop go out of the house as I was coming hither.

Biddy. You might have seen two, Sir Simon, if your eyes had been good.

Sir Sim. Do you hear, Jasper?—Sure the child is possessed!—Pray, Miss, what did they want here?

Biddy. Me, Sir; they wanted me.   420

Sir Sim. What did they want with you, I say?

Biddy. Why, what do you want with me?

Sir Sim. Do you hear, Jasper?—I am thunder-struck! I can't believe my own ears!—Tell me the reason, I say, why—

Tag. I'll tell you the reason why, if you please, Sir Simon. Miss, you know, is a very silly young girl, and having found out (Heaven knows how!) that there is some little difference between sixty-five and twenty-five, she's ridiculous enough to choose the latter; when if she'd take my advice—

Sir Sim. You are right, Tag, she would take me? Eh?

Tag. Yes, Sir, as the only way to have both; for if she marries you, the other will follow of course.   431

Sir Sim. Do you hear, Jasper?

Biddy. 'Tis very true, Sir Simon; from my knowing no better, I have set my heart upon a young man, and a young one I'll have; there have been three here this afternoon.

Sir Sim. Three, Jasper!

Biddy. And they have been quarrelling about me, and one has beat the other two. Now, Sir Simon, if you'll take up the conqueror, and kick him, as he has kicked the others, you shall have me for your reward, and my fifteen thousand pounds into the bargain. What says my hero? Eh?   440

                                                            [*Slaps him on the back.*

Sir Sim. The world's at an end!—What's to be done, Jasper?

Jasper. Pack up and be gone; don't fight the match, Sir.

Sir Sim. Flesh and blood cannot bear it—I'm all over agitation—hugh, hugh!—Am I cheated by a baby, a doll? Where's your aunt, you young cockatrice?—I'll let her know—she's a base woman, and you are—

Biddy. You are in a fine humour to shew your valour. Tag, fetch the Captain this minute, while Sir Simon is warm, and let him know he is waiting here to cut his throat. [*Exit* Tag.] I locked him up in my bed-chamber till you came.

Sir Sim. Here's an imp of darkness! What would I give that my son Bob was here to thrash her spark, while I—ravished the rest of the family.

Jasper. I believe we had best retire, Sir.   452

Sir Sim. No, no, I must see her bully first; and, do you hear, Jasper, if I put him in a passion, do you knock him down.

Jasper. Pray keep your temper, Sir.

Enter Captain, Tag, *and* Puff.

Capt. [*Approaching angrily.*] What is the meaning, Sir?—Ounds! 'tis my father, Puff, what shall I do?   [*Aside.*

Puff. [*Drawing him by the coat.*] Kennel again, Sir.

Sir Sim. I am enchanted!

Capt. There is no retreat, I must stand it!   460

Biddy. What's all this?

Sir Sim. Your humble servant, Captain Fire-Ball.—You are welcome from the wars, noble Captain.—I did not think I should have the pleasure of being knocked o' th' head, or cut up alive by so fine a gentleman.

Capt. I am under such confusion, Sir, I have not power to convince you of my innocence.

Sir Sim. Innocence! Pretty lamb! And so, Sir, you have left the regiment, and the honourable employment of fighting for your country, to come home and cut your father's throat; why you'll be a great man in time, Bob!

Biddy. His father, Tag!   470

Sir Sim. Come, come, 'tis soon done—one stroke does it—or, if you have any qualms, let your 'squire there perform the operation.

Puff. Pray, Sir, don't throw such temptations in my way.

Capt. Hold your impudent tongue!

Sir Sim. Why don't you speak, Mr. Modesty; what excuse have you for leaving the Army, I say?

Capt. My affection to this lady.

Sir Sim. Your affection, puppy!

Capt. Our love, Sir, has been long and mutual; what accidents have happened since my going abroad, and her leaving the country, and how I have most unaccountably met you here, I am a stranger to; but whatever appearances may be, I still am, and ever was, your dutiful son.

Biddy. He talks like an angel, Tag!   483

Sir Sim. Dutiful, Sirrah! Have you not rivalled your father?

Capt. No, Sir, you have rivalled me; my claim must be prior to yours.

Biddy. Indeed, Sir Simon, he can shew the best title to me.

Jasper. Sir, Sir, the young gentleman speaks well, and as the fortune will not go out of the family, I would advise you to drop your resentment, be reconciled to your son, and relinquish the lady.

Sir Sim. Ay, ay, with all my heart—lookye, son, I give you up the girl, she's too much for me, I confess;—and take my word, Bob, you'll catch a Tartar.

                                                                           492

Biddy. I assure you, Sir Simon, I'm not the person you take me for; if I have used you anyways ill, 'twas for your son's sake, who had my promise and inclinations before you; and though I believe I should have made you a most uncomfortable wife, I'll be the best daughter to you in the world; and if you stand in need of a lady, my aunt is disengaged, and is the best nurse—

Sir Sim. No, no, I thank you, child; you have so turned my stomach to marriage, I have no appetite left.—But where is this aunt? Won't she stop your proceedings, think you?   500

Tag. She's now at her lawyer's, Sir, and if you please to go with the young couple, and give your approbation, I'll answer for my old lady's consent.

Biddy. The Captain, and I, Sir—

Sir Sim. Come, come, Bob, you are but an Ensign, don't impose on the girl neither.

Capt. I had the good fortune, Sir, to please my royal general by my behaviour in a small action with the enemy, and he gave me a company.

Sir Sim. Bob, I wish you joy! This is news indeed! And when we celebrate your wedding, son, I'll drink a half-pint bumper myself to your benefactor.

Capt. And he deserves it, Sir; such a general, by his examples and justice, animates us to deeds of glory, and insures us conquest.   511

Sir Sim. Right, my boy—come along then.   [*Going.*

Puff. Halt a little, gentlemen and ladies, if you please: everybody here seems well satisfied but myself.

Capt. What's the matter, Puff?

Puff. Sir, as I would make myself worthy of such a master, and the name of soldier, I cannot put up the least injury to my honour.

Sir Sim. Heyday! What flourishes are these?

Puff. Here is the man; come forth, caitiff. [*To* Jasper.] He hath confessed this day, that, in my absence, he had taken freedoms with my lawful wife, and had dishonourable intentions against my bed; for which I demand satisfaction.—   522

Sir Sim. [*Striking him.*] What stuff is here, the fellow's brain's turned.

Puff. And cracked too, Sir; but you are my master's father, and I submit.

Capt. Come, come, I'll settle your punctilios, and will take care of you and Tag hereafter, provided you drop all animosities, and shake hands this moment.

Puff. My revenge gives way to my interest, and I once again, Jasper, take you to my bosom.

Jasper. I'm your friend again, Puff—but harkye—I fear you not; and if you'll lay aside your steel there, as far as a broken head, or a black eye, I'm at your service upon demand.   532

506 royal general] George II led the 'pragmatic army' of English and German troops against the French at Dettingen, 27 June 1743.

Tag. You are very good at crowing indeed, Mr. Jasper; but let me tell you, the fool that is rogue enough to brag of a woman's favours, must be a dung-hill every way. As for you, my dear husband, shew your manhood in a proper place, and you need not fear these sheep-biters.

Sir Sim. The Abigail is pleasant I confess, he, he!

Biddy. I'm afraid the town will be ill-natured enough to think I have been a little coquettish in my behaviour; but, I hope, as I have been constant to the Captain, I shall be excused diverting myself with pretenders.   540

> Ladies, to fops and braggarts ne'er be kind,
> No charms can warm 'em, and no virtues bind;
> Each lover's merit by his conduct prove,
> Who fails in honour, will be false in love.   [*Exeunt.*

537 Abigail] Woman servant.

EPILOGUE.

By the same HAND as the PROLOGUE.

Spoke by Mrs. PRITCHARD.

Good Folks, I'm come at my young Lady's bidding,
To say, You all are welcome to her Wedding.
Th'Exchange she made, what Mortal here can blame?
Shew me the Maid that would not do the same.
For sure the greatest Monster ever seen,
Is doting Sixty *coupled to* Sixteen!
When wint'ry Age had almost caught the Fair,
Youth, clad in Sunshine, snatch'd her from Despair:
Like a new Semele *the Virgin lay,*
And clasp'd her Lover in the Blaze of Day.   10
Thus may each Maid, the Toils almost intrapt-in,
Change Old Sir Simon *for the* brisk young Captain.

   I love these Men of Arms, they know their Trade:
Let Dastards sue, these Sons of Fire invade!
They cannot bear around the Bait to nibble,
Like pretty, powder'd, patient Mr. Fribble:
To Dangers bred, and skilful in Command,
They storm the strongest Fortress, Sword in Hand!
Nights without Sleep, and Floods of Tears when waking,
Shew'd poor Miss Biddy *was in piteous taking:*   20
She's now quite well; for Maids in that Condition,
Find the young Lover is the best Physician;
And without Helps of Art, or Boast of Knowledge,
They cure more Women, faith, than all the College!

   But to the Point—I come with low Petition,
For, faith, poor Bayes *is in a sad Condition;*
*The huge tall Hangman stands to give the blow,
And only waits your Pleasures—Ay, or No.
If you should—Pit, Box, and Gallery, egad!
Joy turns his Senses, and the Man runs mad: 30

* *Alluding to* Bayes's *Prologue in the* Rehearsal.

But if your Ears are shut, your Hearts are Rock,
And if you pronounce the Sentence—Block to Block,
Down kneels the Bard, and leaves you when he's dead,
The empty Tribute of an Author's Head.

FINIS

THE KEPT MISTRESS

The anonymous *The Kept Mistress, or The Mock Orators* was performed at Drury Lane Theatre on 10 April 1756, for the benefit of the actor Yates.[1] But, like most benefit pieces, it perished quickly thereafter, and has survived only in one MS. in the Larpent collection. There is no clue as to authorship; generally, however, such plays were written by the actor himself or by a well-disposed friend. What distinguishes *The Kept Mistress* from the faceless mass of afterpieces—and to a lesser extent from eighteenth-century comedy as a whole—is its refusal to accept prevailing dramatic conventions. It presents a more thoroughly immoral situation on stage than was then usual, and maintains a hard-nosed realism where most of its brethren resorted to sentimentality, moral didacticism, or improbable recantations. The original audience may have taken exception either to such a presentation or to the play's formlessness: it is excessively unruly in an age of disorderly farces.

The dual title is more than a mere convention. The first title, *The Kept Mistress*, summarizes the main plot, a comedy of the Restoration type, in which we learn (dramatically rather than via direct exposition) of Belladue's dual liaison with Ringworm and Belton. The tone is matter-of-fact and devoid of moral disapprobation. There is unsentimental tough-mindedness in the meeting of old Belladue with Ringworm and in the Hempton-Belton duel scene; also reminiscent of Restoration drama is Belladue's maid's speech on their hedonism (I.ii). In the end all 'love' is brought safely (if belatedly) within the purview of marriage, as the eighteenth century required, but its parallel expectation of fulsome reform scenes is flagrantly violated.

The Mock Orators, on the other hand, refers to the satirical subplot; it is a topical Old Comedy in the style of Aristophanes, Jonson, and Foote, and the play exists chiefly for the sake of this subplot. Romance it disdains, or merely uses to expose a social cancer: in this case, the 'fangled fashion of oratory'. The Widow Lovephrase is sorely infected, and, by way of cure and catharsis, is mocked to her face by Harry, deprived of her only daughter, and at last matched with Ringworm—who comments, 'This comes of logic chopping.' The professional con men who tried to capitalize on the contemporary craze for elocution are exposed in the inquisition scene. Comedy and society teeter here on the brink of chaos; 'the world's mad,' declares the first orator, as indeed it is, while rhetoric rules it. But rhetoric is put down in the end by that incarnation of plain, blunt speech, the Royal Navy (into which the orator is inducted willy-nilly). Underneath the patriotic silliness lies the conviction

[1] Richard Yates (1706–96) was a low comedian famous as a speaking Harlequin.

that these verbal antics run counter to the British traditions of common sense, few words, and creative individual liberty, and must therefore be opposed.

The characters are all familiar types: the main plot triangle from Restoration comedy, the Widow Lovephrase from the humours tradition, Harry and Ringworm from Roman comedy, and the orators from Aristophanic caricature. This profound unoriginality, this unashamed indebtedness to the entire Western comic tradition, was the chief means by which the play helped preserve that tradition for Goldsmith and Sheridan during the lean years of the mid-eighteenth century.

Permission to publish this text, edited from the Larpent MS., has been given by the Trustees of the Henry E. Huntington Library.

THE KEPT MISTRESS,

or

THE MOCK ORATORS.

a comedy of 2 acts.

1756

Sir

   This Farce we have given Mr Yates leave to have perform'd at his Benefit at our Theatre if it meets with the approbation of my Lord Chamberlain

from Y^r

humble Serv^ts

April 7th
1756

J. Lacy

D. Garrick

J. Lacy, D. Garrick] Garrick and Lacy were at this time co-managers of Drury Lane Theatre.

E

Dramatis Personæ

[In order of appearance]

Harry — Belton's servant; college-educated; born above his present condition

Belton — a rake; 'friend' of Belladue

Hempton — a friend of Belton from the country; suitor to Miss Lovephrase

[Betty] Maid to Belladue

Belladue — a belle and *femme libre*; now in Ringworm's keeping

Ringworm — Belladue's keeper

Pedagogue — acquaintance of Ringworm

Widow Lovephrase — a wealthy country woman just arrived in London

Miss Lovephrase — her daughter

Servant to the Widow

Lady Whiffle — an acquaintance of Widow Lovephrase

Old Belladue — Belladue's father

Two ladies and other theatre patrons

Three orators

Doorkeeper at Covent Garden

A press gang

The Cast

Principal parts by: Mr. Yates, Mr. Palmer, Mr. Burton, Mr. Bransby, Mr. Jefferson, Mr. Philips. Miss Haughton, Mrs. Cross, Mrs. Bradshaw.

Song by Champness.

THE

Kept Mistress

OR

The Mock Orators

ACT I. SCENE I. *A chamber.*

Enter Harry.

Har. How my master lives, what he does to live, or what he lives upon, is as much a mystery to me as the longitude. No relations to support him, no estate to supply him, no money in the funds to enable him. Yet he lives gay, keeps gay company, treats [them?], presents high, and all out of nothing. Nothing can come of nothing say the sages, but that I deny, and deny it, I shall.

Enter Belton.

Belt. What shall you deny, Mr. Negative?—Why you look as full of care—

Har. Yes, Sir, as the picture of naked Necessity at the door of an eating house. My imagination, Sir, has turned architect; I have been erecting airy castles, in Fairy Land,—and I wish—but what's that? A wish is no more than a bubble to amuse Miss at the boarding school. I would better myself if I could, but I don't know how to go about it.   13

Belt. Good Mr. Commonplace, tell me what you'd be at. [*Sits down*.] I want a little sleep, come begin—I'll take your opinion by way of opiate; say on; but don't be too dull: for I prefer the chattering of a monkey to the braying of an ass at any time.

Har. Every man has two ears and one tongue, which proves we ought to

---

3 funds] Investments in the stock of the national debt.   4 [them?]] Word obscured by ink blot in MS.

hear twice as much as we say. I am, as the song says, of low degree; dress
makes a wide distinction. Your coat's laced with silver, mine with worsted.
You can cane me; I must not resent it, but if you were to be caned——
    Belt. How, Sir?   22
    Har. I beg pardon, Sir, I was only distinguishing—
    Belt. You're a fool.
    Har. I know it, Sir; wisdom is no more to me than a dead sprat to an angler;
the system of sapience may be a fine study, but the fashion of folly will always
have the most scholars. Wisdom at best is but a schoolboy's task, more overlooked than looked over. A wit is as dangerous to the wearer, as a beautiful
face to a girl without fortune: they are sure to be the ruin of their owners.
    Belt. This may be very pretty, but what is it to the purpose?   30
    Har. I have never purposed much in my life, Sir, and my present purpose I
don't believe I shall bring to bear. I have ambition as well as my betters,
and when I ride behind a coach wish to be in it, instead of waiting at table
would be waited upon.—Ah Sir, many a fine woman have I helped you to in
my time, but a pimp's a poor employment since ladies look out for themselves.
Better be born luckỹ than rich. He who has not what he wants, must be
satisfied with what he has, or go to bed discontented.
    Belt. Where did you pick up all this ribaldry?
    Har. It lay in my way, I found it, Sir, I wish to be what I am not. Like the
rest of mankind, I'm tired with my present condition, and having ruminated
on all the professions, trades and occupations, find nothing will suit me so
well as equipage and independency. Then would I strut like a game cock cut
out of a feather, with a stick as tall as myself, a sword as long as my stick, and
metamorphose myself into Buck, Blood or Jemmy in an instant.   44

                         Enter Mr. Hempton.

    Belt. Mr. Hempton, welcome to town; all friends in the country well, I
hope.
    Hem. All, all Sir, in fine health and high spirits. Oh Frank the country's the
thing, take my word for't.
    Har. Yes, Sir; the country's the thing to be sure, but not quite the thing
neither, the country's very well for country gentlemen; but men of the town,
ay, and women of the town too Sir, think there's no life like a London one.
    Hem. Well, well, one day or other we shall have your master and you love
solitude a little.   53

    19 low degree] *The Squire of Low Degree* was a medieval verse romance. In the eighteenth
century it was known both through Joseph Ritson's *Ancient Metrical Romances* and in
various broadside ballad versions, one of which begins: 'He was a squire of low degree,/And
she was a lass of the high countree'.   44 Jemmy] A common eighteenth-century generic
name for a buck or blood.

Belt. The pleasures of London may leave me, but I shall not leave them in a hurry, I hope.

Har. Keep in that mind, and keep me with you, I beseech you, Sir; your poets may pastoralize as they please, and talk of Pomona, and Flora, and Aurora, but of all gardens, give me Covent Garden. It's a pleasant thing to see the sun rise, to be sure, yet the flambeaux blaze of an opera cuts no contemptible figure. I prefer the choice spirits to a kennel of hounds; and think a country assembly no more to compare to a masquerade, than a medlar is to a pineapple.   62

Hem. Harry's still the same, I see: pertinent as ever.

Belt. Impertinent as ever, I assure you, for since these Orators have exposed themselves, he minds nothing but making speeches.

Hem. Pray what did these Orators, and Inquisitors and Disquisitors (as they called themselves) mean? I read their advertisements in the country, but could make neither head nor tail of them there.

Belt. Nor we here, I promise you.

Hem. Yet upon this oratorizing my hope on a very important point is founded; there is a young lady, Frank, very handsome, very rich, and who I believe I am not indifferent to. But the mother keeps her guarded like a golden fruit. Now it happens luckily that the old lady is far gone in this fangled fashion of oratory, fancies herself a fine speaker, and is resolved, nay, come up to town on purpose to declaim in public. She wants a master to teach Miss oratory. Now, if you can spare your servant, I can get him introduced as such a preceptor, and after he is introduced, I must trust to the goodness of his capacity for the event of my undertaking.   78

Belt. My fellow's at your service. May you have success with him. Make him what you please, for I can't make anything of him.

Hem. I'll make him an oratory-master immediately.

Har. An oratory master! Can I be that without being master of oratory, Sir? I know no more of eloquence than an auctioneer. 'Tis true, I heard the late pretenders to it, but they were no more like orators, than a man's talking in his sleep can be called fair argument. But come, Sir, if you'll trust me, I'll try Sir: if I succeed, so.—If not, Fortune's in fault, and won't work with her eyes open.   87

Belt. Pray how long has this female phoenix been in town?

Hem. Not long enough to be a Ranelagh toast, or a side box beauty;—but

66 Inquisitors and Disquisitors] The craze for elocution was also satirized in Arthur Murphy's *The Apprentice* (1756) and Foote's *The Orators* (1762) and *The Commissary*. The reference here is probably to Charles Macklin, who in 1754 gave a series of lectures and debates known as 'the British Inquisition' (see following speech), with a more general hit at the leading professional elocutionists of the time, Thomas Sheridan and James 'Orator' Henley.

time's precious, you'll excuse compliments. I hope in a few days to bring you
a good account of your servant, by his bringing me one of my mistress.

[*Exeunt.*

Manet Belton.

Belt. A good account? Ay, indeed, it's likely to turn out to a very good
account. A fine woman, a fine fortune, and fond too, s'death why should I
be uneasy at it? He's my friend, I ought to rejoice. I can't, though.—Damned
luck! Why could not I have found her out first? I may find her out still—I
will—but that's villainy—what's villainy?—a word—what meaning has it?—
discovery—   97

Enter Miss Belladue's Maid.

Maid. Oh Mr. Belton, you'll excuse me, I hope, I come in without any
ceremony, but we are all undone at our house. My master has found a letter,
he swears it comes from you, I left them at high words, and stole out to
acquaint you with it, and beg you'll step there immediately.   101

Belt. If I am seen there, 'twill be adding fuel to fire, and only serve to
make the breach wider betwixt 'em.

Maid. Not if you would speak properly to my master, you have schemes
enough to ruin us poor women, do, Sir, pray think of one to save us, bring
my mistress off but this once—

Belt. But how, Betty?

Maid. Ah, Sir, I remember the time when these objections would not have
been raised, but 'tis too true, indeed, when a woman has nothing more to
give, and a man nothing more to expect; your sex are seldom guilty of
gratitude.   111

Belt. A lady in love, child, and a gouty patient are two very fretful beings:
they expect their physicians to perform impossibilities.

Maid. And women, like charitable physicians, are too apt to relieve the
wretched; and patients when cured seldom care what becomes of their
doctors.

Belt. If I thought I could do your mistress any good—

Maid. Do you know anybody else that can, Sir? If she'd take my advice,
I'd try however, if I could not wake your tenderness, I would your pride, I
warrant; I'd make that a more troublesome companion to you than an ill-
natured wife, or a drunken acquaintance.   121

Belt. Hush, hush, Betty, I am ready to attend you. I think instead of
wanting me for an advocate to plead for your mistress, you would [have]
more notably done it yourself. But let us go, and may the genius of good
fortune go along with us.   [*Exeunt.*

123 would [have]] Words inserted in square brackets are not in the MS.

SCENE II. Miss Belladue's *lodgings*.

Enter Miss Belladue, *and old* Ringworm *following
her with a letter in his hand.*

Ring. Only satisfy me so far, say it was not wrote to you; damn it, what an
ass do I make myself: flatter me so far, say you know not anything of it, why
don't you speak to me? When did this letter come? Did it come from Belton?
—if from—tell me dear Bella,—if you don't by all that's dishonest; by yourself, that damned epitome. Bella pray tell me won't you speak to me?—If I
don't part with you—

Bella. Why don't you?—I'll spare you the trouble, Sir, call a chair; I'll
tell you, Sir, I'm not your slave, not the indentured drudge of your pleasures.

Ring. Nay, Bella, don't make such a noise, my dear.

Bella. I don't make a noise, [*Loud.*] nor I won't make a noise. [*Louder.*] I
won't be used ill, Sir. [*Loudest.*] Here you find a letter without either date—
name or direction, and it must come to me, and come to me from Belton,—
from one whom I never could like.—Nay, one whom I always—Belton, pray,
Sir, who ever dared to hint that I granted favours to Belton? To him?

Ring. Well, well, Bella, don't be passionate. I did not say you did, did I? I
only heard so. But it's a damned censorious world, and I'm an ass, and a fool,
and an old fool—but—   17

Bella. But what Sir?—Had you found me exposed in the street, you might
then have presumed upon the prerogative of your money, and used me
accordingly. But I'm as well born as yourself, and as well bred too. But go,
Sir;—go to your widow,—I'm yet, thank Heaven, neither old, nor ugly.—

Ring. What widow, Bella?

Bella. The widow Lovephrase, do you think, Sir, I could not find that
out?—Do you imagine I could be long ignorant of your courtship there?—

Ring. Why Bella, child,—why indeed, that is to say. But I'll conceal nothing
from you, I do intend to have this widow, but it's for thy sake, thou shalt
fare the better for't.

Bella. Well, your wife may be wished joy, indeed, for indeed she'll want
it.—Pray, Sir, after matrimony, leave off your visits to me.—I will not rob
the widow of her mite, I assure you.   30

Ring. Thou shalt live in more splendor than ever Bella. Nothing shall be
wanting to convince thee of my love.

Bella. Of your love, Sir?—I am at present yours, your servant, your
mistress; or what you please to make me. Except making me believe you love,
I could despise you for thinking me weak enough to believe it. No, Sir, your
expense was a pitiful pride to please yourself, and now as pitifully you repent it.

8 indentured] MS.: 'indented'.

Ring. Nay, but Bella,—my dear Bella—

Bella. Let go my hand, Sir; I will go.—You've reproached me with Belton
—I hate him, Sir—I'll tell him so. Nay, I'll send for him, I'll have you face to
face,—who waits there?—bid my maid see for Mr. Belton—I've heard you
say he uses White's, send there for him.—   [*Exit* Maid.

Ring. She's mighty passionate,—but she's mighty pretty, but why Bella,
would you send for Belton?   43

Bella. I chose it. Does it affect you? I am glad of it. Don't say you're
jealous.—That's a jest, your pride's hurt perhaps, I know your sex too well,—
ye are wise in your own conceits, weak in ours, you think us fools, we know
you are so.

Enter Belton. [*They stand silent a moment.*]

Belt. Sir, how odd soever this intrusion may appear, when you have heard
me, you'll find I have a reason sufficient, for thus interrupting you. I come
here to clear up some malicious innuendoes in regard of me, and that
lady.   51

Ring. Sir, all that I,—I,—I have to say, is that—I can't say anything about
it, but you're Mr. Belton, and that lady sent for you, and you are come,—and
come in a moment too.   [*Aside.*

Bella. Your conversation and mine, Mr. Belton, you know never was but
in public. I always looked on you with indifference. You never was anything
more to me than a Bath acquaintance, neither did you ever offer, or I wish
for a nearer intimacy.

Ring. Sir, I am contented—but Sir, I hope you'll excuse me—who could
help thinking? It's all over now indeed, and in return, Sir, I hope soon to
wish you joy of Miss Tulip. I hear you[r] match with her is in great forward-
ness.   62

Bella. Miss Tulip!—What Miss Tulip?—

Ring. The common-council man's daughter of our ward, here, the great
fortune.

Bella. Indeed, Mr. Belton—married to—

Belt. Lord Madam, it's only a report.—

Bella. Sir, it's nothing to me what it is,—only I dote upon fortune-
hunters, extremely.

Belt. About a month ago, Madam, I happened to dance with that young
lady, at a City Ball—and the next day—   71

Bella. Ay, the next night, I suppose,—but you're all alike—your whole sex
is a lie, and man is a villain.

Ring. But Bella, since Mr. Belton is so indifferent to you why should you be
so alarmed?

41 White's] A popular chocolate-house in St. James's Street.

Bella. He is indifferent to me—you are indifferent to me, you are all so.—I despise ye all, I know ye all, and I'll be revenged on you all.

Belt. Madam, if—

Bella. No set speeches now, Sir, I desire you—I'm satisfied; I beg no more I may see you, Sir, that's all the request I ever intend to make you—leave me, your wife wants you, O the comforts of conjugal conversation—Oh the curse—disappointment.—[*Aside, walks about in a fury.*] Oh Belton, Belton, let the man that betrayed me, that brought me to this, but one day feel what I now endure—let me but live to see it, I'll confess my sufferings are satisfied.

[*Sits down and cries.*]

Ring. I think this affair is pretty well cleared up now, yes, yes, if our pictures were drawn now, we should make a very pretty discontented family piece.

Belt. Sir, as I entered abruptly, I shall as abruptly depart.   87

Ring. Sir, if you had spared yourself the trouble of coming here, you would not have wanted such an apology. But your design was good, to be sure. You came to clear yourself, and Miss Belladue, and so you have, faith, like a Dutch politician, made affairs worse by mending 'em, but I forgive you both, I'm an old fool, and can't help it. Tho' as the lady said, just now, but I believe not as much from her heart as I do, I beg hereafter we may be strangers to one another.   [*Exit* Belton.

[Ringworm *stands sometime looking at her.*]

Had I the fortitude of a fly now, I should banish myself from this daughter of double tongues.   96

[*As he speaks, she lets her handkerchief fall
from her face, and leans her head back.*]

She's very handsome!—Why can't she be honest? But I won't look at her.

Bella. Heigh! Ho!

Enter Maid.

Maid. Sir, there's a gentleman at the coffee-house must see you now, he wants you upon very particular business.—   100

Ring. Well, well, I'll come—Bella, my dear Bella.

Bella. Heigh! Ho! Don't tease me so.

Ring. Well, well, I won't tease you—give me one kiss before I go out.— [*Kisses her.*] There's bird-lime in her lips,—now cannot I believe Belton was here—no—nor I won't believe it,—T'other kiss, Bella—and I have no memory. Adieu, Bella, do forget Belton,—do Bella—Ah that face of thine, and this heart of mine has made me a complete grey-headed coxcomb.—

[*Exit.*

---

91 Dutch politician] Cf. 'Dutch uncle'; one whose effect is the opposite of his intent or normal function.

Bella. Forget Belton!—Oh how easy it is to bid us forget, but how impossible to obey! Call me a chair—

Maid. A chair Madam? I thought you was very ill.   110

Bella. So I am—sick at heart—sick of the world.—Sick of myself—sick of Belton, sick for him, call me a chair.

Maid. There's one at the door Madam—but—

Bella. Don't be impertinent and put on your foolish face of advice—I will find out Belton.—I'm wrong I know and I will be so.—I will have my way this once, though I am sure to suffer for it all my life after.   [*Exit.*

Maid. [*Alone.*] There she goes, and go she will, though it was down a precipice, well, the world may call us ladies of pleasure if they please, but they never were more out in their judgments. Our lives are no more than a drunkard's dream, and hurry all our happiness. We are just as fit to have money as sailors, get it in as many dangers, and spend it in as much folly. And yet, though I blame my mistress, I am too much like her, for this love is the devil, and we unhappy women are sure to be troubled with the evil spirit.
                                                                             [*Exit.*

SCENE III. *The Street.*

Enter Ringworm *coming out of the house, and* Pedagogue *meets him.*

Ring. This girl certainly loves Belton, and I as certainly love her, she has run me out considerably, and this widow must recruit me; then will I quit her genteelly—if I can, that is. Well, I will take a bottle of claret in my hand, and immediately to this widow, that when I am at a loss for something to say, I'll give her something to drink.

> For *in vino veritas* quoth Aristotle,
> The fellow was right, there is truth in a bottle.
> Then armed by a bumper, I'll urge my designo
> And prove by my practice, the *verum in vino.*   9

SCENE IV. *The* Widow's *House.*

Enter Widow Lovephrase, *reading a newspaper.*

Wid. 'On Monday next, at the Little Theatre in the Haymarket will be opened *The Female Inquisition.*'—ay, ay, this will do, this is categorical as Mr. Locke says, metaphysically to convince, demonstratively to assert, and by all the predicaments of matter, to shew that as the superficies is equal to the top, and the top is equal to the bottom, and the bottom and the top is equal to the two sides, therefore, by this parity of reasoning, all matter is as broad as 'tis long.

Enter Servant *with a letter.* [*She reads.*]

'Madam Lovephrase,
    According to your request I have found you out an oratory master for Miss, the bearer of this epistle is the person. Etc.'   10
Where is the person who presented this letter?

Ser. Below in the hall, Madam.

Wid. Desire the gentleman then to avail himself of the stairs and momentously make his appearance.

Ser. Anan Madam?

Wid. Why dolt, sophist, savage, hast thou no ideas? Cannot thou apprehend? Petition the gentlemen to perambulate into this repository, dost hear?

Ser. I can't say I do rightly, but if you be pleasen I'll send the gentleman, mayhap he mought understand ye.

Wid. Do so, bullet, hard-head, impenetrable existency—where did I leave off?—oh at matter; for the matter be material, as Mr. Locke says, yet we may syllogize.   22

Enter Harry *as a student.*

Har. Madam, I am come to syllogize from the priori to the posteriori, and through the whole converging series of investigations—mathematically, physically and metaphysically, I am, Madam, while I have an idea existing your most succumbent, and incumbent preponderating humble servant.

Wid. Sir, I am dialectically through the whole circumference of expression, your most obliged, though unknown to command.

Har. Unknown, no, Madam, the Goddess of Fame with her cloud-covered head has expanded her voice in your favour, her speaking trumpet re-echoes with your renown, you are the paragon of phrase, and your lips bear the blossom of eloquence.   32

Wid. Sir, I am essentially your humble servant.

Har. But where's my pupil, Madam? Suffer the retina of my eye to be depicted by the attitude of her form lest the blossom of my wishes, that budded with expectancy, and have put forth the fruit of full hopes, should be blasted by her absence, and my curiosity wither in the famine of a disappointment.

Wid. She shall wait on you, Sir, in the forming of an argument.

[*Whispers a servant.*

Har. You must know, Madam, in oratory, there is a beginning, a middle, and an end.—As for instance—we begin,—very well,—we go on,—well,—

15 Anan] For 'Anon': what? how's that?

we come to the middle, that's halfway, Madam; then we end at the conclusion—but how do we end?—That's periodically, we finish; but where do we
finish?—That's answered hypothetically, for as everything has a beginning
and an ending, and as the beginning, and the end, may be called the head and
tail, so it necessarily follows we must finish at the conclusion.   46

Wid. Well, he's a very great man.

Enter Miss Lovephrase.

Har. Is this young lady the last edition of your works, Madam?

Wid. She is all the books I have, I assure you, Sir.

Har. Permit me to peruse the titlepage Madam. [*Salutes her.*] She's a fine
piece of furniture for a lover's library, a most excellent apparatus to study
natural philosophy with; come, ladies pray be seated. I shall give you a
lecture immediately—Be pleased, Madam, to look over this syllabus, while I
am declaiming.   54

[*Gives* Miss *a letter on the outside of the book
that the audience may see it.*]

I would offer you one Madam, but you are an adept and too well read to
need such childish assistance.

Wid. As you please, Sir.

Har. Hem! Hem! Hem! Metaphor is the whip syllabub of oratory.
Metaphor is divided into two parts, weeds and flowers: the weeds of metaphor
are the roots of rhetoric, and the flowers of phrase compose the nosegay of
eloquence.   61

Wid. Oh he's a fine man! Is he not daughter?

Miss. Yes Madam, indeed, and indeed he is.

Wid. Pray Sir, go on, go on, dear Sir, and recapitulate, as Mr. Locke says.

Har. Man is but a male creature, he is blackened by base desires, 'till he is
made black, even black and all black. He skippeth away from reproof like a
flea, and like a bowl of punch he is full of contradictions. Now as running
waters seldom stand still, and as the making the alphabet is an old invention,
so we may say of oratory, that it is, as it is.—My first lecture ladies is a little
abstruse, but it is not the business of an orator to be always intelligible.

Wid. He is a most learned man, for certain, as Mr. Locke says.   71

Har. And now Miss, give me leave to ask, if you understand what you
have read, and if you approve it?

Miss. I do, indeed, mightily.

Har. Then Miss, with your Mama's leave, retire a moment to your
chamber; write down your observations upon it. I will wait here, 'till you
have done.   [*Exit* Miss.

This Madam, is proper, that I may judge of her genius.

Wid. By all means, most eloquent Sir.

Enter a Servant.

Ser. Madam, Mr. Ringworm.   80
Wid. Dear me, this is vexatious now, Sir, most learned Sir, may I request
with submission, you'll so far condescend to excuse the impertinence of a
visitor, and beg you'll call in the evening, that I may be farther instructed by
so great a master.

Har. Madam, I shall exonerate you immediately from the burthen of my
company Madam, and will wait on you another time. Indefatigably, Lady, I
am yours: transcendently, and supereminently, as you shine afford me a ray
of your illumination—vouchsafe your hand to my salutation, and thus I
greet you,—*vale, vale, vale.*   [*Exit.*

Wid. He's a very great man, metaphysically, as Mr. Locke says.   90

Enter Ringworm *with a bottle in his hand. He sets on the table.*

Ring. Madam, I am happy in the conversation of the learned Lady Lovephrase. Permit me, Madam, to offer to her taste, a fragment or specimen of
that liquidation, which Aristotle in his *Politics* so largely descants upon. Give
me leave, Madam, to declare, that I should rejoice to have to—that is to say—
to—damn this stuff—[*Aside.*] to, to,—drink a glass of wine with you.

Wid. Sir, for me to aver, or equivocate unclassically, would be (as Mr.
Locke says) such a solecism, that argument would not extenuate: I shall only
add, Sir, by way of codicil to your will—that I will not deny your major—
                                                                      [*Drinks.*

Ring. Further, Madam, allow me to illustrate, that I would take thee, as I
would take this glass, and I would comfort and cherish thee, as this wine
doth comfort and cherish me, I would be to thee a protector, a director, and
I,—that is to say—I should say, here's thy health.   [*Drinks.*

Enter a Servant.

Ser. Madam, my Lady Whiffle is at the door in her coach and says, she
promised to call of you, and carry you to the Inquisition.   104
Wid. Oh, I come,—take care of my daughter,—come Mr. Ringworm, you
shall go with us, we intend to speak there.

Ring. You do me honour, Madam, yet give me leave to say, though speaking is pretty, yet saying and doing are two things, and I remember an old
piece of poetry which says:

>   On words or on wind, if too much we depend,   110
>   We seldom security find,
>   A promise is broke though 'tis made by a friend,
>   For the proverb says, words are but wind.

A man full of words is a field full of weeds,
   Thus action alone is the plan.
When you buy an estate, you examine the deeds,
   By the deeds then examine your man.

[ACT II. SCENE I. *The Street.*]

Enter Harry.

Har. So, thus far all goes well, and yet methinks this letter carrying [a] queer sort of a life.—When my father sent me to college he little thought it was to qualify me for a livery, or that all the degrees I should ever take would be from footman to pimp.—In those studies I am Master of Arts however.—Well if I should be reconciled to my father, I mean, if my father should be reconciled to me—

Enter Belton.

Belt. Well Sir, what success?

Har. To our wish—I've seen the lady, delivered the letter, received an answer, [and] now only wait to find out Mr. Hempton to give it him.

Belt. Give it me Sir, I am going to him, and do you hear, if you should meet him before I do, say not a syllable of anything, 'till I see you again.

Har. Shall I tell him I gave you the letter, Sir?   12

Belt. No.

Har. Shall I tell him I had the letter, Sir?

Belt. No.

Har. Shall I tell him I had not the letter, Sir?

Belt. No.

Har. Oh, oh, I understand you Sir, yes, yes, it's as clear as noon-day; no, no, no,—a very pretty negative trio, and set to the tune of Cross-Purposes.

Belt. Go leave me.   [*Exit* Harry.

What business have I with this letter? I promised to give it to Hempton; are all men as good as their words? Suppose I should open it, it may convince me how far I may ground my hopes, or else entirely make me give over my pursuit—so far my curiosity is commendable—he told me she was fond of him.—I'd fain be satisfied—satisfied from under her own hand, and satisfied I will be—   [*Opens the letter, reads.*

  'Dear Sir   27

    My Mama goes this evening to the Inquisition—I have been a prisoner

1, 9 [a], [and]] Words illegible in MS.

for this month past but if you'll be with a ladder this evening at our garden
wall about 7 o'clock you'll find there ready to attend you

M. Lovephrase'

Enter Miss Belladue *behind him who reads as he does and then
snatches the letter out of his hand.*

Bella. Yes Sir, she shall be ready to attend you, oh, Belton, Belton!—but if
I don't—   33
   Belt. Hold Belladue, first return me that letter—or by all—
   Bella. Nay don't exalt your voice, I can be as loud as you.
   Belt. Give me the letter this moment, or—   [*Lays hold on his sword.*
   Bella. What would you, thou man of mighty madness.—

Enter Hempton.

Hemp. Hold Belton, is this the way you treat your ladies, and in the street
too?
   Bella. Oh let him alone, he's a hero indeed—no place is a sanctuary against
his anger—no virgin safe against his wiles—see how intrepid he looks—
mark his magnanimity—I have impertinently spoiled an assignation, and
now—   43
   Hemp. Come, come, the falling out of lovers you know—
   Bella. No, no, let Miss Lovephrase make it up.
   Hemp. Ha! Miss Lovephrase! What Miss Lovephrase Madam?
   Bella. A certain young lady Sir, he is at present in full gallop after. I overlooked him as he was reading a note from her, snatched it out of his hand,
and the discovery has made him desperate.
   Hemp. Is this true Belton?   50
   Bella. True Sir, do you doubt me then? There's my evidence.—[*Throws
the letter down.*] I'll take my oath the goods were found upon him.—

[Hempton *holds the letter to him.*]

Hemp. This letter—
Belt. Well Sir.—
Hemp. I need not explain myself any more upon this head, I believe—
Belt. I desire no more explanations, I am ready to attend you.—
Hemp. Follow me.—   [*Exeunt.*
   Bella. Nay hold Mr. Hempton,—Mr. Belton, nay I'll follow ye, and pre-
vent this.   [*Exit.*

SCENE II. *Piazza's Covent Garden.*

Enter Lady Whiffle, Widow, *and* Ringworm.

Whif. Well, Mem, I protest for all I have been so many years in equipage, as one may say, yet I never met with any accident of this sort before.

Ring. My Lady it's very well as it is, as long as the coach only was broke; it is but an accident not worth reflecting on.

Whif. Well, I am so ashamed, and then indeed if Madam or yourself had been hurt, I should never have forgiven myself.

Ring. All's well, Madam, and well over. I only wish we had taken a hack though.

Wid. Not at all Sir, we are just there, and as the weather is so fine, perambulating as Mr. Locke says is very wholesome exercise.—   10

Enter Harry *and* Old Belladue.

Har. There he is Sir.

O.B. A word in private with you Sir.

Ring. With me Sir?

O.B. Do you know Miss Belladue Sir?

Ring. Ladies, I beg a moment's pardon, I'll wait on you presently.

[*Exeunt ladies to the Inquisition.*
Now Sir, to your question, it is if I know Miss Belladue?

O.B. You do know her Sir, and now know me, I am the unhappy father of that more unhappy child.

Ring. Sir [*To* Harry.] this is your and your master's doing, Mr. Matchiavell is it?—Sir I hired your daughter for my housekeeper, and I don't suppose I am to be called to an account for keeping a servant.   21

O.B. Not if you had only kept her as a servant, but Sir, you have kept her as a slave—a slave to an appetite, a man of your years, ought to blush at attempting (illegally) the gratification of—

Ring. I did not ruin her, Sir.

O.B. I don't tax you with making her wretched, but keeping her so.

Ring. Sir, I saw your daughter, if Miss Belladue is your daughter, in great distress. I took compassion on her.—I relieved her; 'tis true I expected a return.—I did not know who or of what family she was. A man of intrigue would have a fine time on't indeed if he must consult the Herald's Office before he addressed a fine woman.   31

O.B. Sir you look too mean, too little in my eyes, even for me to resent your ribaldry.—From your hands I expect my daughter—what she has cost

s.d. *Piazza's*] i.e. the rival Patent Theatre, situated on Inigo Jones's piazza.

you, I'll repay, though dearly I don't doubt she has earned the bread of infamy.

Ring. Sir, as to infamy, I don't find myself a whit worse than my friend. As to your daughter, you shall have her immediately—I don't care to hear any more on this subject—I have found myself out to be a fool, and I should be very much obliged to you, if you would not make me out a rogue.

Enter Belladue *frightened and out of breath.*

Bella. For heaven's sake gentlemen lend me your assistance—Harry, your master's in danger.—Sir save two gentlemen from killing each other. [*Sees her father [and] offers to run away.*] Oh, my father.   42

O.B. Hold, Bella, don't be frightened—I am your father, your father that forgives you.—Collect yourself child.—I pity, but won't punish you.

Bella. I cannot speak Sir—

O.B. Recover yourself my dear—shew us where these gentlemen are, you were so much frighted about.—Don't look sorrowful, Bella, shew us the way to these combatants.   [*Exeunt.*

Manet Ringworm.

Ring. Well, so much for kept mistresses, I must be in the fashion—forsooth, and be fond too, ay and be fooled too. Let me reflect a little—I have been this day deceived by the woman of my bounty—and lastly documented into a fit of despair, by Signor Seneca the Second—I am old enough to grow wiser, and young enough to reform—and my plan of reformation shall begin with matrimony, and so Madam Lovephrase, or Lady Logic have at you.
                                                                    [*Exit.*

SCENE III. *A Tavern.*

Belton *discovered disarmed by* Hempton.

Hemp. Reproaches now would but ill suit me to make, worse I believe could you bear to them. Live Sir and be better, my time is too precious longer to dally with you. Mend the life you owe me, for your own sake, and I shall then be repaid.   [*Exit.*

Belt. Had I resolution to repent—nay had I shame enough to be sorry for what I have done?—Sorry I am indeed, sorry that it did not succeed—and yet this Hempton's a brave fellow, and has behaved generously to me—what then, I am like other unfortunate schemers a rogue because I am unsuccessful. This I may thank Miss Bella for, now she's even with me. I began with her ruin, she has completed mine, but I must own I have deserved it,—would her father but take her into favour again, I believe he would now have no

objection to my marrying her, and as my circumstances are at present, indeed
I should be glad of it.   13

Enter Old Belladue, Belladue, *and* Harry.

Bella. Oh, Mr. Belton,—are you not hurt Sir?

Belt. Safe child, a little chagrined though.

Bella. Where's Mr. Hempton Sir?

Belt. Didn't you meet him Sir?

Har. No, Sir.

Belt. He went away about a minute before you came in.—But pray Bella,
who may I thank for the honour of that gentleman's company? I never saw
him before I believe.—[*All stand silent a moment.*] I cannot solve this
appearance as I ought to do, and yet something whispers me that gentleman
is one whom, though I wish to know, I dread to be acquainted with. But Sir
if you claim affinity with this lady, and there is something about you that
convinces me I am right—I hope I may at least be forgiven if I declare that
what the heat of appetite has destroyed, my reason shall repair, and any
atonement in my power, I am willing this moment to make to this lady,
whom much I have injured.   28

O.B. Sir, I am indeed her father—a father whom you—but I forgive all
past errors, and hope for future prudence. I undertook this journey in hopes
to find my child, and some way bring you to do her justice.—Accident has
supplied the place of design.—Receive then Mr. Belton, this deluded, as she
ought to be, remember who was her tempter, let not what you have made her
live in your memory, but what you may make her be your hereafter employment. I have enough for you both, and I hope by your future lives you may
convince the world it is sometimes better to know how to repair a fault, than
not to have committed it.   37

Belt. Let me beg you'll excuse me at present Sir, if I don't express myself
as I ought to do. Give me your and your daughter's company to my lodgings.
Then Sir, I hope to convince you I will be worthy your future favour.—
Harry, wait on us home.   41

Har. You'll pardon me Sir, I am at present engaged; am I not going to the
Inquisition? And is it not a scheme laid?—But I forgot Sir, you were not
by at the contrivance. So I wish you all joy, satisfaction, and so forth. Now I
am not Harry your menial, but commence in an instant—Inquisitor General
of Great Britain.   [*Exeunt.*

SCENE *the last. The Inquisition.*

Lady Whiffle, Widow, Ringworm, *and many more seated.*

1st Lady. Lord, Mem, I wish you would not squeeze so.

2nd Lady. I suppose I paid for my place as well as you, Mem.

1st Lady. Excuse me there, Mem, I saw Harris give you a ticket.

2nd Lady. I am sure I would not have so much to do with Harris as some people.

1st Lady. It would be better for some people, that people had less to do with people.

2nd Lady. What do you mean Ma'am?

1st Lady. My meaning's plain enough.

2nd Lady. Not so plain as your face.   10

[*A great noise at the door. 1st* Orator *speaks without.*]

1st Orat. I will come in, I am the oldest orator, they are all hornbooks to me, my oratory's the only one in the universe. [*Enters.*] Who dares dispute me, nay who will dispute with me; I am Disputation itself—I won't pay Sir, I am tolerated.   [Doorkeeper *follows.*
Let's have no words—words are but wind, and a long discourse is like the bellyache, you don't know good manners, you are all black-guards. I am the only scholar in the world, I hate vanity and scandal, I could talk Greek in my go-cart. But I won't be made a Bishop—No I won't.—

2nd Orat. [*Enters.*] Gentlemen I must say, and beg leave to say, that tho' I have been many years President of a Society of Logicians—yet I thinks this is the most rudest behaviour I ever knows in all my life, and I thinks such a parson should be bolted out of this meeting, as bran is from flour: and winnowed away as chaff is from wheat—for a set of disputants is like a well-tied faggot: and when they are lighted up into argument, and put into the oven of education—   25

1st Orat. Education! Sirrah you are as ignorant as pot-ashes.—

3rd Orat. [*Enters.*] Hark ye, Mr. Hubble-bubble, your face and your phrase discover you have been drinking hard; the Roman orators never used potations, or bibations, only libations. I recommend sobriety to you, sup

---

3 Harris] Possibly Thomas Harris (d. 1820), who purchased a share of the Covent Garden Patent in 1767. Little is known of him earlier. 11 hornbooks] i.e. novices, neophytes. A hornbook is a primer. 18 go-cart] A 'walker', or self-propelled perambulator for infants learning to walk. 27 Mr. Hubble-bubble] A nargileh or hookah pipe; hence a bubbling noise; hence confused talk.

small beer for a fortnight, I'll send in some of my own brewing; for *Artemque repono*. My choice spirits I have metamorphosed into malt spirits, my tea into table beer, and as in the town I once had many admirers, I hope now to see as many customers,—more or less, as Tim says.—   33

[Enter Harry *as Inquisitor.]*

1st Orat. Who's this, the Inquisitor? Hark ye Mr. can you form a syllogism? I'll chop logic, or chop wood with you. I am strong both in body and mind.

Har. Gentlemen, and Ladies, Shakespeare was an illiterate fellow;—Milton a pedant, as to Bullinbrooke, I can make nothing of him, Homer was a romance writer, Virgil a translator, and Horace only a maker of ballads. I hate the ancients because they don't write with perspicuity, I despise the moderns, because they don't write at all. All learning's nonsense, and bad luck to the man that invented the alphabet.—But come, shut the door, snuff the candles, and I'll go on to my first question.—The question is, which is most eligible in an orator: to say nothing, or have nothing to say?   45

1st Orat. No man has anything to say except myself.—And I say to say nothing is best, least said is soon amended, when nothing's said, nothing wants amendment; there's wit but the world don't understand it;—three times three is the square root, all roots are good but Hebrew roots: and they are plants, rare work in the plantations: let them send me there, I'll Ohio, Ohio for them, more wit, but what then: the world's mad, not half of it can say their catechise.   52

Enter Doorkeeper *frighted.*

Doorkeeper. Gentlemen, take care of yourselves, here's a press-gang coming upstairs.—

[All the Orators *escape but the first, who is seized by the gang.*
1st Orat. Who do you lay hold of Mr. Grappling Iron—ha? Do you know the Rule of Right Reason Mr. Anchor-Stock? I am infallibility, I can prove anything.

Seaman. Then you're fit to go to sea, friend.

1st Orat. What sea, ha? Why Mr. Bullet-brains, do you think I am a sailor? No, Sirrah, I am an Orator, an Orator of Orators, and the Great Gun of Disputation. You are all amphibious animals, and stink of salt beef and gunpowder. Can you talk Greek, Mr. Spun-yarn? I am fit for an Admiral.

Sailor. Look ye friend, if you don't belay a little, I'll clap a stopper upon

---

30 *Artemque repono*] '(And) I lay aside my skill': Virgil, *Aen.* V. 484.   38 Bullinbrooke] Henry St. John (1678–1751), 1st Viscount Bolingbroke, statesman, historian, philosopher. 50 Ohio] Sing: cf., at end of play, 'The Song' verse 3, last line.

your tongue, who's obliged to bear your foul weather, Mr. Billingsgate, if
you don't understand good manners, I'll teach you.   65

1st Orat. You lie Mr. Kidnapper, I do understand good manners, better
than you do your compass, I won't box your compass, but I'll box you Mr.
Triton. Your souls are all worm-eaten,—I'll sheath them.

Sail. Clap a gag thwart his jaws, and heave off with him.—

[*They gag him and he shakes his head at them.*]

Why don't you speak now Mr. Sensible? What, all becalmed? Why he makes
no way now, see, he stares open-mouthed like a hungry shark. What does he
nod at?—His upper works are out of order. We shall have his head come by
the board by and by;—cast off and away with him.   73

[*As the* Orator *goes, enter* Mr. Hempton *and* Miss Lovephrase.]

Wid. O monstrous! What, art thou here harlotry, and with a man too?

Hem. Madam, this lady is now my wife, therefore good words I beseech
you.

Wid. What, are you conjugated? Thou essence of undutifulness. Hast thou
thrown thyself and thy fortune away ad infinitum? Is the irrevocable deed
concluded? Hast thou tied the Gordian knot, thou Runaway?—

Miss. Indeed, Mama, I hope you'll excuse me, I was told you went to be
married, and I was willing to follow the example of my parent, because you
have said I should do it.   82

Ring. This comes of logic chopping. Come, Widow, don't be uneasy: they
have got the start of us, but it's too good an example, not to be followed.
Let's leave this dry disputing, and proceed to experiment.

Wid. Well Sir, I must submit, give you joy, and may she make you a more
dutiful wife, than she has done me a daughter.

Har. So, now all parties, like the characters, in the last scene of a comedy,
seem provided for: yet methinks, I should not be the only unsuccessful
person in this day's adventure. Some service, I flatter myself, I have performed for you Mr. Hempton; in return, all I ask is your interest with this
gentleman, that he'll accept me as a volunteer. My birth is above my present
condition, my education I hope will entitle me to some respect, and I don't
doubt but my behaviour will be becoming an Englishman and a seaman.

Sail. Give us your hand, my lad, that's hearty, if I don't provide for you,
and a good berth too, may a hard gale of wind, a leaky ship, and a lee shore,
be my portion.   97

Hem. All I can assist you in, command. Receive this as an earnest of my
friendship.—   [*Gives money.*]

Sail. Come lads, bear a hand, but first let's have a song.   100

64 Billingsgate] Foul language.

The Song.

1st.

Our Navy see spread o'er the seas,
What now can our ardour restrain?
Inglorious no longer at ease,
Shall England her offspring detain.
Bear a hand my brave boys step along,
We'll not be enslaved nor enslave,
But jollily join in this song
For Britain, as Britons behave.

2nd.

This island this rocky ribbed coast,
This jewel strong set in the sea,   110
Nor gold-mines, nor vineyards can boast,
But boasts she has sons dare be free;
To the north while the needle shall show,
While canvas can swell to the wind,
To the moon, while the tides ebb and flow,
In Britain we freedom shall find.

3rd.

Britannia's good genius appear,
Appear from your green briny bed.
In your hand freedom's scepter you bear,
And commerce encircles your head;   120
Your harbinger, terror, send out,
To your side conquest buckles his sword;
Hark the Fleet fills the air with a shout:
Ohio! Ohio's the word.

4th.

Reflect on the deeds of brave Drake,
When he sailed the Armada to meet;
Remember the boldness of Blake,
When castles fell down to our Fleet.

110 jewel . . . set in the sea] Cf. *Richard II*, II. i. 40–46 and 61–3.   124 Ohio] The century-old Anglo-French rivalry in the Ohio Valley over land claims and forts culminated in the French and Indian Wars (1754–63). The British fleet's control of the Caribbean and Atlantic proved an important tactical advantage.

Those deeds did our forefathers crown,
Such deeds once again we shall see;   130
Hawke, Warren and Anson have shown,
As Britons we were we can be.

FINIS

---

131 Hawke, Warren·and Anson] Edward, Baron Hawke (1705–81), Admiral of the Fleet;
Sir Peter Warren (1703–52), Vice-Admiral; George, Lord Anson (1697–1762), Admiral of
the Fleet.

POLLY HONEYCOMBE

George Colman

1732–1794

George Colman, lawyer, essayist, editor of Beaumont and Fletcher, and translator of Horace and Terence, was also a playwright and theatre manager. After graduating from Oxford he was called to the bar (1757), but the success of his first play, *Polly Honeycombe*, three years later, pointed him towards the theatre. With Garrick he co-authored two of the most popular comedies of the day: *The Jealous Wife* (1761) and *The Clandestine Marriage* (1766). The early death of his titled patron[1] in 1764 somewhat disappointed Colman's great expectations, and he decided to seek his living in the theatre. He bought into and managed, successively, Covent Garden Theatre (1767–74) and the Little Theatre in the Haymarket (1776–88). Meanwhile he continued to write new plays of his own, and in 1773 had the distinction of producing *She Stoops to Conquer* after Garrick had turned it down at Drury Lane. Colman's last years were marred by physical and mental infirmity.

Altogether about two dozen plays, all comic pieces, came from Colman's somewhat facile pen: seven mainpiece comedies, six short comedies, and about a dozen 'illegitimate' pieces—burlettas, preludes, etc. Financially dependent on his public, Colman tended to give them what they seemed to want, and his longer pieces reveal an understandable preoccupation with the simple but enormous difference between the working and leisure classes. Always versatile, he wrote sentimental comedies and comedies of manners, a Spanish intrigue comedy, and even an early problem play, *The Suicide* (1778). His afterpieces, however, were, as custom dictated, wholly in the laughing tradition. *Polly Honeycombe*, the most successful of these, was first produced (on 5 December 1760, at Drury Lane) during a general upswing in comic activity; long and short comedies in various styles were appearing in greater numbers than at any time since the Licensing Act. Yet even in this context the play stood out, enjoying 31 performances (including two royal commands) in its first season and 17 in its second, then settling down to an unspectacular but steady popularity in the repertoire. The play was, in a sense, the first shot in the laughter *vs.* sentiment warfare (sentimental comedies being often compared to novels) which culminated in the Gold-

[1] William Pulteney, Earl of Bath.

smith–Sheridan broadsides of the seventies. It was one of the major sources of *The Rivals*, Polly serving as a sketch for Lydia Languish, and Scribble, in part, for Beverley, much as Townley's afterpiece *False Concord* had suggested to Colman the outlines of *The Clandestine Marriage*.

Polly Honeycombe is an instance of new wine in old bottles. The venerable comic confrontation of old and young over the marital issue is here made to convey a lively satiric attack upon the debauching effects of novel- and romance-reading. Thus the play fits into an eighteenth-century tradition of moralistic criticism of the early novel which includes Fielding's *Shamela*. But it has a second face: while it purports to castigate the circulating library, it half sympathizes with the Pollys and ridicules their oppressors. As Polly says, with some show of truth, 'You would dispose of your daughter like a piece of merchandise'; to which Honeycombe can only reply, 'Hark ye, hussy!' Colman's ostensible moral would be more convincing if we were shown *early* in the play that Polly is being manipulated and hoodwinked. The outcome of the struggle between these opposing forces is an *anti*-comic stand-off: there is no marriage or climactic revel. Both we and the principals are left dangling—but then the subtitle warns us that this is 'a dramatic novel', not a comedy.

The text is based on the first edition, 1760.

POLLY HONEYCOMBE,

A DRAMATICK NOVEL

OF ONE ACT,

As it is now ACTED at the

THEATRE-ROYAL

IN

DRURY-LANE.

LONDON:

Printed for T. BECKET, at Tully's-Head in the Strand;
and T. DAVIES, in Ruſſel-Street, Covent-Garden.
MDCCLX,

PROLOGUE

Spoken by Mr. KING.

Hither, in days of yore, from Spain or France
Came a dread Sorceress; her name, ROMANCE.
O'er Britain's *Isle her wayward spells she cast,*
And Common Sense in magick chain bound fast.
In mad sublime did each fond lover wooe,
And in Heroicks ran each Billet-Doux:
High deeds of Chivalry their sole Delight,
Each Fair a Maid Distrest, each Swain a Knight.
Then might Statira Orondates *see,*
At Tilts and Tournaments, arm'd Cap-a-pè.   10
She too, on Milk-white Palfrey, Lance in hand,
A Dwarf to guard her, pranced about the land.
  This Fiend to quell, his sword Cervantes *drew.*
A trusty Spanish Blade, Toledo *true:*
Her Talismans and Magick Wand he broke—
Knights, Genii, Castles—vanish'd into smoke.
  But now, the dear delight of later years,
The younger Sister of ROMANCE *appears:*
Less solemn is her air, her drift the same,
And NOVEL *her enchanting, charming, Name.*   20
ROMANCE *might strike our grave Forefathers' pomp,*
But NOVEL *for our Buck and lively Romp!*
Cassandra's *Folios now no longer read,*
See, Two Neat Pocket Volumes in their stead!
And then so sentimental *is the Stile,*
So chaste, yet so bewitching all the while!
Plot, and elopement, passion, rape, and rapture,
The total sum of ev'ry dear—dear—Chapter.
  'Tis not alone the Small-Talk and the Smart,
'Tis NOVEL *most beguiles the Female Heart.*   30
Miss reads—she melts—she sighs—Love steals upon her—
And then—Alas, poor Girl!—good night, poor Honour!

Persons

Honeycombe,	Mr. Yates.
Ledger,	Mr. Bransby.
Scribble,	Mr. King.
[John]	

Mrs. Honeycombe,	Mrs. Kennedy.
Polly,	Miss Pope.
Nurse,	Mrs. Bradshaw.

Polly Honeycombe

A Dramatic Novel of One Act

SCENE I.

An Apartment in Honeycombe's *House.*

Polly, *with a book in her hand.*

Polly. Well said, Sir George!—O the dear man!—But so—'With these words the enraptured baronet [*Reading.*] concluded his declaration of love.'—So!—'But what heart can imagine, [*Reading.*] what tongue describe, or what pen delineate, the amiable confusion of Emilia?'—Well! Now for it!—'Reader, if thou art a courtly reader, thou hast seen at polite tables, iced cream crimsoned with raspberries; or, if thou art an uncourtly reader, thou hast seen the rosy-fingered morning, dawning in the golden east;'—Dawning in the golden east!—Very pretty!—'Thou hast seen, perhaps, [*Reading.*] the artificial vermilion on the cheeks of Cleora, or the vermilion of nature on those of Sylvia; thou hast seen—in a word, the lovely face of Emilia was overspread with blushes.'—This is a most beautiful passage, I protest! Well, a novel for my money! Lord, lord, my stupid papa has no taste. He has no notion of humour, and character, and the sensibility of delicate feeling. [*Affectedly.*] And then mama,—but where was I?—Oh here—'Overspread with blushes. [*Reading.*] Sir George, touched at her confusion, gently seized her hand, and softly pressing it to his bosom, [*Acting it as she reads.*] where the pulses of his heart beat quick, throbbing with tumultuous passion, in a plaintive tone of voice breathed out, "Will you not answer me, Emilia?"'—Tender creature!—'She, half raising [*Reading and acting.*] her downcast eyes, and half inclining her averted head, said in faltering accents—"Yes Sir!"'—Well, now!—'Then gradually recovering with ineffable sweetness she prepared to address him; when Mrs. Jenkinson bounced into the room, threw down a set of china in her hurry, and strewed the floor with porcelain fragments: then turning Emilia round and round, whirled her out of the apartment in an instant, and struck Sir George dumb with astonishment at her appearance. She raved; but the baronet resumed his accustomed effrontery—'

Enter Nurse.

Oh Nurse, I am glad to see you.—Well, and how—

Nurse. Well, Chicken!

Polly. Tell me, tell me all this instant. Did you see him? Did you give him my letter? Did he write? Will he come? Shall I see him? Have you got the answer in your pocket? Have you— 32

Nurse. Blessings on her, how her tongue runs!

Polly. Nay, but come, dear Nursee, tell me, what did he say?

Nurse. Say? Why he took the letter—

Polly. Well!

Nurse. And kissed it a thousand times, and read it a thousand times, and—

Polly. Oh charming!

Nurse. And ran about the room, and blessed himself, and, heaven preserve us, cursed himself, and— 40

Polly. Very fine! Very fine!

Nurse. And vowed he was the most miserable creature upon earth, and the happiest man in the world, and—

Polly. Prodigiously fine! Excellent! My dear dear Nursee! [*Kissing her.*] Come, give me the letter.

Nurse. Letter, Chicken! What letter?

Polly. The answer to mine. Come then!   [*Impatiently.*

Nurse. I have no letter. He had such a *peramble* to write, by my troth I could not stay for it.

Polly. Pshah!
                                                                        50
Nurse. How soon you're affronted now! He said he'd send it some time today.

Polly. Send it some time today!—I wonder now, [*As if musing.*] how he will convey it. Will he squeeze it, as he did the last, into the chicken-house in the garden? Or will he write it in lemon-juice, and send it in a book, like blank paper? Or will he throw it into the house, enclosed in an orange? Or will he—

Nurse. Heaven bless her, what a sharp wit she has!

Polly. I have not read so many books for nothing. Novels, Nursee, novels! A novel is the only thing to teach a girl life, and the way of the world, and elegant fancies, and love to the end of the chapter. 61

Nurse. Yes, yes, you are always reading your simple story-books. The *Ventures* of Jack this, and the *History* of Betsy t'other, and Sir Humphrys, and women with hard Christian names. You had better read your prayer-book, Chicken.

Polly. Why so I do; but I'm reading this now—[*Looking into the book.*] 'She raved, but the baronet'—I really think I love Mr. Scribble as well as Emilia did Sir George.—Do you think, Nursee, I should have had such a good notion of love so early, if I had not read novels?—Did not I make a conquest of Mr. Scribble in a single night at dancing? But my cross papa will hardly ever let me go out.—And then, I know life as well as if I had been in the *beau monde* all my days. I can tell the nature of a masquerade as well as if I had been at twenty. I long for a mobbing scheme with Mr. Scribble to the two-shilling gallery, or a snug party a little way out of town, in a post-chaise—and then, I have such a head full of intrigues and contrivances! Oh, Nursee, a novel is the only thing.   76

Nurse. Contrivances! Ay, marry, you have need of contrivances. Here are your papa and mama fully resolved to marry you to young Mr. Ledger, Mr. Simeon the rich Jew's wife's nephew, and all the while your head runs upon nothing but Mr. Scribble.   80

Polly. A fiddle-stick's end for Mr. Ledger! I tell you what, Nursee. I'll marry Mr. Scribble, and not marry Mr. Ledger, whether papa and mama choose it or no.—And how do you think I'll contrive it?

Nurse. How? Chicken!

Polly. Why, don't you know?

Nurse. No, indeed.

Polly. And can't you guess?

Nurse. No, by my troth, not I.

Polly. O lord, it's the commonest thing in the world.—I intend to elope.

Nurse. Elope! Chicken, what's that?   90

Polly. Why, in the vulgar phrase, run away,—that's all.

Nurse. Mercy on us!—Run away!

Polly. Yes, run away, to be sure. Why there's nothing in that, you know. Every girl elopes, when her parents are obstinate and ill-natured about marrying her. It was just so with Betsy Thompson, and Sally Wilkins, and Clarinda, and Leonora in the *History of Dick Careless*, and Julia in the *Adventures of Tom Ramble*, and fifty others—did not they all elope? And so will I too. I have as much right to elope, as they had, for I have as much love and as much spirit as the best of them.

Nurse. Why, Mr. Scribble's a fine man to be sure, a gentleman every inch of him!   101

Polly. So he is, a dear charming man!—Will you elope too, Nursee?

Nurse. Not for the varsal world. Suppose now, Chicken, your papa and mama—

Polly. What care I for papa and mama? Have not they been married and happy long enough ago? And are not they still coaxing, and fondling, and

---

73 mobbing scheme] A party of pleasure to make a commotion at the playhouse, perhaps by helping to damn or promote a new play on its first night.   74 two-shilling gallery] The first gallery, occupied generally by the middle classes. The upper or 'footman's gallery', to which admission was 1s., was more often the source of playhouse disturbances, and was chiefly responsible for the gallery's bad reputation in the eighteenth century.   103 varsal] Whole.

F

kissing each other all the day long?—'Where's my dear love, [*Mimicking*].
my beauty?' says papa, hobbling along with his crutch-headed cane, and his
old gouty legs: 'Ah, my sweeting, my precious Mr. Honeycombe, d'ye love
your nown dear wife?' says mama; and then they squeeze their hard hands to
each other, and their old eyes twinkle, and they're as loving as Darby and
Joan—especially if mama has had a cordial or two—eh! Nursee!

Nurse. Oh fie, Chicken!   113

Polly. And then perhaps, in comes my utter aversion, Mr. Ledger, with
his news from the Change, and his Change-alley wit, and his thirty per cent
[*Mimicking.*] and stocks have risen one and a half and three eighths.—I'll tell
ye what, Nursee! They would make fine characters for a novel, all three of
them.

Nurse. Ah, you're a graceless bird!—But I must go downstairs, and watch
if the coast's clear, in case of a letter.   120

Polly. Could not you go to Mr. Scribble's again after it?

Nurse. Again! Indeed, Mrs. Hot-upon't!

Polly. Do now, my dear Nursee, pray do! And call at the Circulating
Library, as you go along, for the rest of this novel—*The History of Sir George
Truman and Emilia*—and tell the bookseller to be sure to send me the *British
Amazon*, and *Tom Faddle*, and the rest of the new novels this winter, as soon
as ever they come out.

Nurse. Ah, pise on your naughty novels! I say.   [*Exit.*

Polly. Ay, go now, my dear Nursee, go, there's a good woman!—What an
old fool it is! With her pise on it—and fie, Chicken—and no, by my troth—
[*Mimicking.*]—Lord! What a strange house I live in! Not a soul in it, except
myself, but what are all queer animals, quite droll creatures. There's papa
and mama, and the old foolish nurse.—   133

Re-enter Nurse *with a band-box.*

Oh, Nursee, what brings you back so soon? What have you got there?

Nurse. Mrs. Commode's 'prentice is below, and has brought home your
new cap and ruffles, Chicken!

Polly. Let me see—let me see—[*Opening the box.*] Well, I swear this is a
mighty pretty cap, a sweet pair of flying lappets! Aren't they, Nursee?—Ha!
What's this? [*Looking into the box.*]—Oh charming! A letter! Did not I tell
you so?—Let's see—let's see—[*Opening the letter hastily—it contains three or
four sheets.*] 'Joy of my soul—only hope,—eternal bliss—[*Dipping into different places.*] The cruel blasts of coyness and disdain blow out the flame of
love, but then the virgin breath of kindness and compassion blows it in again.'
—Prodigious pretty! Isn't it, Nursee?   [*Turning over the leaves.*

Nurse. Yes, that is pretty,—but what a deal there is on't! It's an old saying

128 pise] An obscure imprecation, similar to 'fie'.

and a true one, the more there's said the less there's done. Ah, they wrote other guess sort of letters, when I was a girl!   [*While she talks* Polly *reads.*

Polly. Lord, Nursee, if it was not for novels and love-letters, a girl would have no use for her writing and reading.—But what's here? [*Reading.*] Poetry!—'Well may I cry out with Alonzo in *The Revenge*—   150

> Where didst thou steal those eyes? From heaven?
> Thou didst, and 'tis religion to adore them!'

Excellent! Oh! He's a dear man!

Nurse. Ay, to be sure!—But you forget your letter-carrier below, she'll never bring you another, if you don't speak to her kindly.

Polly. Speak to her! Why I'll give her sixpence, woman! Tell her I am coming.—I will but just read my letter over five or six times, and go to her.— Oh, he's a charming man! [*Reading.*] Very fine! Very pretty!—He writes as well as Bob Lovelace—[*Kissing the letter.*] Oh, dear, sweet Mr. Scribble!

[*Exit.*

SCENE *changes to another apartment*.

Honeycombe *and* Mrs. Honeycombe *at breakfast*—Honeycombe *reading the newspaper*.

Mrs. Honey. My dear!   [*Peevishly.*
Honey. What d'ye say, my love?   [*Still reading.*
Mrs. Honey. You take no notice of me.—Lay by that silly paper—put it down—come then—drink your tea.—You don't love me now.
Honey. Ah! My beauty!   [*Looking very fondly.*
Mrs. Honey. Do you love your own dear wife?   [*Tenderly.*
Honey. Dearly.—She knows I do.—Don't you, my beauty?
Mrs. Honey. Ah, you're a dear, dear man! [*Rising and kissing him.*] He does love her—and he's her own husband—and she loves him most dearly and tenderly—that she does.   [*Kissing him.*
Honey. My beauty! I have a piece of news for you.   11
Mrs. Honey. What is it, my sweeting!
Honey. The paper here says, that young Tom Seaton, of Aldersgate-Street, was married yesterday at Bow Church, to Miss Fairly of Cornhill.
Mrs. Honey. A flaunting, flaring hussy! She a husband!—
Honey. But what does my beauty think of her own daughter?
Mrs. Honey. Of our Polly? Sweeting!
Honey. Ay, Polly: what sort of a wife d'ye think she'll make? My love!—I

---

147 other guess sort] A different kind.   150 *The Revenge*] A tragedy by Edward Young, first produced in 1721 at Drury Lane.   159 Bob Lovelace] The rake protagonist in Richardson's *Clarissa*.

concluded everything with Mr. Simeon yesterday, and expect Mr. Ledger
every minute.   20

Mrs. Honey. Think, my sweetings!—Why, I think, if she loves him half
so well as I do my own dear man, that she'll never suffer him out of her sight
—that she'll look at him with pleasure—[*They both ogle fondly.*]—and love
him—and kiss him—and fondle him—oh, my dear, it's impossible to say
how dearly I love you.   [*Kissing and fondling.*

Enter Ledger.

Ledger. Heyday! What now, good folks, what now? Are you so much in
arrear? Or are you paying off principal and interest both at once?

Honey. My dear!—Consider—Mr. Ledger is—

Mrs. Honey. What signifies Mr. Ledger?—He is one of the family, you
know, my sweeting!   30

Ledger. Ay, so I am,—never mind me—never mind me.—Tho' by the by,
I should be glad of somebody to make much of me too. Where's Miss Polly?

Honey. That's right—that's right.—Here, John!

Enter John.

Where's Polly?

John. In her own room, sir.

Honey. Tell her to come here—and hark ye, John! While Mr. Ledger
stays, I am not at home to anybody else.   [*Exit* John.

Ledger. Not at home!—Are those your ways?—If I was to give such a
message to my servant, I should expect a commission of bankruptcy out
against me the next day.   40

Honey. Ay, you men of large dealings—it was so with me, when I was in
business.—But where's this girl? What can she be about?—My beauty, do
step yourself, and send her here immediately.

Mrs. Honey. I will, my sweeting!   [*Offering to kiss him.*

Honey. Nay, my love, not now—

Mrs. Honey. Why not now?—I will. [*Kissing him.*] Goodbye, love.—Mr.
Ledger, your servant!—Bye, dearest!   [*Exit.*

Honey. Ha! Ha! You see, Mr. Ledger! You see what you are to come to—
but I beg pardon—I quite forgot—have you breakfasted?

Ledger. Breakfasted! Ay, four hours ago, and *done* an hundred tickets
since, over a dish of coffee, at Garrayway's.—Let me see, [*Pulling out his
watch.*] bless my soul, it's eleven o'clock! I wish Miss would come.—It's
Transfer-Day.—I must be at the Bank before twelve, without fail.   53

50 tickets] Written notices of the amount of stocks and shares to be delivered by a
broker.   53 Transfer-Day] The day on which transfers of bank stock are registered (at
the Bank of England).

Honey. Oh, here she comes.—

Enter Polly.

—Come, child!—Where have you been all this time?—Well, Sir, I'll leave
you together.—Polly, you'll—ha! ha! ha!—Your servant, Mr. Ledger, your
servant!   [*Exit.*

[Polly *and* Ledger *remain,—they stand at a great distance
from each other.*]

Polly. [*Aside.*] What a monster of a man!—What will the frightful creature
say to me?—I am now, for all the world, just in the situation of poor
Clarissa,—and the wretch is ten times uglier than Soames himself.   60
Ledger. Well, Miss!
Polly. [*Aside.*] He speaks! What shall I say to him?—Suppose I have a
little sport with him.—I will.—I'll indulge myself with a few airs of distant
flirtation at first, and then treat him like a dog. I'll use him worse than Nancy
Howe ever did Mr. Hickman.—Pray, Sir, [*To* Ledger.] did you ever read *The
History of Emilia?*
Ledger. Not I, Miss, not I.—I have no time to think of such things, not I.
I hardly ever read anything, except the *Daily Advertiser*, or the list at Lloyd's
—nor write neither, except it's my name now and then.—I keep a dozen
clerks for nothing in the world else but to write.   70
Polly. A dozen clerks!—Prodigious!
Ledger. Ay, a dozen clerks. Business must be done, Miss!—We have large
returns, and the balance must be kept on the right side, you know.—In
regard to last year now—our returns from the first of January to the last of
December, fifty-nine, were to the amount of sixty thousand pounds, sterling.
We clear upon an average, at the rate of twelve per cent. Cast up the twelves
in sixty thousand, and you may make a pretty good guess at our net
profits.
Polly. Net profits!
Ledger. Ay, Miss, net profits. Simeon and Ledger are names as well
known as any in the Alley, and good for as much at the bottom of a piece of
paper.—But no matter for that—you must know that I have an account to
settle with you, Miss.—You're in the debtor side in my books, I can tell
you, Miss.   84
Polly. I in your debt, Mr. Ledger!
Ledger. Over head and ears in my debt, Miss!
Polly. I hate to be in debt of all things—pray let me discharge you at once
—for I can't endure to be dunned.
Ledger. Not so fast, Miss! Not so fast. Right reckoning makes long friends.

60 Soames] Probably Roger Solmes, Clarissa's unwelcome suitor.   64 Nancy Howe]
Clarissa's confidante.

—Suppose now we should compound this matter, and strike a balance in favour of both parties.   91

Polly. How d'ye mean? Mr. Ledger!

Ledger. Why then in plain English, Miss, I love you—I'll marry you—my uncle Simeon and Mr. Honeycombe have settled the matter between them—I am fond of the match—and hope you are the same.—There's the Sum Total.

Polly. Lord, this is so strange!—Besides, is it possible that I can have any charms for Mr. Ledger?

Ledger. Charms! Miss; you are all over charms.—I like you—I like your person, your family, your fortune—I like you altogether—the Omniums—eh, Miss!—I like the Omniums—and don't care how large a premium I give for them.   102

Polly. Lord, sir!

Ledger. Come, Miss, let's both set our hands to it, and sign and seal the agreement, without loss of time, or hindrance of business.

Polly. Not so fast, sir, not so fast.—Right reckoning makes long friends, you know—Mr. Ledger!

Ledger. Miss!

Polly. After so explicit and polite a declaration on your part, you will expect, no doubt, some suitable returns on mine.   110

Ledger. To be sure, Miss, to be sure—ay, ay, let's examine the *per contra.*

Polly. What you have said, Mr. Ledger, has, I take it for granted been very sincere.

Ledger. Very sincere, upon my credit, Miss!

Polly. For my part then, I must declare, however unwillingly—

Ledger. Out with it, Miss!

Polly. That the passion I entertain for you is equally strong—

Ledger. Oh brave!

Polly. And that I do with equal or more sincerity—   120

Ledger. Thank you, Miss; thank you!

Polly. Hate and detest—

Ledger. How! How!

Polly. Loathe and abhor you—

Ledger. What! What!

Polly. Your sight is shocking to me, your conversation odious, and your passion contemptible—

Ledger. Mighty well, Miss; mighty well!

Polly. You are a vile book of arithmetic, a table of pounds, shillings, and

100 Omniums] The aggregate value of stocks, etc., offered by the Government, in raising loan, for each unit of capital subscribed. The root (Latin) meaning is 'all', 'everything'.

pence—you are uglier than a figure of eight, and more tiresome than the
multiplication-table.—There's the Sum Total.   131
Ledger. Flesh and blood—
Polly. Don't talk to me—get along—or if you don't leave the room, I will.
Ledger. Very fine, very fine, Miss!—Mr. Honeycombe shall know this.
                                                                    [*Exit.*
Polly. [*Alone.*] Ha! Ha! Ha!—There he goes!—Ha! Ha! Ha!—I have out-
topped them all—Miss Howe, Narcissa, Clarinda, Polly Barnes, Sophy
Willis, and all of them. None of them ever treated an odious fellow with half
so much spirit.—This would make an excellent chapter in a new novel.—
But here comes papa—in a violent passion, no doubt.—No matter—it will
only furnish materials for the next chapter.   140

Enter Honeycombe.

Honey. What is the meaning, mistress Polly, of this extraordinary behaviour? How dare you treat Mr. Ledger so ill, and behave so undutifully to
your papa and mama?—You are a spoilt child—your mama and I have been
too fond of you—but have a care, young madam! Mend your conduct, or you
may be sure, we'll make you repent on't.
Polly. Lord, papa, how can you be so angry with me?—I am as dutiful as
any girl in the world.—But there's always an uproar in the family about
marrying the daughter, and now poor I must suffer in my turn.
Honey. Hark ye, Miss!—Why did you not receive Mr. Ledger as your
lover?   150
Polly. Lover!—Oh, dear papa!—He has no more of a lover about him!—
He never so much as cast one languishing look towards me, or struck his
breast, or threw himself at my feet, or—Lord, I read such a delightful
declaration of love in the new novel this morning! First, papa, Sir George
Truman—
Honey. Devil take Sir George Truman!—These cursed novels have turned
the girl's head.—Hark ye, hussy! I could almost find in my heart to—I say,
hussy, isn't Mr. Ledger a husband of your papa and mama's providing? And
aren't they the properest persons to dispose of you?
Polly. Dispose of me!—See there now! Why you have no notion of these
things, papa!—Your head's so full of trade and commerce, that you would
dispose of your daughter like a piece of merchandise—but my heart is my
own property, and at nobody's disposal, but my own.—Sure you would not
consign me, like a bale of silk, to Ledger and Co.—Eh! Papa!   164
Honey. Her impudence amazes me.—Hark ye, hussy, you're an undutiful
slut—

136–7 Miss Howe, . . . Sophy Willis] Miss Anna, or Nancy, Howe: see l. 64 n.; the rest
are generic names for heroines of novels and romances.

Polly. Not at all undutiful, papa!—But I hate Mr. Ledger.—I can't endure the sight of him—

Honey. This is beyond all patience.—Hark ye, hussy, I'll—

Polly. Nay more; to tell you the whole truth, my heart is devoted to another. I have an insuperable passion for him; and nothing shall shake my affection for my dear Mr. Scribble.   172

Honey. Mr. Scribble!—Who's Mr. Scribble?—Hark ye, hussy, I'll turn you out of doors.—I'll have you confined to your chamber—get out of my sight—I'll have you locked up this instant.

Polly. Locked up! I thought so. Whenever a poor girl refuses to marry any horrid creature her parents provide for her, then she's to be locked up immediately.—Poor Clarissa! Poor Sophy Western! I am now going to be treated just as you have been before me.

Honey. Those abominable books!—Hark ye, hussy! You shall have no novel to amuse you—get along, I say—nor no pen and ink to scrawl letters—why don't you go?—nor no trusty companion.—Get along—I'll have you locked up this instant, and the key of your chamber shall be in your mama's custody.   184

Polly. Indeed, papa, you need not give my mama so much trouble.—I have—

Honey. Get along, I say.

Polly. I have read of such things as ladders of ropes—

Honey. Out of my sight!

Polly. Or of escaping out of window, by tying the sheets together—

Honey. Hark ye, hussy—   190

Polly. Or of throwing oneself into the street upon a feather-bed—

Honey. I'll turn you out of doors—

Polly. Or of being catched in a gentleman's arms—

Honey. Zouns, I'll—

Polly. Or of—

Honey. Will you be gone?   [*Exeunt, both talking.*

SCENE *changes to* Polly's *apartment.*

Enter Scribble, *disguised in a livery.*

Scrib. So!—In this disguise mistress Nurse has brought me hither safe and undiscovered.—Now for Miss Polly! Here's her letter: a true picture of her nonsensical self!—'To my dearest Mr. Scribble.' [*Reading the direction.*] And the seal two doves billing, with this motto:

> We two,
> When we woo,
> Bill and coo.

—Pretty!—And a plain proof I shan't have much trouble with her.—I'll make short work on't.—I'll carry her off today, if possible.—Clap up a marriage at once, and then down upon our marrow-bones, and ask pardon and blessing of papa and mama. [*Noise without.*] Here she comes.   11

Honey. [*Without.*] Get along, I say,—Up to your own chamber, hussy!

Polly. [*Without.*] Well, papa, I am—

Scrib. O the devil!—Her father coming up with her!—What shall I do? [*Running about.*] Where shall I hide myself?—I shall certainly be discovered.—I'll get up the chimney.—Zouns! They are just here.—Ten to one the old cuff may not stay with her—I'll pop into this closet.   [*Exit.*

Enter Honeycombe *and* Polly.

Honey. Here, mistress Malapert, stay here, if you please, and chew the cud of disobedience and mischief in private.

Polly. Very well, papa!   20

Honey. Very well!—What! Are you sulky now! Hark ye, hussy, you are a saucy minx, and it's not very well.—I have a good mind to keep you upon bread and water this month. I'll—I'll—but I'll say no more—I'll lock you up, and carry the key to your mama—she'll take care of you.—You will have Mr. Scribble.—Let's see how he can get to you now. [*Showing the key.*]

          [*Exit, locking the door.*

Polly. [*Alone.*] And so I will have Mr. Scribble too, do what you can, Old Squaretoes!—I am provided with pen, ink, and paper, in spite of their teeth.—I remember that Clarissa had cunning drawers made on purpose to secure those things, in case of an accident—I am very glad I have had caution enough to provide myself with the same implements of intrigue, though with a little more ingenuity.—Indeed now they make standishes, and tea-chests, and dressing boxes, in all shorts of shapes and figures—but mine are of my own invention.—Here I've got an excellent ink-horn in my pin-cushion.—And a case of pens, and some paper, in my fan. [*Produces them.*] I will write to Mr. Scribble immediately. I shall certainly see him eavesdropping about our door the first opportunity, and then I'll toss it to him out of the window.   [*Sits down to write.*

Scrib. [*Putting his head out of the door of the closet.*] A clear coast, I find—the old codger's gone, and has locked me up with his daughter—so much the better!—Pretty soul! What is she about? Writing?—A letter to me, I'll bet ten to one—I'll go and answer it *in propria persona.*   40

          [*Comes forward, and stands behind* Polly, *looking over her writing.*

Polly. [*Writing.*] 'Me—in—your—arms.'—Let me see—what have I written? [*Reading.*] 'My dearest dear, Mr. Scribble.'

Scrib. I thought so!

17 cuff] An old man, a miserly old fellow.   31 standishes] Inkstands.

Polly. [*Reading.*] 'I am now writing in the most cruel confinement. Fly then, oh fly to me on the wings of love, release me from this horrid gaol, and imprison me in your arms.'

Scrib. That I will with all my heart.   [*Embracing her.*

Polly. Oh!   [*Screaming.*

Scrib. O the devil!—Why do you scream so?—I shall be discovered in spite of fortune.   [*Running about.*

Polly. Bless me! Is it you? Hush! [*Running to the door.*] Here's my father coming upstairs, I protest.   52

Scrib. What the deuce shall I do?—I'll run into the closet again.

Polly. O no! He'll search the closet.—Lord, here's no time to—he's here— get under the table—[Scribble *hides.*]—Lie still—what shall I say?

[*Sits down by the table.*

Enter Honeycombe.

Honey. How now? Hussy!—What's all this noise?

Polly. Sir!   [*Affecting surprise.*

Honey. What made you scream so violently?

Polly. Scream! Papa?

Honey. Scream? Papa!—Ay, scream, hussy!—What made you scream? I say.   61

Polly. Lord, papa, I have never opened my lips, but have been in a philosophical reverie ever since you left me.

Honey. I am sure I thought I heard—but how now, hussy! What's here?— Pens—ink—and paper!—Hark ye, hussy!—How came you by these?—So! So! Fine contrivances!—[*Examining them.*]—And a letter begun too— 'cruel confinement—wings of love—your arms.' [*Reading.*] Ah, you forward slut!—But I am glad I have discovered this—I'll seize these movables.—So! So! Now write, if you can.—Nobody shall come near you—send to him, if you can.—Now see how Mr. Scribble will get at you.—Now I have you safe, mistress!—and now—ha! ha!—now you may make love to the table.

[*Exit, locking the door.*

Polly. So I will.—We'll turn the tables upon you. Come, Mr. Scribble.

Scrib. Here am I, my love!—This is lucky, and droll too.—Under the table! Ha! ha! ha! This is like making love in a pantomime.—But my dear, you should not have screamed so.   75

Polly. Lord, who thought of you?—I was as much surprised as Sophy Western, when she saw Tom Jones in the looking-glass.—But what brought you here?

Scrib. Love.

Polly. What put you into that habit?   80

Scrib. You and love, my dear Polly, you.—I wear your livery.

Polly. Lord! How well it becomes him!—But why a livery? Mr. Scribble.

Scrib. Only to carry on our affair more securely—a little amour in masquerade.—Do you know me? [*Mimicking*.

Polly. Comical creature!—But how did you get here?

Scrib. Under this disguise, I pretended business to the Nurse, and she brought me hither.

Polly. Admirable!—This is a most charming adventure.

Scrib. Isn't it?

Polly. And have you really a sincere passion for me?   90

Scrib. A sincere passion!—True as the needle to the pole, or the dial to the sun.

Polly. But Mr. Scribble!

Scrib. My dear!

Polly. D'ye think I am as handsome as Clarissa, or Clementina, or Pamela, or Sophy Western, or Amelia, or Narcissa, or—

Scrib. Handsome!—You are a constellation of all their beauties blended together.—Clarissa, and Sophy, and the rest of them, were but mere types of you.—But, my little charmer, what was the meaning of all that uproar I heard just now, and of your being locked up in this manner?   100

Polly. You.

Scrib. I?

Polly. Yes, you. You was the meaning of it. They brought me an odious fellow for an husband; and so I told them that he was my utter aversion; that I was enamoured with you, and you alone, and that my attachment was inviolable to my dear Mr. Scribble.

Scrib. The deuce you did! You need not blush to own your passion for me, to be sure—but things were not quite ripe for that yet.

Polly. Yes, but they were ripe, and ripe enough.—What, d'ye think I don't know how to manage for the best?   110

Scrib. O to be sure! But then this being kept under lock and key, like the old curmudgeon's strong box, spoils the finest scheme.

Polly. What scheme?

Scrib. Why, a scheme to bring matters to issue at once. I was in hopes of securing you for ever, this very day.—I intended to have stolen slily downstairs with you, made a silent escape into the street, have squeezed you into a chair in a twinkling, had you conveyed to my lodging, and have strutted thither with a 'by your leave, gemmin!' before your chair, in this livery.

Polly. A most excellent contrivance!—We must put it in execution—how can we manage it?—Let's make our escape out of the window!

Scrib. I must beg to be excused.   121

95-6 Clarissa . . . Amelia] Clarissa and Pamela are heroines in Richardson's novels, Sophy Western and Amelia in Fielding's.

Polly. Let us force the lock then—or take off the screws of it—or suppose we should contrive to—   [*Noise at the door.*

Scrib. 'Sdeath! Here's somebody coming.

Polly. Hush!—Stay!— [*Running to the door and peeping through the key-hole.*]—O no! It's only Nurse.

After unlocking the door, enter Nurse.

Nurse. Well, Chicken!—Where's Mr. Scribble?

Scrib. O, Mrs. Nurse, is it you?—I am heartily glad to see you.

Polly. Oh Nursee! You frighted us out of our little wits.—I thought it had been papa or mama.   130

Nurse. Ah, Chicken, I've taken care of your mama—but I must not stay long—Mr. Honeycombe brought her the key in a parlous fury, with orders to let nobody go near you, except himself.—But I—I can't choose but laugh —I prevailed on Madam to take a glass extraordinary of her cordial, and have left her fast asleep in her own chamber.

Polly. The luckiest thing in the world!—Now, Mr. Scribble, we may put your stratagem in practice this instant.

Scrib. With all my heart.—I wish we were out of the house.

Polly. Away, away then!

Nurse. Softly, Chicken, softly!—Let me go before, to see that there's nobody in the way. Come gently downstairs. I'll set open the door of your cage, and then you may take wing as fast as you please.—Ah, you're a sweet pair of turtles!—Come along.   143

Scrib. Turtles indeed! Come, my dear!—We two, when we woo, bill and coo.

Polly. Very well!—You're to walk before my chair, remember!—This is the finest adventure I ever had in my life!   [*Exeunt, following the* Nurse.

SCENE *changes to* Mrs. Honeycombe's *apartment.*

Mrs. Honeycombe *alone,—several phials on the table, with labels.*

Mrs. Honey. I am not at all well today.—[*Yawns, as if just waking.*]—Such a quantity of tea in a morning, makes one quite nervous—and Mr. Honeycombe does not choose it qualified.—I have such a dizziness in my head, it absolutely turns round with me.—I don't think neither that the hysteric water is warm enough for my stomach. I must speak to Mr. Julep to order me something rather more comfortable.

Enter Nurse.

143 turtles] Turtle-doves.   Sc. iv, 3 qualified] i.e. diluted.

Nurse. Did you call, Ma'am?

Mrs. Honey. Oh Nurse, is it you?—No, I did not call—where's Mr. Honeycombe?

Nurse. Below stairs in the parlour, Madam.—I did not think she'd have waked so soon—if she should miss the key now, before I've an opportunity to lay it down again! [*Aside.*

Mrs. Honey. What d'ye say? Nurse! 13

Nurse. Say? Ma'am!—Say!—I say, I hope you're a little better, Ma'am!

Mrs. Honey. Oh Nurse, I am perfectly giddy with my nerves, and so low-spirited.

Nurse. Poor gentlewoman! Suppose I give you a sup out of the case of Italian cordials, Ma'am! That was sent as a present from Mr. What-d'ye-call-him, in Crutched-Fryars—the Italian merchant with the long name. 20

Mrs. Honey. Filthy poison! Don't mention it!—Faugh! I hate the very names of them.—You know, Nurse, I never touch any cordials, but what come from the apothecary's.—What o'clock is it?—Isn't it time to take my draught?

Nurse. By my troth, I believe it is—let me see, I believe this is it—[*Takes up a phial, and slips the key upon the table.*] 'The stomachic draught to be taken an hour before dinner. For Mrs. Honeycombe.' [*Reading the label.*]— Ay, this is it.—By my troth, I am glad I've got rid of the key again.

[*Aside.*

Mrs. Honey. Come then!—Pour it into a teacup and give it me.—I'm afraid I can't take it. It goes sadly against me. 30

While she is drinking, Honeycombe *without.*

Honey. Run, John, run!—After them immediately!—Harry, do you run too—stick close to Mr. Ledger—don't return without them for your life!

Nurse. Good lack! Good lack! They're discovered, as sure as the day.

[*Aside.*

Mrs. Honey. Lord, Nurse, what's the matter?

Nurse. I don't know, by my troth.

Enter Honeycombe.

Mrs. Honey. O, my sweeting, I am glad you are come.—I was so frighted about you. [*Rises, and seems disordered.*

Honey. Zouns, my dear—

Mrs. Honey. O don't swear, my dearest!

Honey. Zouns, it's enough to make a parson swear—you have let Polly escape—she's run away with a fellow. 41

Mrs. Honey. You perfectly astonish me, my dear!—I can't possibly conceive—my poor head aches too to such a degree—where's the key of her chamber?   [*Seems disordered.*

Nurse. Here, Madam, here it is.

Honey. Zouns, I tell you—

Mrs. Honey. Why here's the key, my sweeting!—It's absolutely impossible—it has lain here ever since you brought it me—not a soul has touched it —have they, Nurse?   [*Disordered.*

Nurse. Not a creature, I'll take my Bible oath on't.   50

Honey. I tell you, she's gone.—I'm sure on't—Mr. Ledger saw a strange footman put her into a chair, at the corner of the street—and he and John, and a whole posse, are gone in pursuit of them.

Mrs. Honey. This is the most extraordinary circumstance—it's quite beyond my comprehension—but my sweeting must not be angry with his own dear wife—it was not her fault.   [*Fondling.*

Honey. Nay, my love, don't trifle now!—

Mrs. Honey. I must—I will—

Honey. Zouns, my dear, be quiet!—I shall have my girl ruined for ever.

Ledger. [*Without.*] This way—this way—bring them along!   60

Honey. Hark! They're coming—Mr. Ledger has overtaken them—they're here.

Ledger. [*Without.*] Here!—Mr. Honeycombe is in this room—come along!

Enter Ledger, Polly, *and* Scribble, *with servants.*

Ledger. Here they are, Mr. Honeycombe!—We've brought them back again.—Here they are, Madam.

Honey. Hark ye, hussy! I have a good mind to turn you out of doors again immediately.—You are a disgrace to your family.—You're a shame to—

Mrs. Honey. Stay, my dear, don't you put yourself into such a passion!— Polly, observe what I say to you—let me know the whole circumstances of this affair—I don't at all understand—tell me, I say—   [*Disordered.*

Honey. Zouns! I have no patience.—Hark ye, hussy!—Where was you going?—Who does this fellow belong to?—Where does he live?—Who is he?

Polly. That gentleman, papa, is Mr. Scribble.   73

Honey. This! Is this Mr. Scribble?

Scrib. The very man, sir, at your service—an humble admirer of Miss Honeycombe's.

Polly. Yes, papa, that's Mr. Scribble.—The sovereign of my heart—the sole object of my affections.

Mrs. Honey. What can be the meaning of all this?

Honey. Why you beggarly slut!—What, would you run away from your family with a fellow in livery? A footman?   81

Polly. A footman! Ha! ha! ha! Very good; a footman!—

Scrib. A footman, eh, my dear!—An errand boy!—A scoundrel fellow in livery—a good joke, faith!   [*Laughing with* Polly.

Polly. Why, papa, don't you know that every gentleman disguises himself in the course of an amour?—Don't you remember that Bob Lovelace disguised himself like an old man? And Tom Ramble like an old woman?—No adventure can be carried on without it.

Honey. She's certainly mad—stark mad.—Hark ye, sir! Who are you?— I'll have you sent to the compter—you shall give an account of yourself before My Lord Mayor.   91

Scribe. What care I for My Lord Mayor, or the whole court of Aldermen? —Hark ye, old Greybeard, I am a gentleman—a gentleman as well known as any in the city.

Mrs. Honey. Upon my word, I believe so.—He seems a very proper gentleman-like young person.

Ledger. As well known as any in the city!—I don't believe it—he's no good man—I am sure he's not known upon 'Change.

Scrib. Damme, sir, what d'ye mean?

Ledger. Oho! Mr. Gentleman, is it you?—I thought I knew your voice— ay, and your face too.—Pray, sir, don't you live with Mr. Traverse, the attorney, of Gracechurch Street?—Did not you come to me last week about a policy of insurance?   103

Scrib. O the devil! [*Aside.*] I come to you? Sir!—I never saw your face before.   [*To* Ledger.

Nurse. Good lack! He'll certainly be discovered.   [*Aside.*

Honey. An attorney's clerk!—Hark ye, friend—

Scrib. 'Egad, I'd best sneak off before it's worse.   [*Going.*

Honey. Hark ye, woman! [*To* Nurse.]—I begin to suspect—have not I heard you speak of a kinsman, clerk to Mr. Traverse?—Stop him!   110

Scrib. Hands off, gentlemen!—Well then—I do go through a little business for Mr. Traverse—what then? What have you to say to me now? Sir!

Polly. Do pray, mama, take Mr. Scribble's part, pray do! ⎫ *Apart, while*
Nurse. Do, ma'am, speak a good word for him.   ⎬ *they are search-*
Mrs. Honey. I understand nothing at all of the matter.   ⎭ *ing* Scribble.

Honey. Hark ye, woman!—He's your nephew—I'm sure on't—I'll turn you out of doors immediately.—You shall be—

Nurse. I beg upon my knees that your honour would forgive me—I meant no harm, Heaven above knows—   [Nurse *kneeling.*

Honey. No harm! What to marry my daughter to—I'll have you sent to Newgate—and you, [*To* Polly.] you sorry baggage; d'ye see what you was about?—You was running away with a beggar—with your Nurse's nephew, hussy!   123

90 compter] Or counter: debtors' prison.

Polly. Lord, papa, what signifies whose nephew he is? He may be ne'er the worse for that.—Who knows but he may be a foundling, and a gentleman's son, as well as Tom Jones?—My mind is resolved,—and nothing shall ever alter it.

Scrib. Bravo, Miss Polly!—A fine generous spirit, faith!

Honey. You're an impudent slut—you're undone.—

Mrs. Honey. Nay, but, look ye, Polly!—Mind me, child!—You know that I—   131

Polly. As for my poor mama here, you see, sir, she is a little in the nervous way, this morning—when she comes to herself, and Mr. Julep's draughts have taken a proper effect, she'll be convinced I am in the right.

Honey. Hold your impertinence!—Hark ye, Polly—

Polly. You, my angelic Mr. Scribble—   [*To* Scribble.

Scrib. Ma chère adorable!

Polly. You may depend on my constancy and affection. I never read of any lady's giving up her lover, to submit to the absurd election of her parents— I'll have you let what will be the consequence.—I'll have you, though we go through as many distresses as Booth and Amelia.   141

Honey. Peace, hussy!

Polly. As for you, you odious wretch, [*To* Ledger.] how could they ever imagine that I should dream of such a creature? A great He-monster! I would as soon be married to the Staffordshire Giant—I hate you. You are as deceitful as Blifil, as rude as the Harlowes, and as ugly as Doctor Slop.

[*Exit.*

Ledger. Mighty well, Miss, mighty well!

Scrib. Prodigious humour! High fun, faith!

Honey. She's downright raving—mad as a March hare—I'll put her into Bedlam—I'll send her to her relations in the country—I'll have her shut up in a nunnery—I'll—   151

Mrs. Honey. Come, my sweeting, don't make your dear self so uneasy— don't.

Honey. Hark you, woman, [*To the* Nurse.] I'll have you committed to Newgate—I'll—

Nurse. Pray, your dear honour!—   [*Kneeling.*

Honey. As for you, sir! [*To* Scribble.]—Hark ye, stripling—

Scrib. Nay, nay, old gentleman, no bouncing!—You're mistaken in your man, sir! I know what I'm about.

145 the Staffordshire Giant] A short-lived stage phenomenon from the provinces. He played Galligantus the giant in the musical entertainment *Galligantus* (adapted from Henry Brooke's *Jack the Giant Queller*) at the Haymarket Theatre, 1 October 1759, and possibly again in April 1760, at Drury Lane.   146 Blifil, . . . the Harlowes, . . . Doctor Slop] The villain of *Tom Jones*, the family of Clarissa, and the doctor in *Tristram Shandy*.

Honey. Zouns, sir, and I know—   160
Scrib. Yes, sir, and I know that I've done nothing contrary to the twenty-sixth of the King.—Above a month ago, sir, I took lodgings in Miss Polly's name and mine, in the parish of St. George's in the Fields.—The banns have been asked three times, and I could have married Miss Polly today.—So much for that.—And so, sir, your servant.—If you offer to detain me, I shall bring my action on the case for false imprisonment, sue out a bill of Middlesex, and upon a *Non est inventus,* if you abscond, a *Latitat,* then an *Alias,* a *Pluries,* a *Non omittas,* and so on.—Or perhaps I may indict you at the sessions, bring the affair by *Certiorari* into *Bancum Regis, et caetera, et caetera, et caetera*—and now—stop me at your peril.   [*Exit.*

[*While* Scribble *speaks* Nurse *sneaks off.*]

Honey. I am stunned with his jargon, and confounded at his impudence.—I'll put an end to this matter at once—Mr. Ledger, you shall marry my daughter tomorrow morning.   173
Ledger. Not I indeed, my friend! I give up my interest in her.—She'd make a terrible wife for a sober citizen.—Who can answer for her behaviour? —I would not underwrite her for ninety per cent.   [*Exit.*
Honey. See there! See there!—My girl is undone.—Her character is ruined with all the world.—These damned story-books!—What shall we do? Mrs. Honeycombe, what shall we do?
Mrs. Honey. Look ye, my dear! You've been wrong in every particular—
Honey. Wrong!—I! Wrong!—   181
Mrs. Honey. Quite wrong, my dear!—I would not expose you before company—my tenderness, you know, is so great—but leave the whole affair to me—you are too violent—go, my dear, go and compose yourself, and I'll set all matters to rights.—[*Going, turns back.*] Don't you do anything of your own head now—trust it all to me, my dear!—Be sure you do, my love!
                                                                    [*Exit.*

Honey. [*Alone.*] Zouns, I shall run mad with vexation—I shall—was ever man so heartily provoked?—You see now, gentlemen, [*Coming forward to the audience.*] what a situation I am in!—Instead of happiness and jollity,—my friends and family about me,—a wedding and a dance,—and everything as it should be,—here am I, left by myself,—deserted by my intended son-in-law—bullied by an attorney's clerk—my daughter mad—my wife in the vapours—and all's in confusion.—This comes of cordials and novels.—Zouns, your stomachics are the devil—and a man might as well turn his daughter loose in Covent Garden, as trust the cultivation of her mind to
                    A CIRCULATING LIBRARY.   196

161 the twenty-sixth of the King] i.e. the statute passed by Parliament in the twenty-sixth year of King George II's reign (1753), concerning legal marriage.

EPILOGUE.

Written by MR. GARRICK.

Spoken by MISS POPE.

Enter, as POLLY, laughing—*Ha! ha! ha!*—

My poor Papa's in woeful agitation—
While I, the Cause, feel here, [Striking her bosom.] *no palpitation—*
We Girls of Reading, and superior notions,
Who from the fountain-head drink love's sweet potions,
Pity our parents, when such passion blinds 'em,
One hears the good folks rave—One never minds 'em.
Till these dear books infus'd their soft ingredients,
Asham'd and fearful, I was all Obedience.
Then my good Father did not storm in vain,
I blush'd and cry'd—I'll ne'er do so again: 10
But now no bugbears can my spirit tame,
I've conquer'd Fear—And almost conquer'd Shame;
So much these Dear Instructors change and win us,
Without their light *we ne'er should know what's in us:*
Here we at once supply our childish wants—
NOVELS *are Hotbeds for your forward Plants.*
Not only Sentiments refine the Soul,
But hence we learn to be the Smart and Drole;
Each awkward circumstance for laughter serves,
From Nurse's nonsense to my Mother's NERVES: 20
   Tho' Parents tell us, that our genius lies
In mending linnen and in making pies,
I set such formal precepts at defiance
That preach up prudence, neatness, and compliance:
Leap these old bounds, and boldly set the pattern,
To be a Wit, Philosopher, and Slattern—

   O! did all Maids and Wives, my spirit feel,
We'd make this topsy-turvy world to reel:

Let us to arms!—Our Fathers, Husbands, dare!
NOVELS will teach us all the Art of War: 30
Our Tongues will serve for Trumpet and for Drum;
I'll be your Leader—General HONEYCOMBE *!*
  Too long has human nature gone astray,
Daughters should govern, Parents should obey;
Man shou'd submit, the moment that he weds,
And hearts of oak shou'd yield to wiser heads:
I see you smile bold Britons *!—But 'tis true—*
Beat You *the* French *;—But let your* Wives *beat* You.*—*

THE UPHOLSTERER

Arthur Murphy

1727–1805

Arthur Murphy, the son of a Dublin merchant who died when the boy was two, grew up mostly in England and France, finally settling in London (1751), where he engaged in a variety of pursuits. Clerking and banking gave way to journalism, and journalism to play-writing and acting. The stage was a financial expedient suggested by Sam Foote, one of a number of literary friends; like George Colman, Murphy was disappointed of a legacy and had to make his own way. His first play, *The Apprentice*, was written in 1753 and produced by Garrick in 1756, shortly after Murphy's retirement from his brief acting career. For the next twenty years Murphy was at the same time a lawyer and a political writer and also one of the most active and successful of London playwrights: over twenty of his comedies and tragedies were performed at the Patent Theatres. Of his extensive non-dramatic writings, *The Gray's Inn Journal* (1752–4) is notable as an early instance of responsible theatrical criticism in a newspaper, and his *Life of David Garrick* (1801) provides a wealth of not wholly reliable information about Georgian theatre.

The Upholsterer, or What News? was probably written in 1757, and first performed on 30 March 1758 at Drury Lane, with one of the strongest casts ever allotted to a farce. Received with indifference at first, the piece caught on in the repertoire, playing eleven nights its first season (including a command performance) and over a hundred more times before Murphy's retirement in 1777. In print and in principle Murphy denigrated farce as trivial, but in fact he was interested enough to prepare *The Upholsterer* carefully for the reading public (see textual note 24) and to revise it four times (see below).

In an age of dramatic innovation, Murphy's view of comedy was almost wholly traditional. It is the 'business of comedy', he wrote, to

excite . . . laughter and contempt . . . by making striking exhibitions of inconsistent circumstances . . . making us despise and laugh at an object at the same time. . . . It is therefore by placing the humours and foibles of human nature in a ridiculous light that the true comic force is created. (*Gray's Inn Journal*, 17 August 1754.)

The Upholsterer follows Murphy's conservative theories, with both character and plot conforming to hoary archetypes. At its centre is the humour figure of Quidnunc, 'What News', whom Murphy considered 'rather . . . a *passion* than a *man*' (hence this is farce rather than comedy). Quidnunc, along with Razor and Pamphlet, transmits the author's message—the dangers of a 'vicious excess of a propensity to politics'—yet also functions as the classic 'heavy father' who blocks the romance of the young lovers: an economy by which he serves both Old and New Comedy at once. Often enough the humour character has embarrassed the dramatist in the last act: how resolve the play without changing or expelling him? And what about his name if he reforms? Murphy glides gracefully around this obstacle, utilizing Quidnunc's obsession as a device to bring about and lighten the denouement, and at the same time to emphasize his rigidity (which Bergson calls the essence of laughter). Even after he has lost a daughter and gained a son and a pension, Quidnunc remains true to his name: 'What are the Spaniards doing in the Bay of Honduras?' Termagant too, source though she may be for Sheridan's Mrs. Malaprop, has ancestors in Fielding's Mrs. Slipslop and Dogberry of *Much Ado About Nothing*.

Murphy drew upon a number of sources in writing his play, principally two of Addison's papers in the *Tatler* and Fielding's *Coffee-House Politician*. But anyone who looks at the originals will see that he has improved upon the hints he has taken and that his borrowings are not extensive, while no one acquainted with eighteenth-century theories of imitation will find Murphy exceptional in this regard. The derivativeness of Georgian literature and drama was conscious and radical: 'what oft was thought but ne'er so well expressed' is very close to the mark.

Five distinct versions of *The Upholsterer* are extant: the Examiner's copy of 1757;[1] the printed edition of 1758; the Examiner's copy of Murphy's 1763 alteration; the printed version in the 1786 edition of Murphy's *Works*; and the Examiner's copy of Murphy's 1791 alteration. The printings of 1760, 1763, 1765 (two), and 1769 do not differ significantly from these five basic versions. The first two (1757 and 1758) are closely related in outline, although there are many minor differences between them: they represent the play as acted at Drury Lane under Garrick. 1763, the 'Covent Garden version', omits some scenes, rearranges others, and adds new business, but shortens the farce overall. 1786 is somewhat longer, and gives evidence of careful revision for the reader. John Pike Emery edited this text in '*The Way to Keep Him' and Five Other Plays by Arthur Murphy* (New York University Press, New York, 1956), with footnotes indicating the principal variants from the versions of 1769 and 1791. The latter updates the political allusions, and served to protect the theatre by apprising the Examiner's office of almost thirty years of accumulated changes.

Murphy's alteration of 1763 has been taken as the basis of the present edition. It is in my opinion the last true *acting* text of the play: the later versions are literary reworkings aimed at the reading public. It is also the shortest version, and the strength of such a piece on the stage resides in briskness and brevity. The textual notes at p. 194 indicate the major variants from the 1757 and 1758 texts; in some places one of the earlier versions is briefly followed. To note the full extent of these variants would be beyond the scope of this edition, but the notes do illustrate how eighteenth-century plays evolved even after exposure to the public.

The Examiner's copies of the 1757, 1763, and 1791 versions are all among the Larpent MSS., and permission to publish the first two has been kindly granted by the Trustees of the Henry E. Huntington Library.

[1] The Larpent MS. appears to be dated 16 March 1757, but this may be a lapse for '1758'.

THE
UPHOLSTERER,

OR

What NEWS?

A

FARCE,

In Two ACTS.

As it is Performed at the

THEATRE ROYAL,

IN

DRURY-LANE.

——— *O bone (nam te*
Scire, Deos quoniam propius contingis, oportet)
Num quid de Dacis audifti? ——— HOR.

By the Author of the APPRENTICE.

GLASGOW:

Printed in the Year MDCCLVIII.

The UPHOLSTERER; or, What News?

A Farce in Two Acts by Arthur Murphy
1763

Sir:

    This Farce, as here alter'd and added to, is designed to be represented at the Theatre Royal in Covent Garden with the permission of the Right Honourable Earl Gower.

Your humble servants
P. Rich
Jn. Beard[1]

Earl Gower] Granville Leveson-Gower (1721–1803), 1st Marquis of Stafford, 2nd Earl Gower, was Lord Chamberlain April 1763–July 1765.   P. Rich] Probably Priscilla Stevens Rich, widow and executrix of the former manager and famous pantomimist John Rich (d. 1761).   Jn. Beard] John Beard was manager of Covent Garden Theatre in 1763.

[1] Superior figures refer to Textual Notes at p. 194.

PROLOGUE. ²

Spoken by Mr. MOSSOP.

When first, in falling Greece's *evil hour,*
Ambition aim'd at universal pow'r ;
When the fierce man of Macedon *began*
Of a new monarchy to form the plan ;
Each Greek—(*as fam'd* Demosthenes *relates*)
Politically mad !—wou'd rave of states !
And help'd to form, where'er the mob could meet,
An Areopagus *in ev'ry street.*
What news, what news, was their eternal cry ?
Is Philip *sick !*—then soar'd their spirits high,—*   10
Philip *is well !—dejection in each eye.*
Athenian *coblers join'd in deep debate,*
While gold in secret undermin'd the state ;
Till wisdom's bird the vultur's prey was made ;
And the sword gleam'd in Academus' *shade.*

   Now modern Philips *threaten this our land,*
What say Britannia's *sons ?—along the Strand*
What news ye cry ?—with the same passion smit ;
And there at least you rival Attic wit.
A parliament of porters here shall muse   20
On state affairs—'swall'wing a taylor's news,'
For ways and means no starv'd projector sleeps ;
And ev'ry shop some mighty statesman keeps ;
He Britain's *foes, like* Bobadil, *can kill ;*
Supply th' EXCHEQUER, *and neglect his till.*
In ev'ry ale-house legislators meet ;
And patriots settle kingdoms in the Fleet.

---

* Vide the first Philippic.

---

16 *Now modern* Philips *threaten*] A reference to the Seven Years' War (1756–63), more
appropriate in 1758 than in 1763. 21 '*swall'wing . . . news*'] *King John*, IV. ii. 195.
24 Bobadil] The braggart soldier in Jonson's *Every Man in His Humour* (1598).

To shew this phrenzy in its genuine light,
A modern newsmonger appears to night;
Trick'd out from Addison's *accomplish'd page,*   30
Behold! th' Upholsterer *ascends the stage.*

No minister such trials e'er hath stood:
He turns a BANKRUPT for the public good!
Undone himself, yet full of England's *glory!*
A politician!—neither whig nor tory—
Nor can ye high or low the Quixote *call;*
'He's knight o' th' shire, and represents ye all.'

As for the bard,—to you he yields his plan;
For well he knows, you're candid where ye can.
Only one praise he claims,—no party-stroke   40
Here turns a public character to joke.

His Panacaea *is for all degrees,*
For all have more or less of this disease.
Whatever his success, of this he's sure,
There's merit even to attempt the cure.

---

30 Addison's *accomplish'd page*] Murphy's dedication 'To Mr. Garrick' refers to No. 155 of the *Tatler*, but Nos. 403 and 568 of the *Spectator* are also relevant.   37 '*He's Knight . . . ye all*'] Dryden's epilogue to Etherege's *The Man of Mode* (1676), l. 16.

Dramatis Personæ[3]

	[Drury Lane, 1757–8]	[Covent Garden, 1763]
Quidnunc, the Upholsterer	Mr. Yates	Mr. Dunstall
Bellmour	Mr. Usher	Mr. White
Rovewell	Mr. Palmer	Mr. Davis
Pamphlet	Mr. Garrick	Mr. Shuter
Razor, a barber	Mr. Woodward	Mr. Woodward
Feeble	Mr. Blakes	Mr. Hayes
Watchmen	Mr. Clough	Mr. Weller

WOMEN

Harriet	Mrs. Yates	Miss Miller
Termagant	Mrs. Clive	Miss Elliot
Servant Maid to Feeble	Mrs. Simpson	Miss Cokayne

THE

Upholsterer; or, What News?

ACT I. SCENE, *a street*.

Enter Rovewell *and* Bellmour.[4]

Bell. My dear Rovewell, such a girl—ten thousand cupids play about her mouth, you rogue.

Rove. Ten thousand pounds had better play about her pocket—what fortune has she?

Bell. Prithee, Rovewell, how can you be so ungenerous as to ask such a question? You know I don't mind fortune, though by the way she has an uncle who is determined to settle very handsomely on her, and on the strength of that, does she give herself innumerable airs.

Rove. Fortune not to be minded! I'll tell you what, Bellmour, though you have a good one already, there's no kind of inconveniency in a little more. I'm sure if I had not minded fortune, I might have been in Jamaica still, not worth a sugar cane; but the widow Molosses took a fancy to me; Heaven, or a worse deity, has taken a fancy to her, and so after ten years exile, and being turned adrift by my father, here am I again a warm planter, and a widower, most woefully tired of matrimony.—But my dear Bellmour, we were both so overjoyed to meet one another yesterday evening, just as I arrived in town, that I did not hear a syllable from you of your love fit: how, when, and where did this happen?   18

Bell. Oh, by the most fortunate accident that ever was! I'll tell thee, Rovewell: I was going one night from the tavern about six weeks ago.— I had been there with a parcel of blades whose only joy is centred in their bottle, and faith, till this accident I was no better myself.—But ever since I am grown quite a new man.   23

Rove. Ay, a new man indeed! Who in the name of wonder would take thee, sunk as thou art into a musing, moping, melancholy lover, for the gay Charles Bellmour whom I knew in the West Indies?

Bell. Poh, that is not to be mentioned. You know my father took me against my will from the university, and consigned me over to the academic discipline of a man of war, so that to prevent a dejection of spirits, I was obliged to run into the opposite extreme—as you yourself were wont to do.   30

Rove. Why, yes, I had my moments of reflection, and was glad to dissipate them—you know I always told you there was something extraordinary in my story; and so there is still. I suppose it must be cleared up in a few days now —I'm in no hurry about it though; I must see the town a little this evening, and have my frolic first.—But to the point, Bellmour: you was going from the tavern, you say?

Bell. Yes, Sir, about two in the morning, and I perceived an unusual blaze in the air. I was in a rambling humour, and so resolved to know what it was. And oh! Rovewell, my better stars ordained it to light me on to happiness; by sure attraction led, I came to the very street where a house was on fire: water engines playing, flames ascending, all hurry, confusion, and distress, when on a sudden the voice of despair, silver sweet, came thrilling down to my very heart—poor, dear, little soul, what can she do, cried the neighbours? Again she screamed, the fire gathering force, and gaining upon her every instant—here Madam, said I, leap into my arms, I'll be sure to receive you; and would you think it? Down she came—my dear Rovewell, such a girl! I caught her in my arms, you rogue, safe, without harm! The dear naked Venus, just risen from her bed, my boy—her slender waist, Rovewell, the downy smoothness of her whole person, and her limbs 'harmonious, swelled by nature's softest hand'.   50

Rove. Raptures! And Paradise! What seraglio in Covent Garden did you carry her to?

Bell. There again now! Do, prithee, correct your way of thinking, take a *quantum sufficit* of virtuous love, and purify your ideas.—Her lovely bashfulness, her delicate fears, her beauty heightened and endeared by distress, dispersed my wildest thoughts, and melted me into tenderness and respect.

Rove. But Bellmour, surely she has not the impudence to be modest, after you have had possession of her person?

Bell. My views are honourable, I assure you, Sir; but her father is so absurdly positive. The man's distracted about the balance of power, and will give his daughter to none but a politician. Now he's a bankrupt, his head runs upon ways and means, and schemes for paying off the national debt. The affairs of Europe engross all his attention, while the distresses of his lovely daughter pass unnoticed.   65

Rove. Ridiculous enough! But why do you mind him? Why don't you go to bed to the wench at once? Take her into keeping, man.

Bell. How can you talk so affrontingly of her? Have not I told you, though her father is ruined, still she has great expectation from a rich relation?

Rove. Then what do you stand watering at the mouth for? If she is to have

49–50 'harmonious . . . hand'] A slight alteration of line 1316 of James Thomson's *Summer* (1727).   54 *quantum sufficit*] Sufficient quantity.

money enough to pay for her china, her gaming debts, her dogs, and her monkeys, marry her then, if you needs must be ensnared; be in a fool's paradise for a honeymoon, then come to yourself, wonder at what you've done, and mix with honest fellows again.—Carry her off I say, and never stand whining for the father's consent. 75

Bell. Carry her off—I like the scheme—will you assist me?

Rove. No, no, there I beg to be excused. Don't you remember what the satirist says? 'Never marry while there's a halter to be had for money, or a bridge to afford a convenient leap.'

Bell. Prithee leave fooling. 80

Rove. I am in serious earnest, I assure you; I'll drink with you, game with you, go into any scheme of frolic with you, but 'ware matrimony. Nay, if you'll come to the tavern this evening, I'll drink your mistress's health in a bumper; but as to your conjugal scheme, I'll have nothing to do with that business positively.

Bell. Well, well, I'll take you at your word, and meet you at ten exactly at the same place we were at last night; then and there I'll let you know what farther measures I've concerted.

Rove. Till then, farewell.—Apropos, do you know that I've seen none of my relations yet? 90

Bell. Time enough tomorrow.

Rove. Ay, ay, tomorrow will do.—Well, your servant. [*Exit.*

Bell. Rovewell, yours.—I'll write to her this moment, acquaint her with the soft tumult of my desires, and if possible make her mine this very night.

[*Exit repeating:*

Love first taught letters for some wretch's aid,
Some banished lover, or some captive maid.

SCENE II, *the Upholsterer's house.*

Enter Harriet *and* Termagant.

Term. Well, but Madam, he has made love to you these six weeks *success-fully*; he has been as constant in his *'moors*, poor gentleman, as if you had the *subversion* of a *'state* to settle upon him—and if he slips through your fingers now, Madam, you have nobody to *depute* it to but yourself.

Har. Lard, Termagant, how you run on! I tell you again and again, my pride was touched, because he seemed to presume on his opulence and my father's distresses.

78–9 'Never marry ... leap'] A rough translation of lines 30 and 32 of Juvenal's *Satire* VI.
95–6 Love first taught ... maid] A slight alteration of Pope's *Eloisa to Abelard*, 51–2.

Term. La, Miss Harriet, how can you be so *paradropsical* in your *'pinions*?

Har. Well, but you know though my father's affairs are ruined, I am not in so desperate a way; consider, my uncle's fortune is no trifle, and I think that prospect entitles me to give myself a few airs before I resign my person.   12

Term. I grant ye, Ma'am, you have very good pretensions, but then it's waiting for dead men's shoes; I'll venture to be perjured Mr. Bellmour ne'er *disclaimed* an *idear* of your father's distress.

Har. Supposing that—

Term. Suppose, Ma'am! I know it *disputably* to be so.

Har. Indisputably, I guess you mean—but I'm tired of wrangling with you about words.

Term. By my troth you're in the right on't; there's ne'er a she in all old England (as your father calls it) mistress of such *phisiology* as I am. Certain I am, as how you does not know nobody, that puts their words together with such a *curacy* as myself. I once lived with a *Mistus*, Ma'am—Mistus! She was a lady, a great brewer's wife! And she wore as fine clothes as any person of quality, let her get up as early as she will! And she used to call me—Termagant, says she, what's the meaning of such a word—and I always told her, I told her the *importation* of all my words—though I could not help laughing, Miss Harriet, to see so fine a lady such a downright *ignoranimus.*⁵

Har. Well, but pray now, Termagant, would you have me, directly upon being asked the question, throw myself into the arms of a man?   30

Term. O' my conscience you did throw yourself into his arms with scarce a shift on, that's what you did.

Har. Yes, but that was a leap in the dark, when there was no time to think of it.

Term. Well, it does not signify *argyfying*, I wish we were both warm in bed: you with Mr. Bellmour, and I with his coxcomb of a man, instead of being here with an old crazy fool—*axing* your pardon, Ma'am, for calling your father so—but he is a fool, and the worst of fools, with his *policies*—when his house is full of *statues* of *Bangcressy*.

Har. It's too true, Termagant—yet he is still my father, and I can't help loving him.   41

Term. Fiddle faddle—love him! He's an *anecdote* against love.

Har. Hush! Here he comes—

Term. No, it's your Uncle Feeble—poor gentleman, I pity's him, eaten up with *infirmaries*, to be taking such pains with a madman.

Enter Feeble.

Har. Well, Uncle, have you been able to console him?

Feeb. He wants no consolation, child—lackaday, I'm so infirm I can hardly move—I found him tracing, in the map, Prince Charles of Lorraine's passage over the Rhine, and comparing it with Julius Caesar's.

Term. An old blockhead—I've no patience with him, with his fellows coming after him every hour in the day with news. Well, I wishes there was no such thing in the world as a newspaper, with such a pack of lies, and such a deal of *jab-jab* every day.   53

Feeb. Ay, there were three or four shabby fellows with him when I went into the room. Don't be dejected, Harriet—my poor sister, your mother, was a good woman; I love you for her sake, child, and all I am worth shall be yours. But I must be going—I find myself but very ill—good night, Harriet, good night.   [*Exit.*

Har. You'll give me leave to see you to the door, Sir.   [*Exit.*

Term. O' my conscience, this master of mine within here, might have picked up his crumbs as well as Mr. Feeble, if he had any *idear* of his business.[6] I'm sure if I had not hopes from Mr. Feeble, I should not tarry in this house. By my troth, if all who had nothing to say to the *'fairs* of the nation, would mind their own business, and those who should take care of our *'fairs*, would mind their business too, I fancy poor old England (as they call it) would fare the better among 'em. This old crazy pate within here— playing the fool—when the man is past his grand *Clytemnester*.   [*Exit.*

SCENE III *discovers* Quidnunc *at a table, with newspapers, pamphlets, etc., all around him.*

Quid. Six and three is nine—seven and four is eleven, and carry one—let me see, 126 million, 199 thousand, 328—and all this with about—where, where's the amount of the specie? Here, here—with about 15 million in specie, all this great circulation![7] Good, good—why then, how are we ruined? How are we ruined? What says the Land Tax at 4 shillings in the pound? Two million! Now where's my new assessment? Here—here, the 5th part of twenty, 5 in 2 I can't, but 5 in 20 [*Pauses.*]—right, 4 times—why then, upon my new assessment there's 4 million—how are we ruined? What says malt, cider, and mum? Eleven and carry one, naught and go 2—good, good—malt, hops, cider, and mum; then there's the wine licence, and the Gin Act.—The Gin Act is no bad article: if the people will shoot fire down their throats, why in a Christian country they should pay as much as pos- sible for suicide.—Salt, good—sugar, very good—window lights, good again

---

48–9 Prince Charles . . . Rhine] Karl Alexander (1712–80), Prince of Lorraine, won re- nown by his brilliant crossing of the Rhine with the Austrian army in 1744, during the War of the Austrian Succession.   67 grand *Clytemnester*] For 'grand climacteric': the age of seventy.   Sc. iii, 9 mum] Beer brewed in Brunswick.

G

—stamp duty, that's not so well—it will have a bad effect upon the news-papers, and then we shan't have enough of politics—but there's the lottery—where's my new scheme for a lottery? Here it is—now for the amount of the whole—how are we ruined? Seven and carry nought—nought and carry one—   17

Enter Termagant.

Term. Sir, Sir—

Quid. Hold your tongue, you baggage, you'll put me out—nought and carry one—   20

Term. Mr. Razor will be with you presently.

Quid. Prithee be quiet woman—how are we ruined?

Term. Ay, I'm *confidous* as how you may thank yourself for your own *ruination.*

Quid. Ruin the nation! Hold your tongue, you jade—I'm raising the sup-plies within the year—how many did I carry?

Term. Yes, you've carried your pigs to a fine market—

Quid. Get out of the room, hussy—you trollop—get out of the room.

[*Turning her out.*

Enter Razor, *with suds on his hands.*

Quid. Friend Razor, I am glad to see thee—well, hast got any news?

Raz. A budget! I left a gentleman half shaved in my shop over the way; it came into my head of a sudden, so I could not be at ease till I told you.   32

Quid. That's kind, that's kind, friend Razor—never mind the gentleman—he can wait.

Raz. So he can, he can wait.

Quid. Come now, let's hear—what is't?

Raz. I shaved a great man's butler today.

Quid. Did ye?

Raz. I did.

Quid. Ay.   40

Raz. Very true.   [*Both shake their heads.*

Quid. What did he say?

Raz. Nothing.

Quid. Hum—how did he look?

Raz. Full of thought.

Quid. Ay, full of thought—what can that mean?

Raz. It must mean something.   [*Staring at each other.*

Quid. Mayhap somebody may be going out of place.

Raz. Like enough [8]—there's something at the bottom, when a great man's

butler looks grave; things can't hold out in this manner, Master Quidnunc!
Kingdoms rise and fall—luxury will be the ruin of us all—it will indeed.

[Stares at him.

Quid. Pray now, friend Razor, do you find business as current now as
before the war?   53

Raz. No, no, I have not made a wig the Lord knows when; I can't mind it
for thinking of my poor country.

Quid. That's generous, friend Razor—

Raz. Yes, I can't gi' my mind to anything for thinking of my country, and
when I was in Bedlam, it was the same: I could think of nothing else in
Bedlam, but poor old England, and so they said as how I was incurable for it.

Quid. 'Sbodikins, they might as well say the same of me.   60

Raz. So they might—well, your servant, Mr. Quidnunc.[8] I'll go now and
shave the rest of the poor gentleman's face.—Poor old England.

[Sighs, and shakes his head; going.

Quid. But hark ye, friend Razor—ask the gentleman if he has got any news.

Raz. I will, I will.

Quid. And d'ye hear, come and tell me if he has.

Raz. I will, I will—poor old England. [*Going, returns.*] O, Mr. Quidnunc, I
want to ask you—pray now.

Enter Termagant.

Term. Gemini! Gemini! How can the man have so little *difference* for his
customers?

Quid. I tell you, Mrs. Malapert—   70

Term. And I tell you, the gentleman keeps such a bawling yonder; for
shame, Mr. Razor—you'll be a *bankrupper* as well as my master, with such a
house full of children as you have, pretty little things—that's what you will—

Raz. I'm a-coming, I'm a-coming, Mrs. Termagant—I say, Mr. Quidnunc,
I can't sleep in my bed, for thinking what would have come of the Protestants,
if the Papists had got the better in the last war.

Quid. I'll tell you—the geographer of our coffee-house was saying the
other day, that there is an huge tract of land about the Pole, where the
Protestants may retire, and that the Papists never will be able to drive them
thence, if the northern powers hold together, and the grand Turks make a
diversion in their favour.   81

Raz. That makes me easy—I'm glad. [*Going, returns.*] The Protestants
would have had a place to have gone to, if the Papists had got the better in
the late war.[9] I shall now have a night's rest mayhap.   [*Exit.*

<hr>

53 before the war] The Seven Years' War started in 1756. 58 Bedlam] St. Mary of
Bethlehem hospital, London's insane asylum. 80 the northern powers] England and
Prussia.

Quid. I observe in one of the papers, that a certain great potentate—

Term. Fiddle for your potentate—*impair* your ruined fortune, do that. And see where your daughter comes, poor thing, ready to break her heart.

Enter Harriet.

Quid. It may perhaps portend some good to the Protestant powers—

Har. Dear Papa, what are the Protestant powers to people in our situation?

Quid. The Protestant powers? Why if anything should happen to them, we are all undone.   91

Har. Dear Sir, that's our misfortune—we are undone already.

Quid. No, no—here, here, child—I have raised the supplies within the year.

Term. I tell you, you're a *lunadic* man.

Quid. Yes, yes, I'm a lunatic to be sure—I tell you, Harriet, I have saved a great deal out of my affairs for you.

Har. For Heaven's sake, Sir, don't do that—you must give up everything; my uncle's lawyer will be here to talk to you about it.

Quid. Poh, poh,[10] I tell you, I know what I'm about; you shall have my books and pamphlets, and all the manifestos of the powers at war.   101

Har. And so make me a politician, Sir?

Quid. It would be the pride of my heart to find I had got a politician in petticoats—a female Machiavel! 'Sbodikins, you might then know as much as most people that talk in coffee-houses, and who knows but in time you might be a Maid of Honour or a Sweeper of the Mall, or—

Har. Dear Sir, don't you see what you have got by politics?

Quid. Pshaw![10] My country's of more consequence to me, and let me tell you, you can't think too much of your country in these worst of times; for Mr. Monitor has told us, that affairs in the north, and the Protestant interest, begin to grow ticklish.   III

Term. And your daughter's affairs are very ticklish too, I'm sure.

Har. Prithee, Termagant—

Term. I must speak to him—I know you are in a very ticklish situation, Ma'am.

Quid. I tell you, trull—

Term. But I am *convicted* it is so, and the posture of my affairs is very ticklish, too—and so I *imprecate* that Mr. Bellmour would come, and—

Quid. Mr. Bellmour come! I tell you, Mrs. Saucebox, that my daughter shall never be married to a man that has not better notions of the balance of power.   121

Term. But what *purvision* will you make for her now, with your balances?

Quid. There again now! Why do you think I don't know what I'm about?

110 Mr. Monitor] The *Monitor* was a Whig periodical.

I'll look in the papers for a match for you, child; there's often good matches advertised for in the papers.—Evil betide it—evil betide it! I once thought to have struck a great stroke, that would have astonished all Europe—I thought to have married my daughter to Theodore, King of Corsica.

Har. What, and have me perish in a jail, Sir?

Quid. 'Sbodikins, my daughter would have had her coronation day; I should have been allied to a crowned head, and been First Lord of the Treasury of Corsica! But come, I'll go talk over the *London Evening* till the *Gazette* come in[11]—how! Did not I hear the *Gazette*? Yes, yes, it is, it is the *Gazette*—I hear the newsman cry it—Termagant, you jade, run! [*Exit* Termagant.] Harriet, fly—it is the *Gazette*.   134

Har. But Sir, won't you reflect a little upon my situation, and your own— charity begins at home, Sir; don't think any more of the affairs of Europe.

Quid. Not think of the affairs of Europe! It was a law at Athens, that he should be infamous, that did not interest himself for his country.—Here— Termagant—you jade—Termagant—

Enter Termagant.

Term. What do you keep such a bawling for? The newsman says as how the Emperor of *Mocco* is dead.   141

Quid. The Emperor of Morocco!

Term. Yes, Sir.

Quid. That will have some effect upon the stocks, I fear.

Term. Ah! You old Don *Quicksett*! Ma'am—Ma'am! Miss Harriet, go your ways into the next room. There's Mr. Bellmour's man there; Mr. Bellmour has sent you a *billydore*.   [*Aside.*

Har. Oh Termagant, my heart is in an uproar—I don't know what to say— where is he? Let me run to him this instant.   [*Exit.*

Quid. The Emperor of Morocco had a regard for the balance of Europe.[12] [*Sighs.*] Well, well, come, come, give me the paper.   151

Term. The newsman would not trust because you're a *bankrupper*, and so I paid twopence halfpenny for it.

Quid. Let's see, let's see.

Term. Give me money then—   [*Running from him.*

Quid. Give it me this instant, you jade—   [*After her.*

Term. Give me my money, I say—   [*From him.*

Quid. I'll teach you, I will, you baggage—   [*After her.*

Term. I won't part with it till I have my money—   [*From him.*

---

127 Theodore, King of Corsica] Baron Theodor von Neuhof became King of Corsica in 1736, but was driven from the throne by the Genoese and later imprisoned for debt in London. This reference first appears in the 1758 edition.   141 the Emperor of *Mocco*] Moulay Abdullah, Emperor of Morocco, did die in 1757.

Quid. I'll give you no money, hussy—   [*After her.*
Term. Your daughter shall marry Mr. Bellmour—   [*From him.*
Quid. I'll never accede to the treaty—   [*After her.*
Term. Go, you old fool—   [*From him.*
Quid. You vile minx—   [*After her.*
Term. There, you old cracked-brained politic—there's your paper for you.
                                         [*Throws it down and exit.*

Quid. [*Sits down.*] Oh! Heavens! I'm quite out of breath—a jade, to keep
my news from me.—What does it say? What does it say? What does it say?
[*Reads very fast while opening the paper.*] 'Whereas a commission of bankrupt
is awarded and issued forth against Abraham Quidnunc of the parish of St.
Martin's in the Fields, upholsterer, dealer, and chapman, the said bankrupt
is hereby required to surrender himself'—po, what signifies this stuff? I
don't mind myself when the balance of power is concerned.—However, I
shall be read of in the same paper, in the *London Gazette*, by the powers
abroad, together with the Pope, and the French king, and the Mogul, and all
of 'em—good—good—very good! Here's a power of news—let me see.
[*Reads.*] 'Letters from the Vice Admiral, dated *Tyger* off Calcutta.'—
[*Mutters to himself very eagerly.*] Odsheart, those baggages will interrupt me;
I hear their tongues a-going, clack, clack, clack.—I'll run into my closet and
lock myself up.—A vixen—a trollop—to want money from me—when I may
have occasion to buy *The State of the Sinking Fund*, or *Faction Detected*, or
The Barrier Treaty, or—and besides, how could the jade tell but tomorrow
we may have a *Gazette* extraordinary?   [*Exit.*

                        End of the first act.

ACT II

SCENE, *the Upholsterer's house*.

Enter Quidnunc.

Quid. Where, where, where is he? Where's Mr. Pamphlet? Mr. Pamphlet?
Termagant—Mr. a—a—Termagant—Harriet—Termagant, you vile minx,
you saucy—

Enter Termagant.

Term. Here's racket, indeed.
Quid. Where's Mr. Pamphlet? You baggage, if he's gone—

180–81 *The State . . . Treaty*] Obscure political pamphlets. *Some Remarks on the Barrier
Treaty* (1712) is attributed to Jonathan Swift.

Term. Did not I *intimidate* that he's in the next room? Why sure the man's out of his wits.

Quid. Show him in here then.—I would not miss seeing him for the discovery of the North-East passage.

Term. Go, you old Gemini Gomini of a politic.   [*Exit.*

Quid. Show him in, I say—I had rather see him than the whole state of the Peace at Utrecht, or 'the Paris *à-la-main*,' or the votes, or the minutes, or —here he comes—the best political writer of the age.   13

Enter Pamphlet.
[*With a surtout coat, a muff, a long campaign wig out of curl, and a pair of black garters buckled under the knees.*]

Quid. Mr. Pamphlet, I am heartily glad to see you—as glad as if you were an express from the Groyne, or from Berlin, or from Zell, or from Calcutta overland, or from—

Pam. Mr. Quidnunc, your servant—I am come from a place of great importance.

Quid. Look ye there now! Well, where, where?

Pam. Are we alone?   20

Quid. Stay, stay, till I shut the door—how, where do you come from?

Pam. From the Court of Requests.   [*Lays aside his surtout.*

Quid. The Court of Requests! [*Whispers.*] Are they up?

Pam. Hot work!

Quid. Debates arising, maybe.

Pam. Yes—and like to sit late.

Quid. What are they upon?

Pam. Can't say.

Quid. What carried you thither?

Pam. I went in hopes of being taken up.   30

Quid. Look ye there now.   [*Shakes his head.*

Pam. I've been aiming at it these three years.

Quid. Indeed!   [*Stares at him.*

Pam. Indeed—sedition is the only thing an author can live by now. Time has been, I could turn a penny by an earthquake, or live upon a jail distemper, or dine upon a bloody murder; but now that's all over—nothing will do

9 the North-East passage] The sea route between the Atlantic and Pacific Oceans north of Eurasia, first navigated in 1878–9.   12 the Peace at Utrecht . . . the minutes] The Peace of Utrecht in 1713 ended the War of the Spanish Succession; 'Paris *à-la-main*' may be a guide to Paris; the votes and minutes are records of the House of Commons.   15 the Groyne . . . Zell] The Groyne was the English name for La Coruña, a seaport in north-west Spain; Zell (or Radolfzell) is a town on Lake Konstanz in southern Germany. 30 taken up] This can mean 'arrested' or 'summoned as a witness' as well as 'patronized' or 'settled with'.

now but roasting a minister, or telling the people that they are ruined—the people of England are never so happy as when you tell them they are ruined.

Quid. Yes, but they a'n't ruined—I have a scheme for paying off the national debt.   40

Pam. Let's see, let's see—[*Puts on his spectacles.*]—well enough—well imagined—a new thought this—I must make this my own [*Aside.*]—silly, futile, absurd—abominable, this will never do—I'll put it in my pocket, and read it over in the morning for you.—Now look you here—I'll show you a scheme—[*Searches his pockets.*]—no, that's not it: that's my 'Conduct of the Ministry', by a country gentleman—I proved the nation undone here—this sold hugely—and here now, here's my answer to it, 'by a Noble Lord'—this did not move among the trade.

Quid. What, do you write on both sides?

Pam. Yes, both sides—I've two hands, Mr. Quidnunc—always impartial— *ambo dexter*—now here, here's my Dedication to a great man—touched twenty for this—and here—here's my libel upon him.   52

Quid. What, after being obliged to him?

Pam. For that reason—it excites curiosity—whitewash and blacking ball, Mr. Quidnunc! *In utrumque paratus*—no thriving without it.

Quid. What have you here in this pocket?   [*Prying eagerly.*

Pam. That's my account with Jacob Zorobabel, the broker, for writing paragraphs to raise or tumble the stocks, or the price of lottery tickets, according to his purpose.

Quid. Ay, how do you do that?   60

Pam. As thus—today the Protestant interest declines, Madras is taken, and England's undone; then all the long faces in the Alley look as dismal as a blank—and so Jacob buys away and thrives upon our ruin.—Then tomorrow we're all alive again and merry, Pondicherry's taken, a certain northern potentate will shortly strike a blow to astonish all Europe—and then every true-born Englishman is willing to buy a lottery ticket for twenty shillings more than it's worth; so Jacob sells away, and reaps the fruit of our success.

Quid. What, and will the people believe that now?

Pam. Believe it! Believe anything—no swallow like a true-born Englishman's. A man in a quart bottle, or a victory—it's all one to them—they give a gulp, and down it goes—glib, glib.[13]   71

Quid. Yes, but they a'n't at the bottom of things.

Pam. No, not they; they dabble a little, but can't dive—

Quid. Pray now, Mr. Pamphlet, what do you think of our situation?

Pam. Bad, Sir, bad—and how can it be better? The people in power never

55 *In utrumque paratus*] Prepared on both sides. 62 the Alley] For 'Change Alley, the seat of the Stock Exchange in the heart of the eighteenth-century financial district of London.

send to me, never consult me—it must be bad.—Now, here, here—[*Goes to his loose coat.*]—here's a manuscript! This will do the business, a masterpiece! I shall be taken up for this.

Quid. Shall ye?

Pam. As sure as a gun I shall—I know the bookseller's a rogue, and will give me up.   81

Quid. But pray now, what shall you get by being taken up?

Pam. I'll tell you! [*Whispers.*] in order to make me hold my tongue.

Quid. Ay, but you won't hold your tongue for all that?

Pam. Po, po—not a jot of that—abuse 'em the next day.

Quid. Well, well, I wish you success—but do you hear no news? Have you seen the *Gazette*?

Pam. Yes, I've seen that—great news, Mr. Quidnunc! But hark ye! [*Whispers.*] and kiss hands next week.

Quid. Ay!   90
Pam. Certain!
Quid. Nothing permanent in this world.
Pam. All is vanity!
Quid. Ups and downs!
Pam. Ins and outs!   [*Each in deep thought.*
Quid. Wheels within wheels!
Pam. No smoke without fire.
Quid. All's well that ends well.
Pam. It will last our time.
Quid. Whoever lives to see it, will know more of the matter.   100
Pam. Time will tell all.

Quid. Ay, we must leave all to the determination of time. Mr. Pamphlet, I'm heartily obliged to you for this visit.—I love you better than any man in England.

Pam. And for my part, Mr. Quidnunc, I love you better than I do England itself.

Quid. That's kind, that's kind [14]—there's nothing I would not do to serve you, Mr. Pamphlet.

Pam. Mr. Quidnunc—I know you're a man of integrity and honour—I know you are—and now since we have opened our hearts, there is a thing, Mr. Quidnunc, in which you can serve me.—You know, Sir—this in the fullness of our hearts—you know you have my note for a trifle—hard dealing with assignees—now, could not you, to serve a friend, could not you throw that note into the fire?   114

Quid. Hey! Would that be honest?

Pam. Leave that to me—a refined stroke of policy: papers have been destroyed in all governments.

Quid. So they have—it shall be done—it will be political, it will indeed.—¹⁴
Pray now, Mr. Pamphlet, what do you take to be the true political balance of
power?   120

Pam. What do I take to be the balance of power?

Quid. Ay, the balance of power.

Pam. The balance of power is—what do I take to be the balance of power—
the balance of power—[*Shuts his eyes.*] what do I take to be the balance of
power!

Quid. The balance of power I take to be, when the Court of Aldermen sits.

Pam. No, no.

Quid. Yes, yes.

Pam. No, no, the balance of power is, when the foundations of government
and the superstructures are natural.   130

Quid. How d'ye mean natural?

Pam. Prithee be quiet man—this is the language. The balance of power is,
when the superstructures are reduced to proper balances, or when the
balances are not reduced to unnatural superstructures.

Quid. Po, po, I tell you it is when the fortifications of Dunquerque are
demolished.

Pam. But I tell you, Mr. Quidnunc—

Quid. I say, Mr. Pamphlet—

Pam. Hear me, Mr. Quidnunc—

Quid. Give me leave, Mr. Pamphlet—   140

Pam. I must observe, Sir—

Quid. I am convinced, Sir—

Pam. That the balance of power—   [*Both in a*
Quid. That the fortifications of Dunquerque—   *passion.*

Pam. Depends upon the balances and superstructures—

Quid. Constitute the true political equilibrium—

Pam. Nor will I converse with a man—

Quid. And, Sir, I never desire to see your face—

Pam. Of such anticonstitutional principles—

Quid. Nor the face of any man who is such a Frenchman in his heart, and
has such notions of the balance of power.   [*Exeunt.*

Quidnunc *re-enters.*

Quid. Ay, I've found him out—such abominable principles. I never desire
to converse with any man of his notions, no, never while I live.   153

Pamphlet *re-enters.*¹⁵

Pam. Mr. Quidnunc, one word with you, if you please—

Quid. Sir, I never desire to see your face—

Pam. My property, Mr. Quidnunc—I shan't leave my property in the house of a bankrupt [*Twisting his handkerchief round his arm.*], a silly, empty, incomprehensible blockhead. I have been robbed, and the stolen goods are in your possession.

Quid. Blockhead, Mr. Pamphlet!   160

Pam. A blockhead, Mr. Quidnunc! When I have you so much in my power—

Quid. In your power!

Pam. In my power, Sir; it's in my power to hang you.

Quid. To hang me!

Pam. Yes, Sir, to hang you. [*Drawing on his coat.*] Did you not propose but this moment, did not you desire me to combine and confederate to burn a note, and defraud your creditors?

Quid. I desire it!

Pam. Yes, Mr. Quidnunc, but I shall detect you to the world—I'll give your character—you shall have a sixpenny touch next week.   171

Flebit et insignis totâ cantabitur urbe.

[*Exit.*

Quid. Mercy on me—there's the effect of his anti-constitutional principles —the spirit of his whole party. I never desire to exchange another word with him.

Enter Termagant.

Term. Here's a pother, indeed! Did you call me?

Quid. No, you trollop, no.

Term. Will you go to bed?

Quid. No, no, no, no—I tell you, no.

Term. Better go to rest, Sir; I heard a doctor of physic say as how, when a man is past his grand crime—what the deuce makes me forget my word?— his grand *crime-hysteric*, nothing is so good against *indiscompositions* as rest taken in its *prudish natalibus*.   183

Quid. Hold your prating! I'll not go to bed—I'll step to my brother Feeble —I want to have some talk with him, and I'll go to him directly.   [*Exit.*

Term. Go thy ways for an old Hocus Pocus of a newsmonger—you'll have good luck if you find your daughter here when you come back; Mr. Bellmour will be here in the *intrim*, and if he does not carry her off, he's as bad a politician as yourself.   [*Exit.*[16]

---

172 *Flebit . . . urbe*] Horace, *Satires*, II. i. 46: 'He shall lament and his notoriety be sung throughout the town.'   183 *prudish natalibus*] Possibly confused for *puris naturalibus*, 'in a natural state' or 'unclothed' (with a play on 'prudish').

SCENE II, *the street.*

Enter Bellmour *and* Rovewell *in liquor.*[17]

Bell. Women ever were, and ever will be, fantastic beings: vain, capricious, and fond of mischief.—To be insulted thus with such a contemptuous answer to a message of such tender import! She might methinks at least have treated me with good manners, if not with a more grateful return.

Rove. Split her manners, let's go and drink t'other bumper to drown sorrow.

Bell. I'll shake off her fetters—this very night I will—the ingratitude of it touches to the quick—my dear Rovewell, only come and see me take a final leave.

Rove. No, truly, not I, none of your virtuous minxes for me; I'll set you down there, if you've a mind to play the fool.—I know she'll melt you with a tear, and make a puppy of you with a smile; and so I'll not be witness to it.   13

Bell. You're quite mistaken, I assure you; you'll see me most manfully upbraid her with her ingratitude, and with more joy than a fugitive galley-slave, escape from the oar to which I have been chained.

Rove. Well, I'll wait in the coach for you, while you speak to her.

Bell. Her father, by all that's lucky! My dear Rovewell, let's drive off—

Rove. I'll speak to him for you, man—

Bell. Not for the world—prithee come along.   [*Exeunt.*[18]

Enter Quidnunc, *with a dark lantern.*

Quid. If the grand Turk should actually commence open hostilities, and the house-bug Tartars make a diversion on the frontiers, why then 'tis my opinion—time will discover a great deal more of the matter.—[19]

Watchman. [*Within.*] Past eleven o'clock—cloudy night.   24

Quid. Hey! Past eleven o'clock! My brother Feeble will be gone to bed, but he shan't sleep till I have some chat with him.—Hark'ye, watchman, watchman!

Enter Watchman.

Watch. Call, master?

Quid. Ay, step hither, step hither—have you heard any news?

Watch. News, master?

Quid. Ay, about the Prussians or Russians?   30

Watch. Russians, master?

Quid. Yes, or the movements in Pomerania?

Watch. La, master, I knows nothing—poor gentleman. [*Pointing to his head.*] Good night to you, master.—Past eleven o'clock.   [*Exit.*

Quid. That man now has a place under the government, and he won't speak. But I'm losing time. [*Knocks at the door.*] Hazy weather—the wind's fixed in that quarter and we shan't have any mails this week—come about, good wind, do, come about.

Enter a Servant Maid.

Maid. La, Sir, is it you?   40
Quid. Is your master at home, child?
Maid. Gone to bed, Sir.
Quid. Well, well, I'll step up to him.
Maid. Must not disturb him for the world, Sir.
Quid. Business of the utmost importance.
Maid. Pray consider, Sir, my master a'n't well.
Quid. Prithee be quiet, woman, I must see him.   [*Exeunt.*

SCENE III, *a room in* Feeble's *house.*

Enter Feeble *in his nightgown.*

Feeb. I was just stepping into bed—bless my heart—what can this man want? I hope no new misfortunes bring him at this hour!
Quid. [*Within.*] Hold your tongue, you foolish hussy—he'll be glad to see me—brother Feeble, brother Feeble!
Feeb. What can be the matter?

Enter Quidnunc.

Quid. Brother Feeble, I give you joy—the Nabob's demolished.
                    [*Sings,* 'Britons strike home, revenge,' *etc.*
Feeb. Lackaday, Mr. Quidnunc, how can you serve me thus?
Quid. Suraja Dowla is no more.   [*Sings,* 'Rule, Britannia,' *etc.*
Feeb. Poor man! He's stark mad.
Quid. Our men diverted themselves with killing their bullocks and their camels, till they dislodged the enemy from the octagon, and the counter-scarp, and the bunglo.   12
Feeb. I'll hear the rest tomorrow morning—oh, I'm ready to die—
Quid. Odsheart, man, be of good cheer—the new Nabob, Jaffier Ally

---

Sc. iii, 6 s.d. 'Britons strike home . . .'] A song from Purcell's opera *Bonduca* (1695). 8 Suraja Dowla] The Nabob of Bengal, defeated by Clive and killed in 1757.   8 s.d. '*Rule, Britannia*'] From James Thomson's masque *Alfred* (1740), II. v.   12 bunglo] For 'bunga-low', here meaning officers' quarters.

Cawn, has acceded to a treaty; and the English company have got all their
rights restored in the Phirmaud and the Hushbulhoorums.

Feeb. But dear heart, Mr. Quidnunc, why am I disturbed for this?

Quid. We had but two sepoys killed, three chokys, two Zemidars, and four
Gaul walls.   [*Sings, 'Britons never shall be slaves.'*

Feeb. Would not tomorrow morning do as well for this?   20

Quid. Light up your windows, man, light up your windows: Chander-
nagore is taken.

Feeb. Well, well, I am glad of it—oh, I shall certainly faint—

Quid. Ay, ay, sit down—nay, don't run away, I've more news to tell you;
there's an account from Williamsburg in America—the superintendent of
Indian affairs—

Feeb. Dear Sir! Dear Sir!   [*Avoiding him.*

Quid. Has settled matters with the Cherokees—   [*After him.*

Feeb. Enough, enough—

Quid. In the same manner he did before with the Catabaws—   30

Feeb. Well, well, your servant—

Quid. So that the back inhabitants—

Feeb. I wish you'd let me be a quiet inhabitant in my own house.

Quid. So that the back inhabitants will now be secured by the Cherokees
and Catabaws.

Feeb. You'd better go home, and think of appearing before the commis-
sioners.

Quid. Go home! No, no, I'll go and talk the matter over at our coffee-
house.

Feeb. Do so, do so.   40

Quid. [*Returning.*] Mr. Feeble, I had a dispute about the balance of power
—pray now can you tell—

Feeb. I know nothing of the matter—

Quid. Well, another time will do for that—I have a great deal to say about
that. [*Going, returns.*] Right, I had like to have forgot—there's an *erratum* in
the last *Gazette.*

Feeb. With all my heart—

Quid. Page 3rd, line 1, col. 1st and 3rd, for 'bombs' read 'booms'.

Feeb. Read what you will—

---

16 the Phirmaud . . . . the Hushbulhoorums] The corrupted names not of places but of the
documents by which 'the English company have got all their rights restored' by the Nabob,
Jaffier Ali Khan.   18 sepoys] Indians serving in a European army.   18 chokys] Toll col-
lectors.   18 Zemidars] Landowners.   19 Gaul walls] Stable grooms (*gorawallahs*).   19 s.d.
'*Britons never . . .*'] The second line of 'Rule, Britannia' (l. 8).   21 Chandernagore] A
French town near Calcutta. It fell to the English in 1757.   32 back inhabitants] i.e. back-
woodsmen, frontier settlers.

Quid. Nay, but that alters the sense, you know—well now, your servant—
if I hear any more news, I'll come and tell you.   51

Feeb. For Heaven's sake, no more—

Quid. I'll be with you before you're out of your first sleep.

Feeb. Good night, good night.   [*Runs off.*

Quid. I forgot to tell you—the Emperor of Morocco's dead—[*Bawling after
him.*] So, now I've made him happy—I'll go and knock up my friend Razor,
and make him happy too; and then I'll go and see if there's anybody up at the
coffee-houses, and make 'em all happy there too.   [*Exit.*

SCENE IV, *the Upholsterer's house.*

Enter Harriet *and* Bellmour.

Har. Mr. Bellmour, pray Sir—I desire, Sir, you'll not follow me from room
to room.

Bell. Indulge me but a moment—

Har. No, Mr. Bellmour, I've seen too much of your temper; I'm touched
beyond all enduring by your unmanly treatment.

Bell. Unmanly, Madam!

Har. Unmanly, Sir, to presume on the misfortunes of my family, and
insult me with formidable menaces that 'truly you have done'—you'll 'be no
more a slave to me'.—Oh fie, Mr. Bellmour, I did not think a gentleman
capable of it.   10

Bell. But you won't consider—

Har. Sir, I would have Mr. Bellmour to understand, that though my
father's circumstances are embarrassed, I have still an uncle, who can, and
will, place me in a state of affluence, and then, Sir, your declarations—20

Bell. My dearest Harriet, they were but hasty words; let me now entreat
you, suffer me to convey you hence, far from your father's roof, where we
may at length enjoy that happiness, of which we have long cherished the
loved idea—what say you, Harriet?

Har. I don't know what to say—my heart's at my lips—why don't you take
me then?   20

Enter Termagant.[21]

Term. Undone, undone! I am all over in a *flustration*—old Gemini Gomini
is coming.

Har. O Lud, what is to be done now?

Term. The Devil! What can be done? I have it—don't *flustrate* yourself—
I'll find some nonsense news for him—away with you both into that room—
quick, quick, run—[*They go out.*]—let me see—have I nothing in my pocket

for the old Hocus Pocus to read? Pshaw! That's Mr. Bellmour's letter to
Miss Harriet—I *enveloped* that secret for all her pains to *purvent* me—old
Politics must not have an *idear* of that business.—Stay, stay! Is there ne'er
an old trumpery newspaper? This will do—[*Puts it in her pocket.*]—now let
the Gazette of a fellow come as soon as he will.   31

Enter Quidnunc.

Quid. Fie upon it! Fie upon it! All the coffee-houses shut up—where is my
Salmon's *Gazetteer* and my map of the world? In that room, I fancy—I
won't sleep till I see the geography of all these places.   [*Going.*
Term. Sir, Sir, Sir!
Quid. What's the matter?
Term. Here has been Mr.—he with the odd name—
Quid. Mr. Dactyle, that writes the pretty verses upon all public occasions?
Term. Ay! Mr. Reptile—the same. He says as how there are some *assays* of
his in this paper [*Searching her pockets.*] and he desires you will give him
your *idear* of them.   41
Quid. That I will—let me see—
Term. The deuce fetch it—here is some *disintangles* in my pocket—there,
there it is.—[*Gives the paper and drops the letter.*] Pray *amuse* it before you go
to bed—or had not you better go and read it in bed?
Quid. No, I'll read it here.
Term. Do so—he'll call in the morning.—I'll get him to bed, I warrant me,
and then Miss Harriet may elope as fast as she will. [*Aside.*]   [*Exit.*
Quid. Hey! This is an old newspaper, I see.—What's this? [*Takes up the
letter.*] Here may be some news—'To Miss Harriet Quidnunc.'—Let me see—

'My Dearest Harriet: 51
    Why will you keep me in a state of suspense? I have given you every
proof of the sincerest constancy and love. Surely then, now that you see
your father's obstinacy, you may determine to consult your own happiness.
If you will permit me to wait on you this evening, I will convey you to a
family who will take the tenderest care of your person, till you resign it to
the arms of your
                        Eternal admirer,

                           Bellmour'

So! So! Here's policy detected! Why Harriet, daughter, Harriet! She has not
made her escape, I hope.—So, Madam!   61

Enter Harriet *and* Bellmour.

Hey! The enemy in our camp.

33 Salmon's *Gazetteer*] Thomas Salmon's *Modern Gazetteer* (1746).

Har. Mr. Bellmour is no enemy, Sir.

Quid. No? What does he lurk in my house for?

Bell. Sir, my designs are honourable, and you see I am above concealing myself.²²

Quid. Ay! Thanks to Termagant, or I should have been undermined here by you.

Term. [*Within.*] What the Devil is here to do now? I am all over in such a quandary!   70

Quid. Now, Madam! A'n't you a false girl? An undutiful child? But I can get intelligence, you see—Termagant is my friend! And if it had not been for her—

Enter Termagant.

Term. Oh my stars and garters! Here's such a piece of work! What shall I do? My poor Miss Harriet.   [*Cries.*

Quid. What, is there more news? What has happened now?

Term. Oh, Madam, Madam! Forgive me, my dear Ma'am! I did not do it on purpose—I did not, as I hope for mercy I did not.

Quid. Is the woman crazy?

Term. I did not intend to give it him—I would have seen him gibbeted first —I found the letter in your bedchamber—I knew it was the same I delivered to you, and my curiosity did make me peep into it. Says my curiosity, 'Now, Termagant, you may gratify yourself by finding out the contents of that letter which you have such a violent itching for.' My curiosity did say so, and then I own my respect for you did say to me, 'Hussy, how dare you meddle with what does not belong to you? Keep your distance and let your mistress's secrets alone.' And then upon that, in comes my curiosity again: 'Read it, I tell you, Termagant; a woman of spirit should know everything.' 'Let it alone, you jade,' says my respect, 'it's as much as your place is worth.' 'What signification's a place with an old *bankrupper*,' says my curiosity. 'There's more places than one, and so read it, I tell you, Termagant.' I did read it! Heaven help me, what could I do? I did read it! I don't go to deny it! I don't, I don't, I don't!   93

Quid. And I have read it too; don't keep such an uproar, woman.

Term. And then after I had read it—thinks me I—I'll give this to my mistress again, and her old *Germanocus* of a father shall never see it—and so as my ill stars would have it, as I was giving him a newspaper, I run my hand into the lion's mouth.   [*Cries.*

Bell. What an unlucky jade she has been—   [*Aside.*

73 s.d. *Enter* Termagant] Murphy borrowed this servant scene almost verbatim from his own *The Way to Keep Him* (1760), Act III.

Har. Well, well, there's no harm done, Termagant, for I don't want to deceive my father.   101

Quid. Yes, but there is harm done! Hey! What's all that knocking? Step and see, Termagant.

Term. Yes, Sir.   [*Exit.*

Quid. A waiter from the coffee-house, mayhap, with some intelligence.— You shall go to the round-house, friend; I'll carry you there myself—and who knows but I may meet a Parliament-man in the round-house to tell me some politics.

Enter Rovewell.[23]

Rove. But I say I will come in; my friend shan't be murdered amongst you—   110

Bell. 'Sdeath, Rovewell! What brings you here?

Rove. I have been waiting in a hackney coach for you these two hours, and split me but I was afraid they had smothered you between two feather beds.

Enter Termagant.

Term. More misfortunes! Here comes the watch.

Quid. The best news I ever heard.

Enter Watchmen.

Quid. Here, here, thieves, robbery, murder! I charge 'em both, take 'em directly—

Watch. Stand and deliver in the King's name! Seize 'em! Knock 'em down!

Bell. Don't frighten the lady—here's my sword—I surrender.

Rove. You scoundrels—stand off, rascals!   120

Watch. Down with him—down with him!   [*Fight.*

Enter Razor, *in his first dress, the Gazette in his hand.*

Raz. What, a fray at my Master Quidnunc's? [*Folds up the Gazette carefully, then strips to fight.*] Knock him down—down with him.   [*He fights.*

Quid. That's right—that's right, hold him fast.

              [*Watchmen* seize Rovewell, *and* Razor *puts on his clothes.*

Rove. You rascals, you have overpowered me—

Term. I believe as sure as anything as how he's a *highwayrman* and as how it was he that robbed the mail.

Quid. What, rob the mail and stop all the news? Search him, search him, he may have the letters belonging to the mail in his pockets now! Ay! Here's some letter—'To Mr. Abraham Quidnunc'—let's see what it is! 'Your dutiful son, John Quidnunc.'   131

106 round-house] Prison.

Rove. That's my name, and Rovewell was but assumed.

Quid. What, and am I your father?

Raz. [*Looks at him.*] Oh, my dear Sir! [*Embraces and powders him all over.*] 'Tis he, sure enough—I remember the mole on his cheek—I shaved his first beard.

Quid. Just returned from the West Indies, I suppose?

Rove. Yes Sir, the owner of a rich plantation.

Quid. What, by studying politics?

Rove. By a rich planter's widow—and I have now fortune enough to make you happy in your old age.   141

Raz. And I hope I shall shave him again.

Rove. So thou shalt, honest Razor.—In the meantime, let me entreat you to bestow my sister upon my friend Bellmour here.

Quid. He may take her as soon as he pleases.

Term. There, Ma'am—*calcine* your person to him.

Quid. What are the Spaniards doing in the Bay of Honduras?[24]

Rove. Truce with politics for the present, if you please, Sir.

Raz. With all my heart—I am rare happy.

Rove. We'll think of our own affairs first, before we concern ourselves about the balance of power.   151

Term. By my troth, that's what I always said.—And if everybody in the kingdom would do the same, the nation in general would not be in a *flustration* any more.

Then would the passions due proportion bear,
And every Harriet find a father's care.[25]

FINIS

Textual Notes

¹ This request to the Lord Chamberlain's Examiner of Plays for permission to act *The Upholsterer* appears at the end of the 1763 version (Larpent MS. No. 227).

² The Prologue is to the 1758 edition; neither MS. has a prologue.

³ The fact that two characters in the 1758 list—'Codicil, a lawyer' and 'Brisk'—are entirely omitted from the 1763 version, gives an idea of the considerable differences between the two plays. But the 1758 edition also has this note: 'For the sake of brevity, Codicil's scene is omitted in the representation, as are likewise a few passages in the second act.' 'Reading versions' often diverged significantly from 'acting versions'; here, as usual, the printed edition is aimed at readers, while the Examiner's MS. copy is closer to what was acted on stage.

⁴ Both 1757 and 1758 have about two pages of comic business between Bellmour and Brisk prior to this point in the scene. 1763, which omits Brisk entirely, naturally cuts this. In the earlier versions the setting is 'Bellmour's lodging'.

⁵ This speech, from 'I once lived . . .,' first appears in 1758.

⁶ 1757 has here a one-page scene, depicting four newsmongering tradesmen, which is not in either 1758 or 1763.

⁷ 1757 carries this on for ten more lines.

⁸ The speeches from Razor's 'there's something at the bottom . . .' to his '. . . your servant, Mr. Quidnunc' first appear in 1758.

⁹ 1758 inserts here nine lines about India bonds. Such topical references are different in each version, especially 1763, the war then being over.

¹⁰ The lines from 'I tell you . . .' to 'Pshaw!' first appear in 1758.

¹¹ 1757 and 1758 have at this point a four-page scene with Codicil, but they do not have the speeches of Harriet and Quidnunc until Termagant's entrance.

¹² This sentence appears in 1757 and 1758 but not in 1763.

¹³ From this point to the *Exeunt*, 1763 and 1758 differ extensively from 1757.

¹⁴ The material between 'That's kind, that's kind' and 'Pray now, Mr. Pamphlet' first appears in 1758.

¹⁵ Only in 1758 and 1763. In 1757 Quidnunc reads the paper until Termagant's entrance.

¹⁶ 1757 ends the scene thus at this point, while 1758 and 1763 give Termagant 1½ pages in which to read the newspaper and ridicule Quidnunc with many malapropisms. In 1763 she closes by resolving to procure Bellmour's letter to Harriet. I have preferred the 1757 version at this point for its briskness.

¹⁷ The 1763 version resumes. In 1757 Brisk speaks *solus* for one page before Rovewell and Bellmour enter; in 1758 all three enter together.

¹⁸ 1763 begins a new scene here: 'A street—a shabby house with a barber's pole up, and candles burning on the outside'—in other words, Razor's house. But the previous action can as well take place in this locale (if the Razor scene is used at all: see note 19), and a change of scene here will confuse the audience as to how Bellmour can have seen Quidnunc coming. I have therefore followed 1757 and 1758 in continuing the scene.

¹⁹ 1763 alone has at this point a 1½ page 'drunk scene' with Razor. I omit this on the assumption that the audience has by now seen enough of Razor and drunkenness, and follow 1757 and 1758 in passing directly from Quidnunc's first speech to the watchman's call, resuming the 1763 text there.

²⁰ The three versions differ extensively throughout this scene. 1757 and 1758 prolong the Harriet-Bellmour misunderstanding for three more pages by introducing Termagant and Brisk with a misdirected letter.

²¹ The Termagant-Quidnunc business until Harriet and Bellmour's re-entry is not in 1757 or 1758.

²² In 1757 and 1758 Bellmour's tactic is to distract Quidnunc by catering to his passion for news.

²³ This final section is considerably different in each version. In 1757 and 1758 Rovewell enters drunk, in pursuit of a girl (Termagant), and the dialogue is racier. 1757 has Brisk bring in the watchmen and is the longest; 1763 is the shortest.

²⁴ At approximately this point 1758 has Harriet welcome Rovewell home in a speech which appears in *neither* acting MS. (1757 or 1763), and was therefore, we may assume, not spoken in the theatre. It is virtually the only sentimental touch in the play, but was apparently inserted especially for the reading public:

> *Har.* Though your departure from England was too early for my recollection, yet my heart feels a ready inclination to make acquaintance with you; and I shall ever bless the hour that has given to my father so good a son, to Mr. Bellmour so warm a friend, and to me the unexpected happiness of a brother, whom I despaired of ever seeing.

²⁵ This closing couplet is preceded by eight more lines in 1758 and fourteen in 1757, both of which give the speech to Bellmour.

THE WAY TO KEEP HIM

Arthur Murphy

1727–1805

Written in 1758–9, first produced at Drury Lane on 24 January 1760, *The Way to Keep Him* was an immediate success: Garrick had again provided Murphy with a brilliant cast, the play earned fifteen more performances during the spring season, and some critics acknowledged that a genuine short comedy had appeared. But prevailing dramatic theory insisted that a three-act play was farce and a five-act play a comedy, so Murphy rewrote it in five acts (adding a subplot) to gain full accreditation. The resulting comedy held the boards until late in the nineteenth century. The afterpiece had a few private performances in the country (including one with Fanny Burney as Mrs. Lovemore), but otherwise the stage history of *The Way to Keep Him* from 1761 on has been the history of the full-length version.

The obscurity of the afterpiece is, however, undeserved. Granting the merit of the longer play, that it has most or all of what the shorter one contains plus an amusing and smoothly integrated subplot, the original version still exhibits the characteristic virtues of the afterpiece: unity and a brisk pace. In comparison the mainpiece seems diffuse and unwieldy, and more insistently didactic. But whatever the relative merits of the two *Ways*, their relationship shows how little difference in quality there might be between a good afterpiece and a good mainpiece, and how the former could serve as source for the latter.

In *The Upholsterer* Murphy, influenced by Foote's early plays, had been interested chiefly in satire. *The Way to Keep Him* shows a mature, independent playwright exploring the possibilities of his medium, and finally achieving the miniature but recognizable Georgian comedy of manners which had been the *beau idéal* of the *petite comédie* since Garrick's *Miss in Her Teens* (an achievement heightened by the extreme scarcity of even full-length new manners comedy at the time). Comedy within the limits of the afterpiece is realized through tight organization and the eschewal of a subplot. The four central characters are grouped closely around the theme of marital attraction and fidelity; apart from this main concern Murphy allows himself only some topical satire and servant humours. Comedy (as opposed to farce) is also the result of treating the characters as real individuals and the issues as serious and important. But this treatment raises another problem: the moralist may overwhelm the comedian. Once he has undertaken to deal adequately with the erring-husband theme, Murphy will not desist until he has reclaimed *two* philanderers, reproved the abandoned wife for her failure to remain alluring, and twitted the widow Bellmour (a virtuous 'other woman'!) on a point of conduct in the final scene. The play exists to teach the moral that 'it is much more difficult to keep a heart than to win one', and is a comedy only because this is learned in time.

One change made by Murphy in the five-act *Way to Keep Him* deserves comment. In the first interview between Mrs. Lovemore and the widow Bellmour (II. i), he inserted the following exchange after the latter's 'May I beg to know who the gentleman is?' (l. 102):

> *Mrs. L.* The story will be uninteresting to you, and to me it is painful. My grievances . . .   [*Puts her handkerchief to her eyes.*
> *Mrs. B.* [*Aside.*] Her grief affects me. [*Looks at her till she has recovered herself.*] I would not importune too much. . . .

Such tearful sympathy was common with sentimental authors but not with Murphy. That he added it to the full-length *Way to Keep Him* is indicative of one respect in which a mainpiece was expected to differ from an afterpiece.

The text is based on the first edition, 1760. The five-act version of 1761 may be found in '*The Way to Keep Him*' and *Five Other Plays by Arthur Murphy*, edited by John Pike Emery (New York University Press, New York, 1956).

Facing page: Connubio . . . dicabo] *Aeneid*, I. 73: 'I shall join [you] in lasting wedlock and call [her] your own.'

THE
WAY
TO
KEEP HIM,
A
COMEDY
In THREE ACTS:

As it is perform'd at the Theatre-Royal in
Drury-Lane.

Connubio jungam ftabili, propriamque dicabo.
VIRG.

LONDON:
Printed for P. VALLIANT, oppofite *Southampton-ftreet* in the *Strand*, M DCC LX.

(Price One Shilling and Six Pence.)

ADVERTISEMENT.

A poem* of Dr. SWIFT'S, (with all due Deference to the Ladies, that Poem is mentioned) gave the Author the first Idea of a Comedy on this Subject. He had not thought sufficiently of it, to form any regular Plan, when *La Nouvelle Ecole des Femmes*, of Monsieur *De Moissy*, fell into his Hands. There were Circumstances and Sentiments in that Piece, which coincided with his Design; and he also had some Objections. The Husband's visiting a Lady of Fashion, under his own Name, and passing upon her for an unmarried Man; the *Chevalier*'s Attempt upon his Friend's Honour, without a proper Detection of either of them; the Wife singing and dancing about the Stage thro' the whole Last Act, in order to reclaim her Husband, and his Approbation of it; without any other *Denouement*, and without any Situations of Embarassment, which the Story so naturally tended to, were, in his Opinion, palpable Deficiencies. To substitute other Materials, to form a Last Act entirely new, and to work the whole into an *English* Comedy, was the Employment of some vacant Hours in the last Summer. Whether he has been able to do it with any tolerable Spirit, either in the Dialogue, Characters, or Fable, he now submits to the Decision of the candid Reader. He acknowledges the public Candour, and he returns his Thanks to Mr. *Garrick*, for his admirable Acting; and to all the Performers concerned in the following Scenes; and also in THE DESERT ISLAND.

Lincoln's-Inn,   ARTHUR MURPHY.
1st *Feb.* 1760

*STREPHON and CHLOE.

THE DESERT ISLAND] A three-act 'entertainment' by Murphy. It opened on 24 January 1760 at Drury Lane as the companion mainpiece to *The Way to Keep Him*, but lasted for only eleven performances.

Dramatis Personæ

MEN

Lovemore,	Mr. GARRICK.
Sir *Brilliant Fashion*,	Mr. PALMER.
William, Servant to *Lovemore*,	Mr. KING.
[Servant]	

WOMEN

Mrs. *Lovemore*,	Mrs. YATES.
The Widow *Bellmour*,	Miss MACKLIN.
Muslin, Waiting-woman to Mrs. *Lovemore*,	Mrs. CLIVE.
Mignionet, Maid to Mrs. *Bellmour*,	Mrs. BRADSHAW.
Pompey, a black Boy belonging to the Widow.	
[*Jenny*, Maid to Mrs. *Lovemore*]	

Scene LONDON.

THE
Way to Keep Him

ACT I. SCENE I.

The hall in Lovemore's *house,* William *at cards with a brother servant.*

Will. A plague on it! I've turned out my game.—Is forty-seven good?
Serv. Equal.
Will. A plague go with it—tierce to a queen!
Serv. Equal.
Will. I've ruined my game, and be hanged to me.—I don't believe there's a footman in England plays with worse luck than myself.—Four aces is fourteen!
Serv. That's hard; cruel, by Jupiter!
Will. Four aces is fourteen—fifteen.   [*Plays.*
Serv. There's your equality.   10
Will. Very well—sixteen [*Plays.*]—seventeen.   [*Plays.*

Enter Muslin.

Mus. There's a couple of you, indeed! You're so fond of the vices of your betters, that you're scarce out of your beds, when you must pretend to imitate them and their ways, forsooth.
Will. Prithee, be quiet, woman, do.—Eighteen.   [*Plays.*
Mus. Set you up indeed, Mr. Coxcomb.
Will. Nineteen! Clubs.   [*Plays.*
Mus. Have done with your foolery, will ye? And send my mistress word—
Will. Hold your tongue, Mrs. Muslin, you'll put us out.—What shall I play? I'll tell you, woman, my master and I desire to have nothing to say to you or your mistress.—Twenty; diamonds!   [*Plays.*
Mus. But I tell you, Mr. Sauce-box, that my lady desires to know when your master came home last night, and how he is this morning?   23
Will. Prithee, be quiet.—I and my master are resolved to be teased no more by you.—And so, Mrs. Go-Between, you may return as you came.—What the Devil shall I play? We'll have nothing to do with you, I tell you.

s.d. *cards*] The game is piquet.

Mus. You'll have nothing to do with us! But you shall have to do with us, or I'll know the reason why.   [*Snatches the cards out of his hands.*

Will. Death and fury! This meddling woman has destroyed my whole game.   31

Mus. Now, Sir, will you be so obliging as to send my mistress an answer to her questions, how and when your rake-helly master came home last night?

Will. I'll tell you what, Mrs. Muslin—you and my master will be the death of me at last; that's what you will.—In the name of charity, what do you both take me for? Whatever appearances may be, I am but of mortal mould.— Nothing super-natural about me.

Mus. Upon my word, Mr. Powder-Puff!

Will. I have not indeed! And so, do you see, flesh and blood can't hold it always.—I can't be for ever a slave to your whims, and your second-hand airs.

Mus. Second-hand airs!   42

Will. Yes, second-hand airs! You take 'em at your ladies' toilets with their cast gowns, and so you descend to us with them.—And then, on the other hand, there's my master! Because he chooses to live upon the principal of his health, and so run out his whole stock as fast as he can, he must have the pleasure of my company with him in his Devil's dance to the other world.— Never at home, till three, four, five, six in the morning!

Mus. Ay, a vile, ungrateful man, to have so little regard for a wife that dotes upon him.—And your love for me is all of a piece.—I've no patience with you both.—A couple of false, perfidious, abandoned, profligate—   51

Will. Hey, hey—where's your tongue running? My master is, as the world goes, a good sort of a civil kind of a husband, and I, Heaven help me, a poor simpleton of an amorous, constant puppy, that bears with all the follies of his little tyrant here.—Come and kiss me, you jade, come and kiss me.

Mus. Paws off, Caesar.—Don't think to make me your dupe.—I know when you go with him to this new lady, this Bath acquaintance; and I know you're as false as my master, and give all my dues to your Mrs. Mignionet there.

Will. Hush, not a word of that.—I'm ruined, pressed, and sent on board a tender directly, if you blab that I trusted you with that secret.—But to charge me with falsehood—injustice and ingratitude! My master, to be sure, does drink an agreeable dish of tea with the widow—has been there every night this month past.—How long it will last, Heaven knows! But thither he goes, and I attend him.—I ask my master, Sir, says I, what time would you please to want me? He gives me his answer, and then I strut by Mrs. Mignionet, without so much as tipping her one glance; she stands watering at the mouth, and a pretty fellow that, says she.—Ay, ay, gaze on, says I, gaze on; I see what you would be at: you'd be glad to have me, you'd be glad to have me!

59 pressed] Press-ganged.

But sour grapes, my dear! I'll go home and cherish my own lovely wanton; and so I do, you know I do.—Then after toying with thee, I hasten back to my master; later indeed than he desires, but always too soon for him.— He's loath to part; he lingers and dangles, and I stand cooling my heels.— O! To the Devil I pitch such a life.   73

Mus. Why don't you strive to reclaim the vile man then?

Will. Softly, not so fast; I have my talent to be sure! Yes, yes, I have my talent: some influence over my master's mind; but can you suppose that I have power to turn the drift of his inclinations, and lead him as I please—and to whom? To his wife! Pshaw! Ridiculous, foolish, and absurd!

Mus. Mighty well, Sir! Can you proceed?

Will. I tell you a wife is out of date nowadays. Time was—but that's all over—a wife's a drug now; mere tar-water, with every virtue under Heaven, but nobody takes it.   82

Mus. Well, I swear, I could slap your impudent face.

Will. Come and kiss me, I say.

Mus. A fiddlestick for your kisses, while you encourage your master to open rebellion against the best of wives.

Will. I tell you it's her own fault; why don't she strive to please him, as you do me? Come, throw your arms about my neck.

Mus. Ay, as I used to do, Mr. Brazen!

Will. Then must I force you to your own good—[*Kisses her.*]—pregnant with delight! Egad, if my master was not in the next room—   91

Mus. Hush! My mistress's bell rings—how long has he been up?

Will. He has been up—he has been up—'Sdeath, you've set me all on fire.

Mus. There, there, the bell rings again—let me be gone—[*Going.*] well, but what must I say? When did he come home?

Will. At five this morning, rubbed his forehead, damned himself for a blockhead, went to bed in a peevish humour, and is now in tip-top spirits with Sir Brilliant Fashion, in the next room.

Mus. Oh Lud! That bell rings again—there, there, let me be gone.

[She kisses him and exit.

Will. There goes high and low life contrasted in one person; 'tis well I have not told her the whole of my master's secrets: she'll blab that he visits this widow from Bath.—But if they enquire, they'll be told he does not; the plot lies deeper than they think, and so they'll only get into a puzzle.—So, my master's bell rings too.   *[Exit.*

81 tar-water] An infusion of tar in cold water, thought to have medicinal properties.

SCENE [II], *another apartment;* Mrs. Lovemore,
and a maid attending her.

Mrs. L. This trash of tea! I don't know why I drink so much of it.—Heigh ho! I wonder what keeps Muslin—do you step, child, with my compliments to your master, and let him know, I shall be glad of his company to a dish of tea this morning.

Maid. Yes, Ma'am.   [*Exit.*

Mrs. L. Surely, never was any poor woman treated with such cruel indifference; nay, with such an open undisguised insolence of gallantry.

Enter Muslin.

Mrs. L. Well, Muslin, have you seen his Prime Minister?

Mus. Yes, Ma'am, I have seen Mr. William, and he says as how my master came home according to custom, at five this morning, and in a huge pickle.— He's now at breakfast, and has Sir Brilliant Fashion with him.   11

Mrs. L. Is he there again?

Mus. He is, Ma'am; and as I passed by master's study, I overheard them both laughing as loud as anything—

Mrs. L. About some precious mischief, I'll be sworn; and all at my cost, too! Heigh ho!

Mus. Dear Ma'am, why will you chagrin yourself about a vile man, that is not worth, no, as I live and breathe, not worth a single sigh?

Mrs. L. What can I do, Muslin?

Mus. Do, Ma'am! Lard! If I was as you, I'd do for him; as I'm a living Christian, I would.—If I could not cure my grief, I'd find some comforts, that's what I would.   22

Mrs. L. Heigh ho! I have no comfort.

Mus. No comfort, Ma'am? Whose fault then? Would anybody but you, Ma'am? It provokes me to think of it. Would anybody, Ma'am, young and handsome as you are, with so many accomplishments, Ma'am, sit at home here, as melancholy as a poor servant out of place? And all this for what? Why for a husband, and such a husband! What do you think the world will say of you, Ma'am, if you go on this way?

Mrs. L. I care not what they say, I am tired of the world, and the world may be tired of me, if it will: my troubles are my own only, and I must endeavour to bear them.—Who knows what patience may do? If Mr. Lovemore has any feeling left, my resignation may some day or other have its effect, and incline him to do me justice.   34

Mus. But, dear Ma'am, that's waiting for dead mens' shoes—incline him to do you justice! What signifies expecting and expecting? Give me a bird in the hand.—Lard, Ma'am, to be for ever pining and grieving! Dear heart! If all the women in London, in your case, were to sit down and die of the spleen, what would become of all the public places? They might turn Vauxhall to a hop-garden, make a brewhouse of Ranelagh, and let both the playhouses to a Methodist preacher. We should not have the racketting with 'em we have now.—'John, let the horses be put to.'—'John, go to my Lady Trumpabout's, and invite her to a small party of twenty or thirty card tables.'—'John, run to my Lady Cat-Gut, and let her Ladyship know I'll wait on her to the new opera.'—'John, run as fast as ever you can, with my compliments to Mr. Varney, and tell him I shall take it as the greatest favour on earth, if he will let me have a side-box for the new play.—No excuse, tell him.'—They whisk about the town, and rantipole it with as unconcerned looks, and as florid outsides, as if they were treated at home like so many goddesses, though everybody knows possession has ungoddessed them all long ago, and their husbands care no more for them—no, by jingo, no more than they do for their husbands.   52

Mrs. L. You run on at a strange rate.

Mus. [*In a passion.*] Dear Ma'am, 'tis enough to make a body run on.—If everybody thought like you—

Mrs. L. If everybody loved like me—

Mus. A brass thimble for love, if it is not answered by love.—What the deuce is here to do? Shall I go and fix my heart upon a man, that shall despise me for that very reason, and, 'Ay,' says he, 'poor fool, I see she loves me—the woman's well enough, only she has one inconvenient circumstance about her: I'm married to her, and marriage is the Devil.'—And then when he's going a-roguing, smiles impudently in your face, and, 'My dear, divert yourself, I'm just going to kill half an hour at the chocolate-house, or to peep in at the play; your servant, my dear, your servant.'—Fie upon 'em! I know 'em all.—Give me a husband that will enlarge the circle of my innocent pleasures: but a husband nowadays, Ma'am, is no such a thing.—A husband now, as I hope for mercy, is nothing at all but a scarecrow, to show you the fruit, but touch it if you dare.—A husband—the Devil take 'em all—Lord forgive one for swearing—is nothing at all but a bugbear, a snapdragon; a husband, Ma'am, is—   70

Mrs. L. Prithee, peace with your tongue, and see what keeps that girl.

Mus. Yes, Ma'am.—Why, Jenny, why don't you come up to my mistress? What do you stand a-gossiping there for? A husband, Ma'am, is a mere monster; that is to say, if one makes him so; then, for certain, he is a monster indeed; and if one does not make him so, then he behaves like a monster; and of the two evils, by my troth—Ma'am, was you ever at the play of Catherine

41 racketting] Living a gay, social life; 'gadding about'.   45 Mr. Varney] In charge of advance bookings at Drury Lane.   48 rantipole] Behave in a noisy fashion.

H

and Mercutio? The vile man calls his wife his goods, and his cattles, and his household stuff.—There you may see, Ma'am, what a husband is—a husband is—but here comes one will tell you—here comes Sir Brilliant Fashion.—Ask his advice, Ma'am.   80

Mrs. L. His advice! Ask advice of the man who has estranged Mr. Lovemore's affections from me!

Mus. Well, I protest and vow, Ma'am, I think Sir Brilliant a very pretty gentleman.—He's the very pink of the fashion; he dresses fashionably, lives fashionably, wins your money fashionably, loses his own fashionably, and does everything fashionably; and then, he is so lively, and talks so lively, and so much to say, and so never at a loss.—But here he comes.

Enter Sir Brilliant, *singing.*

Sir B. Mrs. Lovemore, your most obedient very humble servant.—But, my dear Madam, what, always in a *vis-à-vis* party with your *suivante*! You will afford me your pardon, my dear Ma'am, if I avow that this does a little wear the appearance of misanthropy.   91

Mrs. L. Far from it, Sir Brilliant—we were engaged in your panegyric.

Sir B. My panegyric! Then am I come most apropos to give a helping hand towards making it complete.—Mr. Lovemore will kiss your hand presently, Ma'am; he has not as yet entirely adjusted his dress.—In the meantime, I can, if you please, help you to some anecdotes, which will perhaps enable you to colour your canvas a little higher.

Mrs. L. I hope you will be sure, among those anecdotes, not to omit the egregious exploit of seducing Mr. Lovemore entirely from his wife. [*She makes a sign to* Muslin *to go.*]   [*Exit* Muslin.

Sir B. I, Ma'am! Let me perish, Madam—   101

Mrs. L. Oh! Sir, I am no stranger to—

Sir B. May Fortune eternally forsake me, and Beauty frown on me, if ever—

Mrs. L. Don't protest too strongly, Sir Brilliant—

Sir B. May I never hold four by honours—

Mrs. L. Nay, but Sir—

Sir B. Ma'am, I am altogether struck with amazement.—May I never taste the dear delight of breaking a Pharaoh bank, or bullying the whole room at a brag-party, if ever I was, in thought, word, or deed, accessory to his infidelity.—I deny all unlawful confederacy.   111

Mrs. L. Oh! Sir, it is vain to deny.

Sir B. Nay, but my dear Mrs. Lovemore, give me leave—I alienate the

77 Mercutio] She means 'Petruchio'. *Catherine and Petruchio* was Garrick's 1756 alteration of *The Taming of the Shrew*.   106 four by honours] Hold the four highest trumps in whist.   109 Pharaoh] Or Faro: a gambling game played with cards.

affections of Mr. Lovemore! Consider, Madam, how would this tell in Westminster Hall? Sir Brilliant Fashion, how say you, guilty of this indictment or not guilty? Not guilty, poss.—Thus issue is joined; you enter the court, and in sober sadness charge the whole plump upon me, without a word as to the how, when, and where.—No proof positive—there ends the prosecution.

Mrs. L. But, Sir, your stating of the case—

Sir B. Dear Ma'am, don't interrupt.   120

Mrs. L. Let me explain this matter.

Sir B. Nay, Mrs. Lovemore, allow me fair play.—I am now upon my defence.—You will please to consider, gentlemen of the jury, that Mr. Lovemore is not a ward, nor I a guardian; that he is his own master to do as he pleases; that Mr. Lovemore is fond of gaiety, pleasure, and enjoyment; that he knows how to live, and if he does not like the bill of fare that is catered for him at home, he very naturally goes abroad to seek for something more palatable.

How say ye, gentlemen of the jury? Not guilty.—There, Ma'am, you see, not guilty.   130

Mrs. L. You run on finely, Sir Brilliant; but don't imagine that this bantering way—

Sir B. Acquitted by my country, Ma'am, you see—fairly acquitted!

Mrs. L. Be it so then.—But you hinted something about Mr. Lovemore's not liking his bill of fare at home.—I should be glad you would explain that matter, Sir—

Sir B. Right, Madam, very right: I did touch upon that head.—It was but slightly—I did not care, in an open court, to enlarge further upon that matter.—But to be plain, upon my word, Mrs. Lovemore, for a fine woman like you to be the dupe of your own false delicacy, an old-fashioned kind of sentiment, a vulgar prejudice, proscribed by custom long ago; an antiquated principle of I know not what: renounce it altogether—*vivez*, Ma'am—do like other people of condition; mix with other amiable ladies, who know how to use the senses nature has given them; pluck the fruit that grows around ye, and bid adieu to the reign of the melancholy pleasures for ever.   145

Mrs. L. After the very edifying counsel you give Mr. Lovemore, this loose strain of yours, Sir Brilliant, is not at all surprising; and, Sir, your late project—

Sir B. My late project!

Mrs. L. Yes, Sir: not content with leading Mr. Lovemore into a thousand dissipations from all conjugal affection and domestic happiness, you have lately introduced him to your Mrs. Bellmour.   152

Sir B. Ma'am, he does not so much as know Mrs. Bellmour.

Mrs. L. Fie upon it, Sir Brilliant! Falsehood is but a poor—

116 poss] 'Defendant' in legal Latin.

Sir B. Falsehood I disdain, Ma'am—and I, Sir Brilliant Fashion, declare, that Mr. Lovemore, your husband, is not acquainted with the widow Bellmour.—And if he was acquainted? What then? No ill consequence could from thence redound to you.—You don't know that lady, Ma'am.— But I'll let you into her whole history, her whole history, Ma'am: pray be seated. The widow Bellmour's history is this; she is one of those ladies—

Love. [*Speaks within.*] William! Is the chariot at the door?

Sir B. We are interrupted.   162

Enter Lovemore.

Love. Very well, let the chariot be brought round directly.—How do you do this morning, my dear? Sir Brilliant, I beg your pardon.—How do you do, my dear?   [*With an air of cold civility.*

Mrs. L. Only a little indisposed in mind, and indisposition of the mind is of no sort of consequence; not worth a cure—

Love. I beg your pardon, Mrs. Lovemore, indisposition of the mind—Sir Brilliant, that is really a mighty pretty ring you have on your finger.

Sir B. A bauble: will you look at it?   170

Mrs. L. Though I have but few obligations to Sir Brilliant, yet I fancy I may ascribe to him the favour of this visit, Mr. Lovemore.

Love. [*Looking at the ring.*]—Nay, now positively you wrong me; I was obliged to you for your civil enquiries concerning me this morning, and so on my part, I came to return the compliment before I go abroad.—Upon my word 'tis very prettily set.   [*Gives it.*

Mrs. L. Are you going abroad, Sir?

Love. A matter of business—I hate business—but business must be done. —[*Examining his ruffles.*]—Pray, is there any news? Any news, my dear?

Mrs. L. It would be news to me, Sir, if you would be kind enough to let me know whether I may expect the favour of your company to dinner.

Love. It would be impertinent in me to answer such a question, because I can give no direct positive answer to it; as things happen, perhaps I may, perhaps may not.—But don't let me be of any inconvenience to you; it is not material where a body eats.—Can I set you down anywhere, Sir Brilliant?

Sir B. I thank you, no—my chariot's in waiting.—I have some visits to make, and shall rattle half the town over presently.   187

Love. As you will—*à ça,* your servant, Mrs. Lovemore.—My dear [*Drawing his gloves on.*]—I kiss your hand.—Who waits there? [*Going, returns.*] Apropos, you have heard what happened?   [*To* Sir Brilliant.

Sir B. When, and where?   191

Love. A word in your ear—Ma'am, with your permission—

Mrs. L. That cold, contemptuous civility, Mr. Lovemore—

Love. Pshaw! Prithee now—how can you, my dear? That's very peevish now, and ill-natured.—It is but about a mere trifle.—Hark ye [*Whispers.*], I lost everything I played for after you went—the foreigner and he understand one another.—I beg pardon, Ma'am, it was only about an affair at the opera.

Mrs. L. The opera, Mr. Lovemore, or anything, is more agreeable than my company.

Love. You wrong me now, I declare you wrong me; and if it will give you any pleasure, I'll sup at home.—Can't we meet at the St. Alban's tonight?
                                                                [*Aside to* Sir Brilliant.

Mrs. L. I believe I need not tell you what pleasure that would give me: but unless the pleasure is mutual, Mr. Lovemore—   203

Love. Ma'am, I—I—I perceive all the delicacy of that sentiment; but—a—a—I shall incommode you, you possibly may have some private party—and it would be very impolite in me, to obstruct your schemes of pleasure.—Would it not, Sir Brilliant?   [*Laughs.*

Sir B. It would be gothic to the last degree.—Ha! Ha!

Love. Ha! Ha! To be sure, for me to be of the party, would look as if we lived together like our friend Sir Jealous Hotbrain and his scolding wife, who are for ever like two gamecocks, ready armed to goad and wound one another most heartily.—Ha! Ha!   212

Sir B. The very thing—Ha! Ha!

Love. So it is—so it is.   [*Both stand laughing.*

Mrs. L. Very well, gentlemen; you have it all to yourselves.

Love. Odso! [*Looking at his watch.*] I shall be beyond my time.—Any commands into the city, Madam?

Mrs. L. Commands! I have no commands, Sir.

Love. I have an appointment there at my banker's; Sir Brilliant, you know old Discount?   220

Sir B. What, he that was in Parliament?

Love. The same—Entire Butt, I think, was the name of the borough.—Ha! Ha! Ha! Ma'am, your most obedient; Sir Brilliant, yours.—Who waits there? No ceremony.—Your servant.   [*Exit singing.*

Sir B. Bon voyage!

Enter Muslin.

Mus. Did you call, Ma'am?

Mrs. L. Come hither, Muslin [*Whispers her.*]; mind what I say.

Mus. I'll do it, Madam; I'll do it.   [*Exit.*

Mrs. L. He's gone to visit this Mrs. Bellmour, I suppose.

Sir B. Dear Ma'am, how can you take such a notion in your head? But apropos—that brings us back to the little history I was just going to give you of the widow Bellmour.   232

201 St. Alban's] A tavern near Pall Mall.   208 gothic] i.e. barbaric.

Mrs. L. Proceed, Sir.

Sir B. The widow Bellmour, Ma'am, is a lady, who to all the charms of external beauty, has added such an elegance of understanding, and such a vivacity of wit, that it is no wonder the pretty fellows are all on their knees to her.—Her person youthful, blooming, and graceful—and then her manner! And so entertaining! Such quickness in her transition from one thing to another; and everything she does, does so become her! Does she sit still? 'Tis an indolent Venus before ye.—Does she move? 'Tis Beauty walking in conscious triumph! To see her smile, and hear her talk—I shall glow up into rapture, and fall a-raving if I talk a moment longer about her.

Mrs. L. Pray, finish your picture, Sir.   243

Sir B. 'Tis from the real life, I assure ye.—In short, Ma'am, she is a lady that has been abroad, has ever kept the best company, and has such a variety of talents, that upon my soul, she knows the whole theory of agreeable sensations better than all the philosophers in Europe.

Mrs. L. And to this theory, she has joined the practice, I presume.

Sir B. She has.

Mrs. L. I imagined as much.   250

Sir B. Ma'am!

Mrs. L. You need not affect to be surprised, Sir—there is no mighty secret in the affair.—My accounts of the lady inform me, that she is as you say, young and handsome; has lived a great deal abroad, buried her husband there, is lately come to town, has taken a house, lives at great expense, receives all the men of rank and fortune.—We all know what the world is apt to infer from these appearances.

Sir B. I am no stranger to the way of the world.—Every object has its different aspects, its side-lights; and the world is generally good-natured enough to fix upon the most unfavourable points of view.   260

Mrs. L. So then, this is another antiquated prejudice of mine.

Sir B. Nothing more certain.

Mrs. L. Oh! Mighty well, Sir! She is a very Vestal; come, exhibit your portrait.—A Vestal from your school of painting will, no doubt, be very curious.

Sir B. My dear Madam, consider what you are saying! What is your charge against this lady? That she is amiable! Surely Mrs. Lovemore should be the last person in the world, to reproach her with a quality, which [she] so eminently possesses herself.

Mrs. L. The gallantry of that compliment, Sir Brilliant, added to your other favours—   271

Sir B. What next? That she has agreeable talents! What then? As nature is liberal of talents to but very few, she makes a kind of recompense to those who have none, by conducing to their entertainment.—But she is young and handsome! So perishable a quality might, methinks, be suffered to bloom without reproach.—Ay, but she has taken a house, and sees company.—It is what she is entitled to, and a fine picture should be seen by people of rank and taste; and surely, Madam, your sex entrenches upon your own happiness, by not allowing that a woman may partake of the innocent pleasures of life, unless she has resigned her person to a man, and parted with her liberty!

Mrs. L. And so you would persuade me that Mr. Lovemore is not acquainted with her?   282

Sir B. Absolutely ignorant of him! And I'll tell you further, she has such a generosity of temper, and such a feeling heart, that were she to know him, and to know that his visits gave you pain, she would never be at home for him again.

Mrs. L. Then give me leave, Sir—if you have so exalted an opinion of the lady, how comes it that you desist from paying your addresses in that quarter?

Sir B. Compulsion, Ma'am—it is not voluntary.—The garrison, I thought, was upon the point of surrendering, but up came my Lord Etheridge with his honourable forces to relieve the town.—I thought he was out of the kingdom, but it seems he is returned.—I bribed the chambermaid yesterday, and I find he has supplanted me; and so all that remains for me, is to do justice to the lady, and console myself in the best way I can for my demerits, and the insufficiency of my pretensions.   296

Mrs. L. And am I really to believe all this?

Sir B. May the first woman I put the question to, strike me to the centre with a supercilious eyebrow, if every syllable is not minutely true—so that you see, Ma'am, I am not the cause of your inquietude.—There is not on earth a man that could be more averse from such a thing, nor a person in the world who more earnestly aspires to prove the tender esteem he bears ye— and, Ma'am, I have long panted for an opportunity.—By all that's soft she hears me. [*Aside.*]—I have long panted, Ma'am, for a tender moment like this, with all the ardour of love, which charms like yours alone could kindle. —[*She rises disconcerted.*] Were it even at the expense of my life—[*She walks about uneasy.*]—You see, my dear Ma'am, we both have cause of discontent; we are both disappointed, both crossed in love, and so, Ma'am, the least we can do is, both heartily to join to sweeten each other's cares.   309

Mrs. L. Sir Brilliant, I don't understand.   [*Angrily.*

Sir B. If you will pour the balm of love on this poor wounded heart, you may have the most delicious revenge against a husband who, from his own perverse inclination, his own inhumanity of temper, has for a long time—I have seen it, Madam, with vexation seen it—yes—he has long been false to honour, love, and you.   315

278 entrenches] Encroaches.

Mrs. L. This usage, Sir—you take my wrongs too much to heart, Sir—
[*Walking about.*]—I myself, Sir, can remedy my own afflictions.—But this
presumption of yours—upon my word! This is the most unparalleled—

[*Walks about and flutters her fan.*

Sir B. Pray, Ma'am, don't break your fan—don't break it, Ma'am—I beg
you won't.   320

Mrs. L. This is the most affronting—come to a fine pass, indeed! [*She
stands looking at her fan.*]—Intolerable assurance!

Sir B. Now am I in a sweet condition.—The poet has touched it most
exquisitely.—

> She views the *Sory* with attentive eyes,
> And pities *Procris*, while her lover dies.

Mrs. L. Sir, I must desire you will quit my house immediately.

Sir B. Don't overheat yourself—consider, my dear Madam—

Mrs. L. Sir, I desire—was ever such rudeness!   [*Rings the bell.*

Sir B. Ma'am, I desist—I have done—but when you're in a better humour,
pray recollect.   331

Mrs. L. Will nobody answer there?

Sir B. I retire.—

> Those eyes that tell us what the sun is made of;
> Those hills of driven snow.

Enter Muslin *hastily.*

Sir B. Ma'am, your most obedient.   [*Exit.*

Mus. Did you call, Ma'am?

Mrs. L. To show the gentleman out.   [*Walking angrily.*

Mus. The servants are all in the hall.

Mrs. L. To be insulted thus by his loose confident carriage!   340

Mus. As I live and breathe, Ma'am, if I was as you, I would not flutter
myself about it.

Mrs. L. About what?

Mus. La! What signifies mincing matters? I overheard it all.

Mrs. L. You did, did you?   [*Angrily.*

Mus. Ma'am!

Mrs. L. It does not signify at present.

Mus. No, Ma'am, it does not signify, and revenge is sweet, I think; and
by my troth, I don't see why you should stand on ceremony with a husband
that stands upon none with you.   350

334-5 Those eyes . . . snow] Edward Young, *The Revenge* (1721), I. i. 142, 144.

Mrs. L. Again—prithee, Mrs. Malapert, none of your advice.—How dare you talk in this manner to me? Let me hear no more of this impertinent freedom. [*Walks about.*

Mus. No, Ma'am.—It's very well, Ma'am.—I have done, Ma'am.—[*Disconcerted, and then she speaks aside.*]—What the Devil is here to do? An unmannerly thing to go for to huff me in this manner!

Mrs. L. [*Still walking about.*] [*Aside.*] To make his character public, and render him the subject of every tea-table throughout this town, would only serve to widen the breach, and instead of his neglect, might call forth his anger, and settle at last into a fixed aversion.—Lawyers, parting, and separate maintenance would ensue.—No, I must avoid that, if possible; I will avoid that.—What must be done? 362

Mus. What can she be thinking of now? The sulky thing, not to be communicative with such a friend as I am! What can she mean? Did you speak to me, Ma'am?

Mrs. L. Suppose I were to try that! Muslin—

Mus. Ma'am! Now for it. [*Aside.*

Mrs. L. Did John follow your master's chariot, as I ordered?

Mus. He did, Ma'am.

Mrs. L. Where is he? 370

Mus. He's below, Ma'am; he followed it as far as the chocolate house in St. James's Street.

Mrs. L. Are you sure of that?

Mus. You may rely upon it.

Mrs. L. You heard Sir Brilliant deny that Mr. Lovemore visits at this widow Bellmour's.

Mus. Lard, Ma'am, he's as full of fibs as a French milliner—he does visit there—I know it all from William—I'll be hanged in my own garters if he does not.

Mrs. L. I know not what to do! Heigho! I think I'll venture.—Let my chair be got ready instantly. 381

Mus. Your chair, Ma'am! Are you going out, Ma'am?

Mrs. L. Don't tease me with your talk, but do as I bid you—and bring my capuchin down to the parlour immediately. [*Exit.*

Mus. What is in the wind now? An ill-natured puss, not to tell me what she is about! It's no matter—she does not know what she is about.—Before I'd lead such a life, I'd take a lover's leap into Rosamond's Pond.—I love to see company for my part.—But, Lord bless me! I had like to have forgot, Mrs. Sugar-Key comes to my rout tonight.—I had as live she had stayed away, she's nothing but mere lumber! So formal, that she won't play above a

384 capuchin] A cloak and hood. 387 Rosamond's Pond] A pond in St. James's Park, London (filled in in 1770). 389 live] For 'lief': 'I had as soon'.

shilling-whist.—How the Devil does she think I'm to make a shilling party for her? There's no such a thing to be done nowadays—nobody plays shilling-whist now.   [*Exit in a passion.*

End of the First Act.

ACT II

SCENE, *a room at the* Widow Bellmour's, *in which are disposed up and down, several chairs, a toilette, a bookcase, and a harpsichord;* Mignionet, *her maid, is settling the toilette.*

Enter Mrs. Bellmour, *reading a volume of Pope.*

Mrs. B.   Oh! Blest with temper, whose unclouded ray,
Can make tomorrow cheerful as today;
She who can own a sister's charms, and hear
Sighs for a daughter, with unwounded ear;
That never answers till a husband cools,
And if she rules him, never shows she rules;

Sensible, elegant Pope!

Charms by accepting, by submitting sways,
Yet has her humour most when she obeys;
                                        [*Seems to read on.*
Mig. Lord love my mistress! She's always so happy, and so gay.   10
Mrs. B. These charming characters of women! 'Tis like a painter's gallery, where one sees the portraits of all one's acquaintance! Here, Mignionet, put this book in its place.
Mig. Yes, Ma'am.—There, Ma'am, you see your toilette looks most charmingly.
Mrs. B. Does it? I think it does.—Apropos, where's my new song? Here it lies—I must make myself mistress of it.—[*Plays and sings a little.*]—I believe I shall conquer it presently. [*Rises and goes towards her toilette.*]—This hair of mine is always tormenting me; always in disorder, and straggling out of its place: I must absolutely subdue this lock.—Mignionet, do you know that this is a very pretty song? 'Tis written by my Lord Etheridge; I positively must learn it before he comes.—[*Sings a line.*]—Do you know, Mignionet, that I think my Lord not wholly intolerable?   23

1–9 Oh! Blest . . . obeys] *Moral Essays*, Epistle II, 'To a Lady' (1735), 257–64.

Mig. Yes, Ma'am, I know that.

Mrs. B. Do you?

Mig. And if I have any skill, Ma'am, I fancy you think him more than tolerable.

Mrs. B. Really! Then you think I like him, I suppose.—Do ye think I like him? I don't well know how that is, and yet I don't know but I do like him; no—no—I don't like him neither, not absolutely like; but I could like, if I had a mind to humour myself.—The man has a softness of manner, an elegant turn of thinking, and has a heart—has he a heart? Yes, I think he has; and then he is such an observer of the manners, and shows the ridiculous of them with so much humour—   34

Mig. I'll be whipped, if you don't get into the noose before the long nights are over.—Without doubt, Ma'am, my Lord is a pretty man enough; but lackaday, what o' that? You know but very little of him—your acquaintance is but very short; [*Mrs. Bellmour hums a tune.*] do, pray my dear Madam, mind what I say, for I am at times, I assure you, very speculative, very speculative indeed; and I see very plainly.—Lord, Ma'am, what am I doing! I'm talking to you for your own good, and you're all in the air, and no more mind one, no, no more than if I was nothing at all.   42

Mrs. B. [*Hums a tune still.*] Why indeed you talk wonderfully well upon the subject; but as I know how the cards lie, and can play the game myself, and as I don't know my song—why a body is inclined to give that the preference.   [*Sings.*

Mig. Ma'am, I assure you, I am none of those servants that bargain for their mistress's inclinations; but I see you are going to take a leap in the dark. —I don't know what to make of his manner of coming here, with his chair always brought into the hall, and the curtains drawn close about his ears, as if —may I never be married, if I don't believe there is something amiss in the affair.—Dear heart, Ma'am, if you won't listen to me, what signifies my living with you? I am of no service to you.   53

Mrs. B. I believe I have conquered the song. [*Runs to her glass.*] How do I look today? Well enough, I think.—Do you think I shall play the fool, Mignionet, and marry my Lord?

Mig. You have it, Ma'am, through the very heart of you—I see that.

Mrs. B. Do you think so? Maybe I may marry, and maybe not.—Poor Sir Brilliant Fashion, what will become of him? But I won't think about it.

Enter Pompey.

Mrs. B. What's the matter, Pompey?   60

Pom. There's a lady below in a chair, that desires to know if you are at home, Madam.

35 the long nights] The play opened on 24 January.

Mrs. B. Has the lady no name?

Pom. She did not tell her name.

Mrs. B. How awkward you are! Well, show her up.   [*Exit* Pompey.

Mig. Had not you better receive the lady in the dining-room, Ma'am? Things here are in such confusion.

Mrs. B. No, 'twill do very well here. I dare say it is somebody I am intimate with, though the boy does not recollect her name.—Here she comes.

Enter Mrs. Lovemore.

[*They both look with a grave surprise at each other, then curtsey with an air of distant civility.*]

Mrs. B. Ma'am, your most obedient.   [*With a kind of reserve.*

Mrs. L. Ma'am, I beg your pardon for this intrusion.   [*Disconcerted.*

Mrs. B. Pray, Ma'am, walk in—won't you please to be seated? Mignionet, reach a chair.   73

Mrs. L. This chair will do mighty well.

Mrs. B. I beg you'll sit from the door—I beg you'll sit here, Ma'am.

          [Mrs. Lovemore *crosses the stage and they salute each other.*

Mrs. L. I'm afraid this visit from one unknown to you, will be inconvenient and troublesome.

Mrs. B. Not at all, I dare say; you need not be at the trouble of an apology: would you choose a dish of chocolate?

Mrs. L. Much obliged to you, not any.   80

Mrs. B. Mignionet, you may withdraw.   [*Exit* Mignionet.

Mrs. L. Though I have not the pleasure of your acquaintance, Ma'am, there is a particular circumstance which has determined me to take this liberty with you; for which I entreat your pardon beforehand.

Mrs. B. The request is wholly unnecessary; but a particular circumstance, you say.—Pray Ma'am, to what circumstance am I indebted for this honour?

Mrs. L. I shall appear perhaps very ridiculous, and indeed I am afraid I have done the most absurd thing.—But Ma'am, from the character you bear for tenderness of disposition, and generosity of sentiment, I easily incline to flatter myself, that you will not take offence at anything; and that if it is in your power, you will afford me your assistance.   91

Mrs. B. You may depend upon me.

Mrs. L. I will be very ingenuous; pray Ma'am, a'n't you acquainted with a gentleman whose name is Lovemore?

Mrs. B. Lovemore! No, no such person in my list.—Lovemore! I don't know him, Ma'am.

Mrs. L. Ma'am, I beg your pardon—I am but where I was.—I won't trouble you any further.   [*Going.*

Mrs. B. 'Tis mighty odd, this.[*Aside.*] Madam, I must own my curiosity is

a good deal excited.—[*Takes her by the hand.*]—Pray Ma'am, give me leave—
I beg you will sit down—pray don't think me impertinent—may I beg to
know who the gentleman is?   102

Mrs. L. You have such an air of frankness and generosity, that I will open
myself to you: I have been married to him these two years; I admired him
for his understanding, his sentiment, and spirit; I thought myself as
sincerely loved by him, as my fond heart could wish, but there is of late such
a strange revolution in his temper, I know not what to make of it: instead of
the looks of affection, and expressions of tenderness with which he used to
meet me, 'tis nothing now but cold, averted, superficial civility.—While
abroad he runs on in a wild career of pleasure; and to my deep affliction, has
fixed his affections upon another object.   111

Mrs. B. If you mean to consult with me in regard to this case, I am afraid
you have made a wrong choice; there is something in her appearance that
affects me. [*Aside.*]—Pray excuse me, Ma'am, you consider this matter too
deeply.—Men will prove false, and if there is nothing in your complaint but
mere gallantry on his side, upon my word, I can't think your case the worse
for that.

Mrs. L. Not the worse!

Mrs. B. On the contrary, much better. If his affections, instead of being
alienated, had been extinguished, he would have sunk into a downright
stupid, habitual insensibility; from which it might prove impossible to recall
him.—In all love's bill of mortality there is not a more fatal disorder—but
your husband is not fallen into that way.—By your account, he still has
sentiment, and where there is sentiment, there is still room to hope for an
alteration.—But in the other case, you have the pain of seeing yourself
neglected, and for what? For nothing at all; the man has lost all sense of
feeling, and is become to the warm beams of wit and beauty, as impenetrable
as an icehouse.

Mrs. L. I am afraid, Ma'am, he is too much the reverse of this, too
susceptible of impressions from every beautiful object.   130

Mrs. B. Why, so much the better, as I told you already; some new idea has
struck his fancy, and he will be for a while under the influence of that.

Mrs. L. How light she makes of it!   [*Aside.*

Mrs. B. But it is the wife's business to bait the hook for her husband with
variety; and to draw him daily to herself: that is the whole affair, I would not
make myself uneasy, Ma'am.

Mrs. L. Not uneasy! When his indifference does not diminish my regard
for him! Not uneasy, when the man I dote on, no longer fixes his happiness at
home!

Mrs. B. Ma'am, you'll give me leave to speak my mind freely.—I have
often observed, when the fiend Jealousy is roused, that women lay out a

wonderful deal of anxiety and vexation to no account, when perhaps, if the
truth were known, they should be angry with themselves instead of their
husbands.   144

Mrs. L. Angry with myself, Madam! Calumny can lay nothing to my
charge—the virtue of my conduct, Madam—

Mrs. B. Look ye there now, I would have laid my life you would be at that
—that's the folly of us all.—But virtue is out of the question at present.—I
mean the want of address, and proper management! It is there that most
women fail.—Virtue alone cannot please the taste of this age.—It is *La Belle
Nature*—Nature embellished by the advantages of art, that the men expect
nowadays.   152

Mrs. L. But after being married so long, and behaving all that time with
such an equality—

Mrs. B. Ay, that equality is the rock so many split upon.—The men are
now so immersed in luxury, that they must have eternal variety in their
happiness.

Mrs. L. She justifies him.   [*Aside.*

Mrs. B. I'll tell you what; I would venture to lay a pot of coffee, that the
person who now rivals you in your husband's affection, does it without your
good qualities, and even without your beauty, by the mere force of agreeable
talents, and assiduity to please.   162

Mrs. L. I am afraid that compliment—

Mrs. B. Let me ask you, Ma'am, have you ever seen this formidable person?

Mrs. L. I think I have.

Mrs. B. What sort of a woman, pray?

Mrs. L. Formidable indeed! She was described to me as one of charming
and rare accomplishments: and that is fatally too true! I can see in her the
sensible, the spirited, the—in short, in her I see my ruin.   170

Mrs. B. Never throw up the cards for all that.—Really, Ma'am, without
compliment, you seem to have all the qualities that can dispute your husband's heart with anybody; but the exertion of those qualities, I am afraid, is
suppressed.—You'll excuse my freedom.—You should counterwork your
rival, by the very same arts she employs.—I know a lady now in your very
situation, and what does she do? She consumes herself with eternal jealousy; whereas, if she would but employ half the pains she uses in teasing
herself, to vie with the creature that has won her husband from her—to vie
with her, I say, in the arts of pleasing, for it is there a woman's pride should
be piqued—would she do that, take my word for it, victory would declare in
her favour.   181

Mrs. L. Do you think so, Ma'am?

Mrs. B. Think so! I am sure of it—for there is this advantage on her side, that virtue is an auxiliary in her cause, and virtue is the best beautifying fluid for the complexion; it gives a lustre to the features, that cannot be equalled by any artifice whatever.

Mrs. L. What can this mean? I begin to doubt.   [*Aside.*

Mrs. B. But even virtue herself must condescend to call in external aid.— Her own native charms would do, if men were perfect, but that is not the case; and since vice can assume allurements, why should not truth and innocence have additional ornaments also?   191

Mrs. L. I begin to think Sir Brilliant has told me truth.   [*Aside.*

Mrs. B. I have been married, Ma'am, and am a little in the secret.—It is much more difficult to keep a heart than win one.—After the fatal words 'for better or worse', the general way with wives is to relax into indolence, and while they are guilty of no infidelity, they think that is enough: but they are mistaken, there is a great deal wanting—an address, a manner, a desire of pleasing—an agreeable contrast in their conduct, of grave, and gay; a favourite poet of mine, Prior, has expressed this very delicately:

> Above the fixed and settled rules   200
> Of vice, and virtue, in the schools,
> The better part should set before 'em
> A grace, a manner, a decorum.

Mrs. L. But when the natural temper—

Mrs. B. The natural temper must be forced, home must be made a place of pleasure to the husband, and the wife must throw infinite variety into her manner; in short, she must, as it were, multiply herself, and appear to him sundry different women on different occasions.—And this, I take to be the whole mystery; the way to keep a man.—But I run on at a strange rate.— Well, to be sure, I'm the giddiest creature.—Ma'am, will you now give me leave to enquire, how I came to have this favour? Who recommended me to your notice? And pray who was so kind as to intimate that I was acquainted with Mr. Lovemore?   213

Mrs. L. I beg your pardon for all the trouble I have given you, and I assure you, 'tis entirely owing to my being told that his visits were frequent here.

Mrs. B. His visits frequent here! They have imposed upon you, I assure you—and they have told you, perhaps, that I have robbed you of Mr. Lovemore's heart! Scandal is always buzzing about, but, I assure you, I have not meddled with his heart.—Oh! Lud, I hear a rap at the door; I positively won't be at home.   [*Rings a bell.*

Enter Mignionet.

200–203 Above the fixed . . . decorum] A slight alteration of 'Paulo Purganti and His Wife: an Honest, But a Simple Pair' (1708), 1–2, 5–6.

Mig. Did you call, Madam?

Mrs. B. I am not at home.

Mig. 'Tis Lord Etheridge, Ma'am—he's coming upstairs; the servants told him you were within.

Mrs. B. Was ever anything so cross? Tell him there is company with me, and he won't come in. Mignionet, run to him.

Mrs. L. Ma'am, I beg I mayn't hinder you.

Mrs. B. Our conversation begins to grow interesting, and I would not have you go for the world. I won't see my Lord.   230

Mrs. L. I beg you will, don't let me prevent, I'll step into another room.

Mrs. B. Will you be so kind? There is a study of books in that room; if you will be so obliging as to amuse yourself there, I shall be glad to resume this conversation again.—He sha'n't stay long.

Mrs. L. I beg you will be in no hurry, I can wait with pleasure.

Mrs. B. This is a lover of mine; and a husband and a lover should be treated in the same manner; perhaps it will divert you to hear how I manage him. I hear him on the stairs, for Heaven's sake, make haste. Mignionet, show the way.   240

Mig. This way, Madam, this way.

                              [*Exeunt* Mrs. Lovemore *and* Mignionet.

Mrs. B. Let me see how I look to receive him.   [*Runs to her glass.*

Enter Lovemore, *with a star and ribbon, as Lord Etheridge.*

Mrs. B. [*Looking in her glass.*] Lord Etheridge! Walk in, my Lord.
Love. [*Repeats.*]

> A heav'nly image in the glass appears,
> To that she bends, to that her eyes she rears,
> Repairs her smiles—

Mrs. B. Repairs her smiles, my Lord! I don't like your application of that phrase.—Pray, my Lord, are my smiles out of repair, like an old house in the country, that wants a tenant?

Love. Nay now, that's wresting the words from their visible intention.—You can't suppose I thought you want repair, whatever may be the case, Ma'am, with regard to the want of a tenant.   252

Mrs. B. And so you think I really want a tenant! And perhaps you imagine too, that I am going to put up a bill [*Looking in her glass.*] to signify to all passers-by, that here is a mansion to be let.—Well, I swear, I don't think it would be a bad scheme.—I have a great mind to do so.

Love. And he who has the preference—

244-6 A heav'nly image . . . smiles] Pope, *The Rape of the Lock*, Canto I, 125–6, 141.

Mrs. B. Will be very happy, I know you mean so. But I'll let it to none but a single gentleman, that you may depend upon.

Love. What the Devil does she mean by that? She has not got an inkling of the affair, I hope. [*Aside.*] None else could presume, Madam, to—

Mrs. B. And then it must be a lease for life—but nobody will be troubled with it—I shall never get it off my hands.—Do you think I shall, my Lord?

Love. Why that question, Madam? You know I am devoted to you, even if it were to be bought with life.   265

Mrs. B. Heavens! What a dying swain you are! And does your Lordship really intend to be guilty of matrimony? Lord, what a question have I asked? Well, to be sure, I am a very madcap! My Lord, don't you think me a strange madcap?

Love. A wildness like yours, that arises from vivacity and sentiment together, serves only to exalt your beauty, and give new poignancy to every charm.   272

Mrs. B. Well, upon my word you have said it finely! But you are in the right, my Lord.—I hate your pensive, melancholy beauty, that sits like a well-grown vegetable in a room for an hour together, till at last she is animated to the violent exertion of saying yes or no, and then enters into a matter-of-fact conversation: 'Have you heard the news? Miss Beverly is going to be married to Captain Shoulderknot.—My Lord Mortgage has had another tumble at Arthur's; Sir William Squanderstock has lost his election. They say, short aprons are coming into fashion again.'   280

Love. Oh, Lord! A matter-of-fact conversation is insupportable.

Mrs. B. Pray, my Lord, have you ever observed the manner of one lady's accosting another at Ranelagh? She comes up to you with a demure look of insipid serenity—makes you a solemn salute—'Ma'am, I am overjoyed to meet you—you look charmingly.—But dear Madam, did you hear what happened to us all the other night? We were going home from the opera, Ma'am; you know my Aunt Roly-Poly—it was her coach—there was she, and Lady Betty Fidget—your most obedient servant, Ma'am [*Curtseying to another, as it were going by.*]—Lady Betty, you know, is recovered—everybody thought it over with her, but Doctor Snakeroot was called in, no not Doctor Snakeroot, Doctor Bolus it was, and so he altered the course of the medicines, and so my Lady Betty recovered; well, there was she and Sir George Bragwell—a pretty man Sir George, finest teeth in the world.— Your Ladyship's most obedient.—We expected you last night, but you did not come—He! He!—And so there was he and the rest of us—and so turning the corner of Bond Street, the villain of a coachman—how do you do, Madam?—the villain of a coachman overturned us all; my Aunt Roly-Poly

279 Arthur's] A London club, presumably White's, where Arthur was the keeper until his death in 1761. Arthur's (his namesake) did not open until 1765.

was frightened out of her wits, and Lady Betty has been *nervish* ever since:
only think of that—such accidents in life.—Ma'am, your most obedient—I
am proud to see you look so well.'   300

Love. An exact description—the very thing.—Ha! Ha!

Mrs. B. And then from this conversation they all run to cards—'Quadrille
has murdered wit.'

Love. Ay, and beauty too; for upon these occasions, 'the passions in the
features are'—I have seen many a beautiful countenance change in a moment,
into absolute deformity; the little loves and graces that before sparkled in the
eye, bloomed in the cheek, and smiled about the mouth, all fly off in an
instant, and resign the features which they before adorned, to fear, to anger,
to grief; and the whole train of fretful passions.

Mrs. B. Ay, and the rage we poor women are often betrayed into on these
occasions—   311

Love. Very true, Ma'am; and if by chance, they do bridle and hold in a
little, the struggle they undergo is the most ridiculous sight imaginable.—I
have seen an oath quivering upon the pale lip of a reigning toast, for half an
hour together; yes, and I have seen an uplifted eye blaspheming Providence
for the loss of an odd trick; and then at last, when the whole room burst out
into one loud universal uproar, 'My Lord, you flung away the game.'—'No,
Ma'am, it was you.'—'Sir George, why did not you rough the diamond?'
'Capt. Hazard, why did not you lead through the honour?' 'Ma'am, it was
not the play.'—'Pardon me, Sir'—'But Ma'am'—'But Sir'—'I would not
play with you for straws.'—'Don't you know what Hoyle says? If A and B
are partners against C and D, and the game nine-all, A and B have won three
tricks, and C and D four tricks; C leads his suit, D puts up the King then
returns the suit, A passes, C puts up the Queen, B roughs the next': and so A
and B, and C and D are banged about; and all is jargon, confusion, uproar,
and wrangling, and nonsense, and noise.—Ha! Ha!   326

Mrs. B. Ha! Ha! A fine picture of a rout; but one must play sometimes—
we must let our friends pick our pockets sometimes, or they'll drop our
acquaintance.—Pray my Lord, do you never play?

Love. Play, Ma'am!—I must lie to the end of the chapter [*Aside.*]—play!
Now and then out of necessity; otherwise, I never touch a card.   331

Mrs. B. Oh! Very true, you dedicate your time to the Muses; a downright
rhyming Peer.—Do you know, my Lord, that I am charmed with your song?

Love. Are you?

Mrs. B. I am indeed; I think you'd make a very tolerable Vauxhall poet.

Love. You flatter me, Ma'am.

---

318 rough] To ruff, to trump.   321 Hoyle] Edmund Hoyle (1672–1769), writer on games,
first published his book on whist in 1742.

Mrs. B. No, as I live and breathe, I don't; and do you know that I can sing it already? Come, you shall hear me—you shall hear it.　　　　　[*Sings.*

I

Attend all ye fair, and I'll tell ye the art
To bind every fancy with ease in your chains,　　　　　340
To hold in soft fetters the conjugal heart,
And banish from Hymen his doubts and his pains.

II

When Juno accepted the cestus of Love,
At first she was handsome; she charming became;
With skill the soft passions it taught her to move,
To kindle at once, and to keep up the flame.

III

'Tis this gives the eyes all their magic and fire;
The voice melting accents; impassions the kiss;
Confers the sweet smiles that awaken desire,
And plants round the fair each incentive to bliss.　　　　　350

IV

Thence flows the gay chat, more than reason that charms;
The eloquent blush, that can beauty improve;
The fond sigh, the fond vow, the soft touch that alarms,
The tender disdain, the renewal of love.

V

Ye fair take the cestus, and practise its art;
The mind unaccomplished, mere features are vain,
Exert your sweet power, you conquer each heart,
And the Loves, Joys, and Graces, shall walk in your train.

Love. My poetry is infinitely obliged to you, for the embellishments your voice and manner confer upon it.　　　　　360
Mrs. B. Oh fulsome! I sing horridly, and I look horridly. [*Goes to the glass.*]
—How do I look, my Lord? But don't tell me, I won't be told.—I see you are studying a compliment, and I hate compliments; well, what is it? Let's hear your compliment, why don't you compliment me? I won't hear it now.
—But pray now, how came you to choose so grave a subject as connubial happiness?

343 cestus] A belt or girdle, especially that of a bride, or of Aphrodite/Venus.

Love. Close and particular that question. [*Aside.*] Why Ma'am, in general, one does not see the talents of a wife, dedicated to the happiness of the husband.—I have known ladies, who on the eve of their wedding appeared like the very Graces, in a few weeks after the ceremony become very slatterns, both in their persons and understandings: no solicitude on their side to appear amiable.—Distaste insinuates itself by degrees into the husband's mind, the bands of Hymen grow loose; and thus with perhaps the best disposition in the world, he is obliged to start wild, and away he urges where youth and a career of spirits hurry him; and so goodnight to all real and solid happiness.—But with one accomplished as you are, Ma'am—   376

Mrs. B. To be sure, with me nobody could be otherwise than happy; was not that what you was going to say? I know it was.—Well, upon my word you have drawn your picture so well, that one would imagine you had a wife at home to sit for it.   380

Love. Ma'am [*Embarrassed.*], the compliment—a—you are but laughing at me; I—I—I—Zouns, I am afraid she begins to smoke me. [*Aside.*]—A very scanty knowledge of the world will serve: and—and there is no need of one's own experience in these cases: nor had I talked so, were I not persuaded you will make an exception to the general rule.

Mrs. B. O lard, you are going to plague me again with your odious solicitations, but I won't hear 'em; you must be gone.—If I should be weak enough to listen to you, what would become of Sir Brilliant Fashion?

Love. Sir Brilliant Fashion!

Mrs. B. Yes, don't you know Sir Brilliant Fashion?   390

Love. No, Ma'am, I don't know the gentleman: I beg pardon if he is your acquaintance, but from what I have heard of him, I should not choose him to be among my intimates.

Enter Mignionet *in a violent hurry.*

Mig. O Lud! I am frighted out of my senses—the poor lady—where's the hartshorn-drops?

Love. The lady! What lady?

Mig. Never stand asking what lady—she has fainted away, Ma'am, all of a sudden. Give me the drops.

Mrs. B. Let me run to her assistance. Adieu, my Lord—I shall be at home in the evening; Mignionet, step this way. My Lord, you'll excuse me; I expect you in the evening.   [*Exit [with* Mignionet].

Love. I shall wait on you, Ma'am. What a villain am I to carry on this scheme against so much beauty, innocence, and merit! Ay, and to have the impudence to assume this badge of honour, to cover the most unwarrantable purposes! But no reflection, have her I must; and that quickly too.—If I

395 hartshorn-drops] Ammonia solution; smelling salts.

don't prevail soon, I'm undone—she'll find me out: egad, I'll be with her betimes this evening, and press her with all the vehemence of love.—Women have their soft, unguarded moments, and who knows? But to take the advantage of the openness and gaiety of her heart! And then my friend Sir Brilliant, will it be fair to supplant him? Prithee be quiet, my dear conscience; don't you be meddling; don't interrupt a gentleman in his amusements.—Don't you know, my good friend, that love has no respect of persons, knows no laws of friendship? Besides 'tis all my wife's fault—why don't she strive to make home agreeable? 414

> For foreign pleasures, foreign joy, I roam,
> No thought of peace or happiness at home. [*Going.*

[Sir Brilliant *is heard singing within.*]

What the Devil is Madam Fortune at now? Sir Brilliant, by all that's odious! No place to conceal in! No escape! The door is locked! Mignionet, Mignionet, open the door—

Mig. [*Within.*] You can't come in here, Sir. 420

Love. This cursed star, and this ribbon, will ruin me.—Let me get off this confounded tell-tale evidence. [*Takes off the ribbon in a hurry.*

Enter Sir Brilliant.

Sir B. My dear Madam, I most heartily rejoice—ha! Lovemore!

Love. Your slave, Sir Brilliant, your slave. [*Hiding the star with his hat.*

Sir B. How is this? I did not think you had been acquainted here!

Love. I came to look for you—I thought to have found you here; and so I have scraped an acquaintance with the lady, and made it subservient to your purposes.—I have been giving a great character of you.

Sir B. Well, but what's the matter? What are you fumbling about?
[*Pulls the hat.*

Love. 'Sdeath, have a care! For Heaven's sake— 430
[*Crams his handkerchief there.*

Sir B. What the Devil ails you?

Love. Taken so unaccountably—my old complaint—Sir Brilliant, yours.

Sir B. Zouns man, you had best sit down.

Love. Here's a business—[*Aside.*]—pray let me pass—my old complaint.

Sir B. What complaint?

Love. I must have a surgeon—occasioned by the stroke of a tennis ball; my Lord Racket's unlucky left hand: let me pass, there is certainly something forming there, let me pass.—To be caught is the Devil [*Aside.*]—don't

415–6 For foreign . . . home] A slight alteration of Pope, *Moral Essays*, Epistle II, 223–4.

name my name, you'll ruin all that I said for you, if you do.—Sir Brilliant, your servant.—There is certainly something forming. [*Exit.*

Sir B. What can this mean? I must have this explained.—Then Mrs. Lovemore's suspicions are right; I must come at the bottom of it.—Ay, ay— there is something forming here!   443

Enter Mrs. Bellmour.

Sir B. My dear Mrs. Bellmour.

Mrs. B. Heavens! What brings you here?

Sir B. I congratulate with myself upon the felicity of meeting you thus at home.

Mrs. B. Your visit is unseasonable, you must be gone.

Sir B. Madam, I have a thousand things—

Mrs. B. Well, well, another time.   450

Sir B. Of the tenderest import.

Mrs. B. I can't hear you now; fly this moment: I have a lady taken ill in the next room.

Sir B. Ay, and you have had a gentleman taken ill here too.

Mrs. B. Do you dispute my will and pleasure? Fly this instant! [*Turns him out.*] So, I'll make sure of the door.

Enter Mrs. Lovemore, *leaning on* Mignionet.

Mig. This way, Madam, here's more air in this room.

Mrs. B. How do you find yourself, Ma'am? Pray sit down.

Mrs. L. My spirits were too weak to bear up any longer, against such a scene of villainy.   460

Mrs. B. Villainy! What villainy?

Mrs. L. Of the blackest dye! I see, Madam, you are acquainted with my husband.

Mrs. B. Acquainted with your husband!   [*Angrily.*

Mrs. L. A moment's patience, Madam.—That gentleman that was here with you is my husband.

Mrs. B. Lord Etheridge your husband!

Mrs. L. Lord Etheridge, as he calls himself, and as you have been made to call him also, is no other than Mr. Lovemore.

Mrs. B. And has he then been base enough to assume that title, to ensnare me to my undoing?   471

Mig. Well, for certain, I believe the Devil's in me, I am certainly a witch, for I always thought him a sly one.

Mrs. L. To see my husband carrying on this dark business, to see the man I have loved, the man I have esteemed, the man, I am afraid, I must still love, though esteem him again I cannot, to be a witness to his complicated wickedness—it was too much for sensibility like mine—I felt the shock too severely, and sunk under it.

Mrs. B. I am ready to do the same myself now. I sink into the very ground with amazement. The first time I ever saw him was at old Mrs. Loveit's—she introduced him to me; the appointment was of her own making.

Mrs. L. You know her character, I suppose, Madam.   482

Mrs. B. She's a woman of fashion, and sees a great deal of good company.

Mrs. L. Very capable of such an action for all that.

Mrs. B. Well, I could never have imagined that any woman would be so base as to pass such a cheat upon me. Step this moment, and give orders never to let him within my doors again. [*To her maid* [Mignionet], *who goes out.*] I am much obliged to you, Ma'am, for this visit. To me it is highly fortunate, but I am sorry for your share in't, as the discovery brings you nothing but a conviction of your husband's baseness.   490

Mrs. L. I'm determined to be no further uneasy about him, nor will I live a day longer under his roof.

Mrs. B. Hold, hold, make no violent resolutions.—You'll excuse me, I can't help feeling for you, and I think this incident may be still converted to your advantage.

Mrs. L. That can never be—I am lost beyond redemption.

Mrs. B. Don't decide that too rashly.—Come, come, a man is worth thinking a little about, before one throws the hideous thing away for ever. Besides, you have heard his sentiments. Perhaps you are a little to blame yourself.— We will talk this very coolly. Ma'am, you have saved me, and I must now discharge the obligation.—You shall stay and dine with me.   501

Mrs. L. I can't possibly do that—I won't give you so much trouble.

Mrs. B. It will be a pleasure, Ma'am—you shall stay with me, I will not part with you, and I will lay such a plan, as may ensure him yours for ever.— Come, come, my dear Madam, don't you still think he has some good qualities to apologize for his vices?

Mrs. L. I must own, I still hope he has.

Mrs. B. Very well then, and he may still make atonement for all; and let me tell you, that a man who can make proper atonement for his faults should not be entirely despised.—*Allons!*   [*Exeunt.*

End of the Second Act.

ACT III

SCENE, *an apartment at* Mr. Lovemore'*s.*

Enter Mrs. Lovemore *elegantly dressed;* Muslin *following her.*

Mus. Why to be sure, Ma'am, it is so for certain, and you are very much in the right of it.

Mrs. L. I fancy I am: I see the folly of my former conduct, and I am determined never to let my spirits sink into a melancholy state again.

Mus. Why, that's the very thing, Ma'am, the very thing I have been always preaching up to you.—Did not I always say, see company, Ma'am, take your share of pleasure, and never break your heart for any man? This is what I always said.

Mrs. L. It's very well, you need not say any more now.

Mus. I always said so! And what did the world say? Heaven bless her for a sweet woman! And a plague go with him for an inhuman, barbarous, bloody, murdering brute.   12

Mrs. L. No more of these liberties, I desire.

Mus. Nay, don't be angry, they did say so indeed.—But dear heart, how everybody will be overjoyed, when they find you have plucked up a little— as for me, it gives me new life to have so much company in the house, and such a racketing at the door with coaches and chairs, enough to hurry a body out of one's wits.—Lard, this is another thing, and you look quite like another thing, Ma'am, and that dress so becomes you—I suppose, Ma'am, you'll never wear your négligée again. It is not fit for you indeed, Ma'am.—It might pass very well with some folks, Ma'am, but the like of you—

Mrs. L. Prithee truce with your tongue, and see who is coming upstairs.

Enter Mrs. Bellmour.

Mrs. L. Mrs. Bellmour, I revive at the sight of you. Muslin, do you step downstairs, and do as I have ordered you.   24

Mus. What the deuce can she be at now?   [*Exit.*

Mrs. B. You see I am punctual to my time.—Well, I admire your dress of all things.—Did you buy this silk on Ludgate Hill? It's mighty pretty.

Mrs. L. I am glad you like it—but under all this appearance of gaiety, I have at the bottom but an aching heart.

Mrs. B. Be ruled by me, and I'll answer for the event.—Why really, now you look just as you should do.—Why should you neglect so fine a figure?

Mrs. L. You are so civil, Mrs. Bellmour—   32

Mrs. B. And so true too! What was beautiful before, is now heightened by

the additional ornaments of dress; and if you will but animate and inspire the
whole, by those graces of the mind, which I am sure you possess, the impres-
sion cannot fail of being effectual upon all beholders, and even upon the
depraved mind of Mr. Lovemore.—You have not heard anything of him
since—have you?

Mrs. L. No—no account at all of him.

Mrs. B. I can tell you something—he has been at my house. You know I
had promised to be at home for him—not being let in, my servants tell me, he
was strangely disconcerted, knit his brow, stormed, raved, wondered, and
expostulated, and then at last, went off as sulky as a Russian general, when a
garrison refuses to capitulate.   44

Mrs. L. If he has no other haunts, he may perhaps come home.

Mrs. B. I wish he may.—Well, and have you got together a deal of company?

Mrs. L. Pretty well.

Mrs. B. That's right—show him that you will consult your own pleasure.—
Is Sir Brilliant of the party?   50

Mrs. L. Apropos, as soon as I came home I received a letter from him; my
maid had taken it in.—He there presses his addresses with great warmth,
begs to see me again, and has something particular to tell me—you shall see
it.—Oh! Lud, I have not it about me—I left it in my dressing room, I
believe; you shall see it by and by. I took your advice, and sent him word
he might come; that lure brought him hither immediately—he makes no
doubt of his success with me.

Mrs. B. Well! Two such friends as Sir Brilliant and Mr. Lovemore, I
believe, never existed!

Mrs. L. Their falsehood to each other is unparalleled.—I left Sir Brilliant
at the whist-table; as soon as the rubber's out, he'll certainly quit his
company in pursuit of me.—[*A rap at the door.*] As I live, I believe this is
Mr. Lovemore.   63

Mrs. B. If it is, everything goes on swimmingly.

Mrs. L. I hear his voice, it is he.—How my heart beats!

Mrs. B. Courage, and the day's our own.—Where must I run?

Mrs. L. In there, Ma'am.—Make haste, I hear his step on the stair-head.

Mrs. B. Success attend you—I am gone.   [*Exit.*

Mrs. L. [*Alone.*] I am frightened out of my senses—what the event may be
I fear to think, but I must go through with it.   70

Enter Lovemore.

Mrs. L. Mr. Lovemore, you're welcome home.

Love. Mrs. Lovemore, your servant.   [*Without looking at her.*

Mrs. L. It's somewhat rare to see you at home so early.

Love. I said I would come home, did not I? I always like to be as good as my word.—What could she mean by this usage? To make an appointment, and break it thus abruptly!   [*Aside.*

Mrs. L. He seems to muse upon it.   [*Aside.*

Love. I can't tell what to make of it—she does not mean to do so infamous a thing as to jilt me. [*Aside.*] Oh, Lord! I am wonderfully tired.

[*Yawns, and sinks into an armchair.*

Mrs. L. You a'n't indisposed, I hope, my dear.   80

Love. No, my dear, I thank you, I am very well; a little fatigued only, with jolting over the stones all the way from the city. I stayed to dine with the old banker—I have been there ever since I went out in the morning.—Confoundedly tired.—Where's William?

Mrs. L. Did you want anything?

Love. Only my cap and slippers.—I am not in spirits, I think.   [*Yawns.*

Mrs. L. You are never in spirits at home, Mr. Lovemore.

Love. I beg your pardon—I never am anywhere more cheerful. [*Stretching his arms.*] I wish I may die, if I a'n't very happy at home—very [*Yawns.*]—very happy!   90

Mrs. L. I can hear otherwise.—I'm informed that Mr. Lovemore is the inspirer of mirth and good humour wherever he goes.

Love. Oh! You overrate me; upon my soul you do.

Mrs. L. I can hear, Sir, that no person's company is so acceptable to the ladies; that 'tis your wit that inspirits everything, that you have your compliment for one, your smile for another, a whisper for a third, and so on, Sir— you divide your favours, and are everywhere, but at home, all whim, vivacity, and spirit.

Love. No, no—[*Laughing.*]—how can you talk so? I swear, I can't help laughing at the fancy.—I all whim, vivacity, and spirit! I shall burst my sides.—How can you banter one so? I divide my favours too! Oh, Heavens! I can't stand this raillery—such a description of me! I that am rather saturnine, and of a serious cast, and inclined to be pensive! I can't help laughing at the oddity of the conceit.—Oh Lord! Oh Lord!   [*Laughs.*

Mrs. L. Just as you please, Sir.—I see that I am ever to be treated with indifference.   [*Walks across the stage.*

Love. [*Rises and walks the contrary way.*] I can't put this widow Bellmour out of my head.   [*Aside.*

Mrs. L. If I had done anything to provoke this usage, this cold, insolent contempt—   110

Love. I shall never be at rest till I know the bottom of it.—I wish I had done with that business entirely; but my desires are kindled, and must be satisfied.   [*Aside.*

[*They walk for some time silently by each other.*]

Mrs. L. What part of my conduct gives you offence, Mr. Lovemore?

Love. Still harping upon that ungrateful string! But prithee don't set me a-laughing again.—Offence! Nothing gives me offence, child: you know I am very fond.—[*Yawns and walks.*]—I like you of all things, and think you a most admirable wife; prudent, managing, careless of your own person and attentive to mine; not much addicted to pleasure, grave, retired, and domestic; govern the house, pay the tradesmens' bills [*Yawns.*], scold the servants, and love your husband: upon my soul, a very good wife! As good a sort of a wife [*Yawns.*] as a body might wish to have.—Where's William? I must go to bed.   123

Mrs. L. To bed so early! Had not you better join the company?

Love. I shan't go out tonight.

Mrs. L. But I mean the company in the dining-room.

Love. What company?   [*Stares at her.*

Mrs. L. That I invited to a rout.

Love. A rout in my house! And you dressed out too! What is all this?

Mrs. L. You have no objection, I hope.   130

Love. Objection! No, I like company, you know, of all things; I'll go and join them: who are they all?

Mrs. L. You know 'em all; and there's your friend Sir Brilliant there.

Love. Is he there? I'm glad of it.—But pray now, how comes this about?

Mrs. L. I intend to do it often.

Love. Do ye?

Mrs. L. Ay, and not look tamely on, while you revel luxuriously in a course of pleasure; I shall pursue my own plan of diversion.

Love. Do so, do so, Ma'am, the change in your temper will be very pleasing.

Mrs. L. I shall indeed, Sir—I'm in earnest.   140

Love. By all means follow your own inclinations.

Mrs. L. And so I shall, Sir, I assure ye.   [*Sings.*

> No more I pine,
> Content is mine;
> That sunshine of the breast!
> The pangs of love
> No more I prove;
> No cares disturb my rest.

Love. What the Devil is come over her? And what in the name of wonder does all this mean?   150

Mrs. L. Mean, Sir! It means—it means—it means—how can you ask me what it means? Well to be sure, the sobriety of that question! Do you think a woman of spirit can have leisure to tell her meaning, when she is all air, alertness, pleasure, and enjoyment?

Love. She's mad! Stark mad!

Mrs. L. You're mistaken, Sir—not mad, but in spirits, that's all; no offence, I hope.—Am I too flighty for you? Perhaps I am—you are of a saturnine disposition, inclined to think a little, or so.—Well, don't let me interrupt you; don't let me be of any inconvenience—that would be the impolitest thing—for a married couple to interfere and encroach on each other's pleasures—oh hideous! It would be gothic to the last degree. Ha! Ha! Ha!

Love. [*Forcing a laugh.*] Ha! Ha! Ma'am—you—Ha! Ha! You are perfectly right.   163

Mrs. L. Nay, but I don't like that laugh now—I positively don't like it; can't you laugh out as you were used to do? For my part, I'm determined to do nothing else the rest of my life.

Love. This is the most astonishing thing! Ma'am, I don't rightly comprehend—

Mrs. L. Oh Lud! Oh Lud!—with that important face.—Well but come now, what don't you comprehend?   170

Love. There is something in this treatment that I don't so well—

Mrs. L. Oh! Are you there, Sir? How quickly they, who have no sensibility for the peace and happiness of others, can feel for themselves, Mr. Lovemore! But that's a grave reflection, and I hate reflection.

Love. What has she got into her head? This sudden change, Mrs. Lovemore, let me tell you, is a little alarming, and—

Mrs. L. Nay, don't be frightened—there is no harm in innocent mirth, I hope; never look so grave upon it.—I assure ye, Sir, that though on your part, you seem determined to offer constant indignities to your wife, and though the laws of retaliation would in some sort exculpate her, if, when provoked to the utmost, exasperated beyond all enduring, she should in her turn, make him know what it is to receive an injury in the tenderest point—   182

Love. Madam!   [*Angrily.*

Mrs. L. Well, well, don't be frightened I say, I shan't retaliate: my own honour will secure you there; you may depend upon it.—You won't come and play a game at cards? Well, do as you like; well, you won't come? No, no, I see you won't.—What say you to a bit of supper with us? Nor that neither? Follow your inclinations, 'it is not material where a body eats.'—The company expects me; your servant, Mr. Lovemore, yours, yours.

                                                                    [*Exit, singing.*

Love. [*Alone.*] This is a frolic I never saw her in before! Laugh all the rest of my life! Laws of retaliation! An injury in the tenderest point! The company expects me—your servant, my dear, yours, yours! [*Mimicking her.*] What the Devil is all this? Some of her female friends have been tampering with her.—Zouns! I must begin to look a little sharp after Madam.—I'll go

188 'it is not material . . . eats'] Cf. Act I, sc. ii, l. 184.

this moment into the card-room, and watch whom she whispers with, whom she ogles with, and every circumstance that can lead to—   [*Going*.

Enter Muslin *in a hurry*.

Mus. Madam, Madam—here's your letter—I would not for all the world that my Master—   198
Love. What, is she mad too? What's the matter, woman?
Mus. Nothing, Sir, nothing—I wanted a word with my lady, that's all, Sir.
Love. You would not for the world that your Master—what was you going to say? What paper's that?   202
Mus. Paper, Sir!
Love. Let me see it.
Mus. Lard, Sir! How can you ask a body for such a thing? It's a letter to me, Sir—a letter from the country—a letter from my sister, Sir—she bids me buy her a *Shiver de Fize* cap, and a sixteenth in the lottery; and tells me of a number she dreamt of, that's all, Sir—I'll put it up.
Love. Let me look at it—give it me this moment! [*Reads*.] 'To Mrs. Lovemore'! 'Brilliant Fashion.' This is a letter from the country, is it?
Mus. That, Sir—that is—no, Sir—no—that's not sister's letter.—If you'll give me that back, Sir, I'll show you the right one.   212
Love. Where did you get this?
Mus. Sir?
Love. Where did you get it? Tell me truth.
Mus. Dear heart, you fright a body so—in the parlour, Sir—I found it there.
Love. Very well! Leave the room.
Mus. The Devil fetch it, I was never so out in my politics, in all my days.
                                                            [*Exit*.

Love. [*Alone*.] A pretty epistle truly this seems to be—let me read it.

'Permit me, dear Madam, to throw myself on my knees (for on my knees I must address you), and in that humble posture, to implore your compassion.'—Compassion with a vengeance on him.—[*Walks about*.]— 'Think you see me now with tender, melting, supplicating eyes, languishing at your feet.'—Very well, Sir—'Can you find it in your heart to persist in cruelty? Grant me but access to you once more, and in addition to what I already said to you this morning, I will urge such 'motives'—urge motives, will ye—'as will suggest to you, that you should no longer hesitate in gratitude, to reward him, who still on his knees, here makes a vow to you of eternal constancy and love.   230
                                                  Brilliant Fashion'

207 *Shiver de Fize*] For *chiveret de Frise*, Friesland wool.

So; so! So! Your very humble servant, Sir Brilliant Fashion! This is your
friendship for me, is it? You're mighty kind indeed, Sir, but I thank you as
much as if you had really done me the favour—and, Mrs. Lovemore, I'm
your humble servant too.—She intends to laugh all the rest of her life! This
letter will change her note.—Odso, yonder she comes along the gallery, and
Sir Brilliant in full chase of her.—They come this way—could I but detect
them both now! I'll step aside, and who knows but the Devil may tempt 'em
to their undoing—at least I'll try—a polite husband I am—there's the coast
clear for you, Madam.   [*Exit*.

Enter Mrs. Lovemore, Sir Brilliant *after her*.

Mrs. L. I tell you, Sir Brilliant, your civility is odious, your compliments
fulsome, and your solicitations impertinent, Sir.—I must make use of harsh
language, Sir, you provoke me to it and I can't refrain.   243

Sir B. By all my hopes, we are now conveniently alone. [*Aside*.] Not
retiring to solitude and discontent again, I hope, Madam! Have a care, my
dear Mrs. Lovemore, of a relapse.

Mrs. L. No danger of that, Sir, don't be solicitous about me.—Why would
you leave the company? Let me entreat you to return, Sir.

Sir B. By Heaven, there is more rapture in being one moment *vis-à-vis*
with you, than in the company of a whole drawing-room of beauties. Round
you are melting pleasures, tender transports, youthful loves, and blooming
graces, all unfelt, neglected, and despised, by a tasteless, cold, languid,
unimpassioned husband, while they might be all so much better employed
to the purposes of ecstasy and bliss.   254

Mrs. L. I am amazed, Sir, at this liberty—what action of my life has
authorized such barefaced assurance? And for what reason do you think so
meanly of me, as to imagine that I have not a greater regard for my reputation, and for what the world may say, Sir?

Sir B. The world, Ma'am, the world will justify you—she served him right
—they will all agree in it, there will be but one opinion about it—that is,
Ma'am, if the world should know it; but our loves may be as concealed, as
secrets undiscovered yet by mortal eye.—By all that's soft, it goes down with
her like a dish of tea. [*Aside*.] And so, Madam, since I have convinced you,
and since the time, the place, and mutual ardour all concur—   264

Mrs. L. Sir, I am not to be treated in this manner, and, I assure you,
Sir, that were I not afraid of the evil consequences that might follow, I
should not hesitate a moment to acquaint Mr. Lovemore with your whole behaviour.

Sir B. She won't tell her husband then—a charming creature, and blessings
on her for so convenient a hint—she yields, by all that's wicked! What shall I
say to overwhelm her senses in a flood of nonsense?   [*Aside*.

Go my heart's envoys, tender sighs make haste,   272
Still drink delicious poison from thy eye—
Raptures and paradise
Pant on thy lip, and to thy heart be pressed.

[Forcing her all this time.

Enter Mr. Lovemore.

Love. Zoons, this is too much.

Sir B. What the Devil's the matter now? [*Kneels down to buckle his shoe.*] This confounded buckle is always plaguing me.—My dear boy, Lovemore, I rejoice to see thee.   [*They stand looking at each other.*

Love. And have you the confidence to look me in the face?   280

Sir B. I was telling your lady here, of the most whimsical adventure—

Love. Don't add the meanness of falsehood, to the black attempt of invading your friend's happiness.—I did imagine, Sir, from the long intercourse that has subsisted between us, that you might have had delicacy enough, feeling enough, honour enough, Sir, not to meditate an injury like this.

Sir B. Ay, ay, it's all over, I'm detected. [*Aside.*] Mr. Lovemore, if begging your pardon for this rashness will any ways atone—

Love. No, Sir, nothing can atone. The provocation you have given me, would justify my drawing upon you this instant, did not that lady and this roof protect you.   290

Sir B. But Mr. Lovemore—

Love. But, Sir—

Sir B. I only beg—

Love. Pray, Sir—Sir, I insist—I won't hear a word.

Sir B. I declare, upon my honour—

Love. Honour! For shame, Sir Brilliant, don't use the word.

Sir B. If begging pardon of that lady—

Love. That lady! I desire you will never speak to that lady.

Sir B. Nay, but prithee, Lovemore.

Love. No, Sir, no—I have done with you for the present.—As for you, Madam, I am satisfied with your conduct. I was, indeed, a little alarmed, but I was a witness of your behaviour, and I'm above harbouring low suspicions.

Sir B. Allow me but a word—   303

Love. No more, Sir, I have done—

Sir B. Let me but explain—

Love. Zoons! I'll go into another room to avoid you.

[Going, sees Mrs. Bellmour.

272–5 Go my heart's ... pressed] Line 1: Sir Richard Steele, *The Tender Husband* (1705), I. i. 221. Lines 2 and 4: Pope, 'Eloisa to Abelard', 122–3. Line 3 is Sir Brilliant's own contribution.

Hell and destruction, what fiend is conjured up here? Zounds, let me make
my escape out of the house.   [*Runs to the other door.*

Mrs. L. I'll secure this door—you must not go, my dear.   [*Stops him.*

Love. S'death, Madam, let me pass.   310

Mrs. L. Nay, you shall stay, I want to introduce an acquaintance of mine to
you.

Love. I desire, Madam—

Enter Mrs. Bellmour.

Mrs. B. My Lord, my Lord Etheridge; I am heartily glad to see your
Lordship.   [*Taking hold of him.*

Mrs. L. Do, my dear, let me introduce this lady to you.
                                             [*Turning him to her.*

Love. Here's the Devil and all to do!   [*Aside.*

Mrs. B. My Lord, this is the most fortunate encounter—

Love. I wish I was fifty miles off.   [*Aside.*

Mrs. L. Mrs. Bellmour, give me leave to introduce Mr. Lovemore to you.
                                             [*Turning him to her.*

Mrs. B. No, my dear Ma'am, let me introduce Lord Etheridge to you.
[*Pulling him.*] My Lord—   322

Sir B. In the name of wonder, what is all this?

Mrs. L. My dear Ma'am, you're mistaken; this is my husband.

Mrs. B. Pardon me, Ma'am, 'tis my Lord Etheridge.

Mrs. L. My dear, how can you be so ill-bred in your own house? Mrs.
Bellmour, this is Mr. Lovemore.

Love. Are you going to toss me in a blanket, Madam? Call up the rest of
your people, if you are.

Mrs. B. Pshaw! Prithee now, my Lord, leave off your humours; Mrs.
Lovemore, this is my Lord Etheridge, a lover of mine, who has made
proposals of marriage to me.   332

Love. Confusion! Let me get rid of these two furies.

                                             [*Breaks away from them.*

Mrs. B. [*Follows him.*] My Lord, I say! My Lord Etheridge! Won't your
Lordship know me?

Love. This is the most damnable accident!   [*Aside.*

Mrs. B. I hope your Lordship has not forgot your appointment at my
house this evening.

Love. Ay, now my turn is come.   [*Aside.*

Mrs. B. Prithee, my Lord, what have I done, that you treat me with this
coldness? Come, come, you shall have a wife, I will take compassion on you.

Love. Damnation! I can't stand this.   [*Aside.*

Mrs. B. Come, cheer up, my Lord; what the deuce, your dress is altered!

What's become of the star and the ribbon? And so the gay, the florid, the *magnifique* Lord Etheridge, dwindles down into plain Mr. Lovemore, the married man! Mr. Lovemore, your most obedient, very humble servant, Sir.

Love. I can't bear to feel myself in so ridiculous a circumstance.   [*Aside.*

Mrs. B. I beg my compliments to your friend Mrs. Loveit; and I am much obliged to you both for your very honourable designs.—

[*Curtseying to him.*

Love. I never was so ashamed in all my life!   350

Sir B. So, so, so, all his pains were to hide the star from me.—The discovery is a perfect cordial to my dejected spirits.

Mrs. B. Mrs. Lovemore, I cannot sufficiently acknowledge the providence that directed you to pay me a visit, though I was wholly unknown to you; and I shall henceforth consider you as my deliverer.

Love. Zoons! It was she that fainted away in the closet, and be damned to her jealousy.   [*Aside.*

Sir B. By all that's whimsical, an odd sort of adventure this—my Lord [*Advances to him.*], my Lord—my Lord Etheridge, as the man says in the play, 'Your Lordship's right welcome back to Denmark.'   360

Love. Now he comes upon me. Oh! I'm in a fine situation.   [*Aside.*

Sir B. My Lord, I hope that ugly pain in your Lordship's side is abated.

Love. Absurd and ridiculous.   [*Aside.*

Sir B. There is nothing forming there I hope, my Lord.

Mrs. L. [*Apart with* Mrs. Bellmour.] I begin now to feel for him, and to pity his uneasiness.

Sir B. Pray, my Lord, don't you think it a base thing to invade the happiness of a friend? Or to do him a clandestine wrong? Or to injure him with the woman he loves?

Love. To cut the matter short with you, Sir, we are both rascals.

Sir B. Rascal!   371

Love. Ay, both! We are two very pretty fellows indeed!

Mrs. B. I am glad to find that you are at length awakened into a sense of your error.   [*To* Lovemore.

Love. I am, Madam, and I am frank enough to own it.—I am above attempting to disguise my feelings, when I am conscious they are on the side of truth and honour; and Madam, with a true remorse, I ask your pardon.

Mrs. B. Upon certain terms, I don't know but I may sign and seal your pardon.

Love. Terms! What terms?   380

Mrs. B. That you make due expiation of your guilt to that lady.

Love. That lady, Ma'am! That lady has no reason to complain.

Mrs. L. No reason to complain, Mr. Lovemore!

360 'Your Lordship's . . . Denmark'] *Hamlet*, V. ii. 81–2.

I

Love. No Madam, none! For whatever may have been my imprudences, they have had their source in your conduct.

Mrs. L. In my conduct, Sir!

Love. In your conduct! I here declare before this company—and I am above palliating the matter—I here declare, that no man in England could be better inclined to domestic happiness, if you, Madam, on your part, had been willing to make home agreeable.   390

Mrs. L. There I confess he touches me.   [*Aside.*

Love. You could take pains enough before marriage, you would put forth all your charms, practice all your arts, and make your features please by rule; for ever changing, running an eternal round of variety: and all this to win my affections.—But when you had won them, you did not think them worth your keeping.—Never dressed, pensive, silent, melancholy; and the only entertainment in my house was the dear pleasure of a dull conjugal *tête-à-tête*; and all this insipidity, because you think the sole merit of a wife consists in her virtue: a fine way of amusing a husband truly!

Sir B. Upon my soul, and so it is!   [*Laughing.*

Enter Muslin.

Mus. O Gemini! Gemini! Here's such a piece of work—what shall I do? My poor dear lady!   [*Crying bitterly.*

Love. Is the woman crazy?   403

Mus. Oh! Madam—forgive me, my dear Madam—I did not do it on purpose—as I hope for mercy, I did not.

Mrs. L. What did not you do?

Mus. I did not intend to give it him, I would have seen him gibbeted first. —I found the letter in the parlour, Madam—I knew it was the same letter I had delivered to you, and my curiosity did make me peep into it.—Says my curiosity, 'Now, Muslin, you may gratify yourself by finding out the contents of that letter, which you have such a violent itching for.'—My curiosity said so, Ma'am, and then, I own, Ma'am, my respect for you did say to me, 'Hussy, how dare you meddle with what does not belong to you? Keep your distance, and let your Mistress's secrets alone.'—But then upon that, in comes my curiosity again, and says my curiosity, 'Read it, I tell you, Muslin, a woman of spirit should know everything.'—'Let it alone, you jade,' says my respect. 'It's as much as your place is worth.'—'There's more places than one,' says my curiosity, 'and so read it, I tell you, Muslin.'—I did read it— what could I do? Heaven help me, I did read it—I don't go to deny it, I don't, I don't.   [*Crying.*

Love. Don't keep such an uproar, woman.   421

401–425] Murphy used these speeches by Muslin again almost word for word at the end of *The Upholsterer* (1763).

Mus. And then, after I read it, thinks me, I, I'll give this to my Mistress directly, and that perfidious thing her husband shall not see it; and so as my ill stars would have it, as I was looking for you, I run my hand full in the lion's mouth.   [*Crying.*

Sir B. What an unlucky jade it has been!   [*Aside.*

Mrs. L. Well, have done, Muslin; this is too much.

Mrs. B. Upon my word but she gives him his own.—I suppose you own the truth of what she says, Mr. Lovemore.

Love. Pray, Madam, does that lady own the truth of what I have said?

Mrs. L. Sir, I am sensible there is too much truth in what you say; this lady has opened my eyes, and convinced me that there was a mistake in my former conduct.   433

Love. Come, come, you need not say any more—I forgive you, I forgive you.

Mrs. L. Forgive me! I like that air of confidence, when you know, that on my side, it is, at worst, an error in judgment, whereas on yours—

Mrs. B. Come, come, you know each other's faults and virtues, and so you have nothing to do but to mend the former, and enjoy the latter.—There, there, kiss and friends.—There, Mrs. Lovemore, take your reclaimed libertine to your arms.   441

Love. It is in your power, Madam, to make a reclaimed libertine of me indeed.

Mrs. L. From this moment it shall be our mutual study to please each other.   [*They embrace.*

Sir B. Lovemore, may I presume to hope for pardon at that lady's hands?

Love. My dear confederate in vice, your pardon is granted.—Two sad dogs we have been, but come, give us your hand—we have used each other damnably—for the future we will endeavour to make each other amends.

Sir B. And so we will.—Ma'am, since my Lord decamps from before the town, may I presume to hope—   451

Mrs. B. I positively forbid you the least grain of hope; whenever I take to myself a husband, I must be convinced first that he will answer the trouble of keeping him.

Sir B. My dear Ma'am, by all that's—

Mrs. B. No swearing—I positively will have my own way; you shall perform quarantine before I speak to you again.

Love. She's yours, man, she's yours—she'll throw herself into your arms in a day or two.—And now I heartily congratulate the whole company, that this business has had so happy a tendency to convince each of us of our folly.   461

Mrs. B. Pray, Sir, don't draw me into [a] share of your folly.

Love. Come, come, my dear Ma'am, you are not without your share of it.

This will teach you for the future, to be content with one lover at a time, without listening to a fellow you know nothing of—because he assumes a title, and reports well of himself.

Mrs. B. The reproof is just, I grant it.

Love. Come, let us join the company cheerfully, keep our own secrets, and not make ourselves a town-talk; though, I don't know but if this transaction were sent abroad into the world, it might prove a very useful lesson. The men would see how their passions may carry them into the danger of wounding the bosom of a friend—the ladies would learn, that after the marriage rites, they should not suffer their powers of pleasing to languish away, but should still remember to sacrifice to the Graces.   474

> To win a man, when all your pains succeed,
> The Way to Keep Him, is a task indeed.

FINIS

THE COMMISSARY

Samuel Foote

1720–1777

Samuel Foote, actor, dramatist, and theatre patentee, is one of the most irresistible of eighteenth-century characters. He is the man who inherited two fortunes and dissipated each in a couple of years; dined with a sullen Sam Johnson and was 'so very comical' that the Great Lexicographer was obliged to lay down his knife and fork, throw himself back in his chair, and 'fairly laugh it out'; lost his leg in a riding accident and at once began writing plays about cripples, starring himself; sent his most irreligious play to the Archbishop of Canterbury in hopes of having it 'corrected and approved for the press' by His Grace; outmanoeuvred the Lord Chamberlain's Office for many years; and profitably mimicked on the stages of London his talented friends even more readily than he did his enemies. The anecdotes about him are almost endless, and in them he appears extravagant, vain, and witty, though it is clear there was more to him than that. Foote's stage career extends from his acting début with Macklin at the Haymarket in 1744 (he had just run through the first fortune) to the sale of his theatre patent to Colman in 1777. In the interim, when not doing outright mimicry, giving comic lectures, or heckling more serious orators, he was writing and staging more than twenty satires, and acting in them and in other plays indefatigably. Foote cheerfully evaded or violated the Licensing Act from 1747—when he began to produce his amorphous entertainment *Diversions of a Morning* (or *Chocolate*, or *Tea*, or *The Auction of Pictures*, or *Taste*, as the Examiner caught up with each)—off and on until 1766, when he acquired his own royal patent after his accident.

The Commissary, one of Foote's most popular satirical farces (or comedies, as he called them), opened at the Haymarket Theatre on 10 June 1765, and had thirty performances before the regular season commenced in the fall. It became a summer staple, playing well over a hundred times during Foote's life. The portraits of Catgut, Gruel, and the *bourgeois gentilhomme* Zach Fungus illustrate the kind of topical satire that gave Foote his nickname— the 'English Aristophanes'—and frequently made him an object of controversy. Foote has always been criticized for his libellous caricatures and extreme topicality, in disregard of his repeated claims to be writing Old

Comedy. 'The original purpose of comedy', he wrote in *The Comic Theatre* (1762), 'was to expose particular follies for the punishment of individuals, and as an example to the whole community.' Later dramatists had to sweeten this recipe by adding 'plot, incident, and all the mechanical parts', producing New Comedy, but Foote insisted that satire remained the quintessential ingredient. He declared himself 'a rebel to this universal tyrant', Love, naming his target as 'affectation' and his weapon as 'ridicule'. Seen in this light, 'a comedy's being local or temporary is so far from being a moral or critical fault, that it constitutes its chiefest merit,' he argued. To sigh about Shakespeare and universality is to refuse the challenge on his own ground— as most of Foote's detractors have done. The fact remains that Foote stated his critical principles and worked by them with evident conviction for twenty years. In theory and in practice he was the Garrick era's staunchest upholder of the oldest western comic tradition.

The text is based on the first edition, 1765.

Facing page : The two epigraphs from Juvenal are translated by Ramsey (who reads '*quis*' for '*queis*' in the first): 'Those to whom it comes easy to take contracts for temples, rivers or harbours, for draining floods, or carrying corpses to the pyre' (*Satire* III, ll. 31–2); and 'It is to their crimes that men owe their pleasure-grounds and palaces, their fine tables and old silver goblets with goats standing out in relief' (*Satire* I, ll. 75–6).

THE
COMMISSARY.

A
COMEDY
IN THREE ACTS.

As it is Performed at the

THEATRE in the HAY-MARKET.

By SAMUEL FOOTE, Efq;

Queis facile eft ædem conducere flumina portus,
Siccandum eluviem, portandum ad bufta cadaver.
JUV. Sat. III.

Criminibus debent hortos, prætoria, menfas,
Argentum vetus, & ftantem extra pocula Caprum.
Ibid. Sat. I.

LONDON,
Printed for P. VAILLANT, facing Southampton-ftreet,
in the Strand. MDCCLXV.

[Price One Shilling and Six-pence.]

Dramatis Personæ

Mr. Zac Fungus,	Mr. FOOTE.
Mr. Isaac Fungus,	Mr. COSTOLLO.
Mr. Gruel,	Mr. SHUTER.
Young Loveit,	Mr. DAVIS.
Dr. Catgut,	Mr. PARSONS.
Simon,	Mr. PRESTON.
Mr. Bridoun,	Mr. GARDNER.
Mr. Paduasoy,	Mr. KEEN.
Mr. Harpy,	Mr. TINDAL.
La Fleur,	Mr. JOHNSON.
John,	Mr. MARSHALL.
A Hackney-Coachman,	Mr. PARSONS.

WOMEN

Mrs. Mechlin,	Miss CHENEY.
Mrs. Loveit,	Mr. SHUTER.
Dolly,	Miss REYNOLDS.
Jenny,	Mrs. GRANGER.

THE
Commissary

ACT I. SCENE I.

Mrs. Mechlin's *House*.

[Loud knocking at the door.]

Enter Jenny.

Jenny. Rap, rap, rap, upstairs and down, from morning to night; if this same commissary stays much longer amongst us, my mistress must e'en hire a porter. Who's there?

Simon. [*Without.*] Is Mrs. Mechlin at home?

Jenny. No. [*Opens the door.*] Oh, what is it you, Simon?

Enter Simon.

Simon. At your service, sweet Mrs. Jane.

Jenny. Why you knock with authority; and what are your commands, Master Simon?

Simon. I come, Madam, to receive those of your mistress. What, Jenny, has she any great affair on the anvil? Her summons is most exceedingly pressing; and you need not be told, child, that a man of my consequence does not trouble himself about trifles. 12

Jenny. Oh, Sir, I know very well you principal actors don't perform every night.

Simon. Mighty well, Ma'am, but notwithstanding your ironical sneer, it is not every man that will do for your mistress; her agents must have genius and parts: I don't suppose, in the whole Bills of Mortality, there is so general and extensive a dealer as my friend Mrs. Mechlin.

Jenny. Why, to be sure, we have plenty of customers; and for various kinds of commodities it would be pretty difficult I fancy to— 20

Simon. Commodities! Your humble servant, sweet Mrs. Jane; yes, yes, you have various kinds of commodities, indeed.

17 Bills of Mortality] The districts of London for which official bulletins of births and deaths were periodically published.

Jenny. Mr. Simon, I don't understand you; I suppose it is no secret in what sort of goods our dealing consists.

Simon. No, no, they are pretty well known.

Jenny. And to be sure, though now and then to oblige a customer, my mistress does condescend to smuggle a little—

Simon. Keep it up, Mrs. Jane.

Jenny. Yet there are no people in the Liberty of Westminster that live in more credit than we do.　　　　　　　　　　　　　　　　　30

Simon. Bravo.

Jenny. The very best of quality are not ashamed to visit my mistress.

Simon. They have reason.

Jenny. Respected by the neighbours.

Simon. I know it.

Jenny. Punctual in her payments.

Simon. To a moment.

Jenny. Regular hours.

Simon. Doubtless.

Jenny. Never misses the sarmant on Sundays.　　　　　　　　　　　　40

Simon. I own it.

Jenny. Not an oath comes out of her mouth, unless, now and then, when the poor gentlewoman happens to be overtaken in liquor.

Simon. Granted.

Jenny. Not at all given to lying, but like other tradesfolks, in the way of her business.

Simon. Very well.

Jenny. Very well! Then pray, Sir, what would you insinuate? Look you, Mr. Simon, don't go to cast reflections upon us; don't think to blast the reputation of our—　　　　　　　　　　　　　　　　　50

Simon. Hark ye, Jenny, are you serious?

Jenny. Serious! Ay, marry am I.

Simon. The devil you are!

Jenny. Upon my word, Mr. Simon, you should not give your tongue such a licence; let me tell you, these airs don't become you at all.

Simon. Hey-day! Why where the deuce have I got, sure I have mistaken the house; is not this Mrs. Mechlin's?

Jenny. That's pretty well known.

Simon. The commodious, convenient Mrs. Mechlin, at the sign of the Star, in the parish of St. Paul's?　　　　　　　　　　　　　　60

Jenny. Bravo.

Simon. That commercial caterpillar?

29 Liberty of Westminster] The area around Westminster proper which was still subject to its municipal authority.　40 sarmant] Sermon.

Jenny. I know it.

Simon. That murderer of manufactures?

Jenny. Doubtless.

Simon. That walking warehouse?

Jenny. Granted.

Simon. That carries about a greater cargo of contraband goods under her petticoats than a Calais cutter?

Jenny. Very well.   70

Simon. That engrosser and seducer of virgins?

Jenny. Keep it up, Master Simon.

Simon. That forestaller of bagnios?

Jenny. Incomparable fine.

Simon. That canting, cozening, money-lending, match-making, pawn-broking—   [*Loud knocking.*

Jenny. Mighty well, Sir; here comes my mistress, she shall thank you for the pretty picture you have been pleased to draw.

Simon. Nay, but dear Jenny—

Jenny. She shall be told how highly she stands in your favour.   80

Simon. But my sweet girl—   [*Knock again.*

Jenny. Let me go, Mr. Simon, don't you hear?

Simon. And can you have the heart to ruin me at once!

Jenny. Hands off.

Simon. A peace, a peace, my dear Mrs. Jane, and dictate the articles.

> *Enter Mrs.* Mechlin, *followed by a hackney coachman,*
> *with several bundles, in a capuchin, a bonnet, and*
> *her clothes pinned up.*

Mech. So, hussy, what must I stay all day in the streets? Who have we here? The devil's in the wenches, I think—one of your fellows I suppose—oh, is it you! How fares it, Simon?

Jenny. Madam, you should not have waited a minute, but Mr. Simon—   90

Simon. Hush, hush! You barbarous jade—

Jenny. Knowing your knock, and eager to open the door, flew upstairs, fell over the landing-place, and quite barred up the way.

Simon. Yes, and I am afraid I have put out my ankle. Thanks, Jenny; you shall be no loser, you slut.   [*Aside.*

Mech. Poor Simon.—Oh, Lord have mercy upon me, what a round I have taken!—Is the wench petrified, why don't you reach me a chair, don't you see I am tired to death?

Jenny. Indeed, Ma'am, you'll kill yourself.

73 bagnios] Prisons or brothels, as well as baths.

Simon. Upon my word, Ma'am Mechlin, you should take a little care of yourself; indeed you labour too hard.   101

Mech. Ay, Simon, and for little or nothing: only victuals and clothes, more cost than worship.—Why does not the wench take the things from the fellow? Well, what's your fare?

Coach. Mistress, it's honestly worth half a crown.

Mech. Give him a couple of shillings and send him away.

Coach. I hope you'll tip me the tester to drink?

Mech. Them there fellows are never contented: drink! Stand farther off; why you smell already as strong as a beer-barrel.

Coach. Mistress, that's because I have already been drinking.   110

Mech. And are you not ashamed, you sot, to be eternally guzzling? You had better buy you some clothes.

Coach. No, mistress, my honour won't let me do that.

Mech. Your honour! And pray how does that hinder you?

Coach. Why, when a good gentlewoman like you, cries, 'Here coachman, here's something to drink'—

Mech. Well!

Coach. Would it be honour in me to lay it out in anything else? No, mistress, my conscience won't let me, because why, it's the will of the donor, you know.   120

Mech. Did you ever hear such a blockhead?

Coach. No, no, mistress; tho' I am a poor man, I won't forfeit my honour; my cattle, tho'f I love 'em, poor beastesses, are not more dearer to me than that.

Mech. Yes, you and your horses give pretty strong proofs of your love and your honour; for you have no clothes on your back, and they have no flesh. Well, Jenny, give him the sixpence; there there, lay it out as you will.

Coach. It will be to your health, mistress; it shall melt at the Meuse, before I go home; I shall be careful to clear my conscience.

Mech. I don't doubt it.   130

Coach. You need not. Mistress, your servant.   [*Exit* Coachman.

Mech. Has there been anybody here, Jenny?

Jenny. The gentleman, Ma'am, about the Gloucestershire living.

Mech. He was, oh oh! What, I suppose his stomach's come down. Does he like the incumbrance? Will he marry the party?

Jenny. Why that article seems to go a little against him.

Mech. Does it so? Then let him retire to his Cumberland curacy: that's a fine keen air, it will soon give him an appetite. He'll stick to his honour too, till his cassock is wore to a rag.

107 tester] A sixpence.   123 tho'f] Though.   128 melt at the Meuse] Be spent on drink at the Meuse tavern.

Jenny. Why, indeed, Ma'am, it seems pretty rusty already. 140

Mech. Devilish squeamish, I think; a good fat living, and a fine woman into the bargain! You told him a friend of the lady's will take the child off her hands?—

Jenny. Yes, Madam.

Mech. So that the affair will be a secret to all but himself. But he must quickly resolve, for next week his wife's month will be up.

Jenny. He promised to call about four.

Mech. But don't let him think we are at a loss for a husband; there is to my knowledge a merchant's clerk in the city, a comely young man, and comes of good friends, that will take her with but a small place in the custom-house. 151

Jenny. He shall know it.

Mech. Ay, and tell him, that the party's party has interest enough to obtain it whenever he will. And then the bridegroom may put the purchase-money too of that same presentation into his pocket.

Jenny. Truly, Ma'am, I should think this would prove the best match for the lady.

Mech. Who doubts it? Here, Jenny, carry these things above stairs. Take care of the aigrette, leave the watch upon the table, and be sure you don't mislay the pearl necklace; the lady goes to Mrs. Cornelly's tonight, and if she has any luck, she will be sure to redeem it tomorrow. [*Exit* Jenny.

Simon. What a world of affairs! It is a wonder, Madam, how you are able to remember them all. 163

Mech. Trifles, mere trifles, Master Simon.—But I have a great affair in hand—such an affair, if well managed, it will be the making of us all.

Simon. If I, Ma'am, can be of the least use—

Mech. Of the highest! There is no doing without you.—You know the great—

Enter Jenny.

Jenny. I have put the things where you ordered, Ma'am.

Mech. Very well, you may go. [*Exit* Jenny.
I say, you know the great commissary, that is come to lodge in my house. Now they say this Mr. Fungus is as rich as an Indian governor; heaven knows how he came by it: but that you know is no business of ours. Pretty pickings, I warrant, abroad. [*Loud knocking.*
Who the deuce can that be? But let it be who it will, you must not go till I speak to you. 176

Enter Jenny.

Jenny. The widow Loveit, Ma'am.

Mech. What, the old liquorish dowager from Devonshire Square? Show her in. [*Exit* Jenny.] You'll wait in the kitchen, Simon; I shall soon dispatch her affair.   [*Exit* Simon.

Enter Mrs. Loveit.

Love. So, so, good morning to you, Mrs. Mechlin. John, let the coach wait at the corner.   182

Mech. You had better sit here, Madam.

Love. Anywhere. Well, my dear woman, I hope you have not forgot your old friend—ugh, ugh, ugh—[*Coughs.*] Consider I have no time to lose, and you are always so full of employment.

Mech. Forgot you! You shall judge, Mrs. Loveit. I have, Ma'am, provided a whole cargo of husbands for you of all nations, complexions, ages, tempers, and sizes: so you see you have nothing to do but to choose.

Love. To choose! Mrs. Mechlin; Lord help me, what choice can I have? I look upon wedlock to be a kind of a lottery, and I have already drawn my prize; and a great one it was! My poor dear man that's gone, I shall never meet with his fellow.   193

Mech. 'Pshaw! Madam, don't let us trouble our heads about him, it's high time that he was forgot.

Love. But won't his relations think me rather too quick?

Mech. Not a jot; the greatest compliment you could pay to his memory; it is a proof he gave you reason to be fond of the state. But what do you mean by quick! Why he has been buried these three weeks—

Love. And three days, Mrs. Mechlin.   200

Mech. Indeed! Quite an age!

Love. Yes; but I shall never forget him; sleeping, or waking, he's always before me. His dear swelled belly, and his poor shrunk legs. Lord bless me, Mrs. Mechlin, he had no more calf than my fan.

Mech. No!

Love. No, indeed; and then, his bit of a purple nose, and his little weezen face as sharp as a razor—don't mention it, I can never forget him.   [*Cries.*

Mech. Sweet marks of remembrance, indeed. But Ma'am, if you continue to be so fond of your last husband, what makes you think of another?

Love. Why, what can I do, Mrs. Mechlin? A poor lone widow woman as I am; there's nobody minds me; my tenants behind-hand, my servants all careless, my children undutiful—ugh, ugh, ugh—   ⸱ [*Coughs.*

Mech. You have a villainous cough, Mrs. Loveit; shall I send for some lozenges?   214

Love. No, I thank you, it's nothing at all; mere habit, just a little trick I've got.

206 weezen] Wizened.

Mech. But I wonder you should have all those vexations to plague you, Madam, you, who are so rich, and so—

Love. Forty thousand in the four per cents every morning I rise, Mrs. Mechlin, besides two houses at Hackney; but then my affairs are so weighty and intricate; there is such tricking in lawyers, and such torments in children, that I can't do by myself; I must have a helpmate; quite necessity, no matter of choice. 223

Mech. Oh, I understand you, you marry merely for convenience; just only to get an assistant, a kind of a guard, a fence to your property?

Love. Nothing else.

Mech. I thought so; quite prudential; so that age is none of your object; you don't want a scampering, giddy, sprightly, young—

Love. Young! Heaven forbid. What, do you think, like some ladies I know, that I want to have my husband taken for one of my grandchildren! No, no; thank Heaven, such vain thoughts never entered my head. 231

Mech. But yet, as matters stand, he ought not to be so very old neither; for instance now, of what use to you would be a husband of sixty?

Love. Sixty! Are you mad, Mrs. Mechlin, what do you think I want to turn nurse?

Mech. Or fifty-five?

Love. Ugh, ugh, ugh—

Mech. Or fifty?

Love. Oh! that's too cunning an age; men, nowadays, rarely marry at fifty, they are too knowing and cautious. 240

Mech. Or forty-five, or forty, or—

Love. Shall I, Mrs. Mechlin, tell you a piece of my mind?

Mech. I believe, Ma'am, that will be your best way.

Love. Why then, as my children are young and rebellious, the way to secure and preserve their obedience, will be to marry a man that won't grow old in a hurry.

Mech. Why I thought you declared against youth?

Love. So I do, so I do; but then, six or seven and twenty is not so very young, Mrs. Mechlin.

Mech. No, no, a pretty ripe age; for at that time of life, men can bustle and stir, they are not easily checked, and whatever they take in hand they go through with. 252

Love. True, true.

Mech. Ay, ay, it is then they may be said to be useful; it is the only tear and wear season.

Love. Right, right.

Mech. Well, Ma'am, I see what you want, and tomorrow about this time, if you'll do me the favour to call—

Love. I shan't fail.

Mech. I think I can suit you.   260

Love. You'll be very obliging.

Mech. You may depend upon't, I'll do my endeavours.

Love. But, Mrs. Mechlin, be sure don't let him be older than that, not above seven or eight and twenty at most; and let it be as soon as you conveniently can.

Mech. Never fear, Ma'am.

Love. Because you know, the more children I have by the second venter, the greater plague I shall prove to those I had by the first.

Mech. True, Ma'am. You had better lean on me to the door; but indeed, Mrs. Loveit, you are very malicious to your children, very revengeful, indeed.   271

Love. Ah, they deserve it; you can't think what sad whelps they turn out; no punishment can be too much; if their poor father could but have foreseen they would have—why did I mention the dear man! It melts me too much. Well, peace be with him.—Tomorrow about this time, Mrs. Mechlin, will the party be here, think you?

Mech. I can't say.

Love. Well, a good day, good Mrs. Mechlin.

Mech. Here, John, take care of your mistress.   [*Exit* Mrs. Loveit. A good morning to you, Ma'am. Jenny, bid Simon come up.—A husband! There now is a proof of the prudence of age; I wonder they don't add a clause to the act to prevent the old from marrying clandestinely as well as the young. I am sure there are as many unsuitable matches at this time of life as the other.   284

Enter Simon.

Shut the door, Simon. Are there any of Mr. Fungus's servants below?

Simon. Three or four strange faces.

Mech. Ay, ay, some of that troop, I suppose; come, Simon, be seated.— Well, Simon, as I was telling you: this Mr. Fungus, my lodger above, that has brought home from the wars a whole cartload of money, and who (between you and I) went there from very little better than a driver of carts—

Simon. I formerly knew him, Ma'am.   291

Mech. But he does not know you?

Simon. No, no.

Mech. I am glad of that—this spark, I say, not content with being really as rich as a lord, is determined to rival them too in every other accomplishment.

267 second venter] In the second marriage.   289 the wars] The Seven Years' War in Germany.

Simon. Will that be so easy? Why he must be upwards of—

Mech. Fifty, I warrant.

Simon. Rather late in life to set up for a gentleman.

Mech. But fine talents you know, and a strong inclination— 300

Simon. That, indeed.

Mech. Then I promise you he spares for no pains.

Simon. Diligent?

Mech. Oh, always at it. Learning something or other from morning to night; my house is a perfect academy, such a throng of fencers, dancers, riders, musicians—but, however, to sweeten the pill, I have a fellow-feeling for recommending the teachers.

Simon. No doubt, Ma'am; that's always the rule.

Mech. But one of his studies is really diverting; I own I can't help laughing at that. 310

Simon. What may that be?

Mech. Oratory.—You must know that his first ambition is to have a seat in a certain assembly; and in order to appear there with credit, Mr. What d'ye Call'em, the man from the city, attends every morning to give him a lecture upon speaking, and there is such haranguing and bellowing between them—Lord have mercy upon—but you'll see enough on't yourself; for do you know, Simon, you are to be his valet de chambre?

Simon. Me, Madam!

Mech. Ay, his privy counsellor, his confidant, his director in chief.

Simon. To what end will that answer? 320

Mech. There I am coming.—You are to know, that our 'Squire Would-be is violently bent upon matrimony; and nothing forsooth will go down but a person of rank and condition.

Simon. Ay, ay, for that piece of pride he's indebted to Germany.

Mech. The article of fortune he holds in utter contempt, a grand alliance is all that he wants; so that the lady has but her veins full of high blood, he does not care twopence how low and empty her purse is.

Simon. But, Ma'am, won't it be difficult to meet with a suitable object? I believe there are few ladies of quality that—

Mech. Oh, as to that, I am already provided. 330

Simon. Indeed!

Mech. You know my niece Dolly?

Simon. Very well.

Mech. What think you of her?

Simon. Of Miss Dolly, for what?

Mech. For what? You are plaguily dull; why a woman of fashion, you dunce.

Simon. To be sure Miss Dolly is very deserving, and few ladies have a

K

better appearance; but, bless me, Madam, here people of rank are so generally known, that the slightest enquiry would poison your project.

Mech. Oh, Simon, I have no fears from that quarter; there, I think, I am pretty secure.   342

Simon. If that, indeed, be the case—

Mech. In the first place, Mr. Fungus has an entire reliance on me.

Simon. That's something.

Mech. Then to baffle any idle curiosity, we are not derived from any of your new-fangled gentry, who owe their upstart nobility to your Harrys and Edwards. No, no, we are scions from an older stock; we are the hundred and fortieth lineal descendant from Hercules Alexander, Earl of Glendowery, prime minister to King Malcolm the First.   350

Simon. Odso! A qualification for a canon of Strasbourg. So then it seems you are transplanted from the banks of the Tweed; cry you mercy! But how will Miss Dolly be able to manage the accent?

Mech. Very well; she was two years an actress in Edinburgh.

Simon. That's true. Is the overture made, has there been any interview?

Mech. Several; we have no dislike to his person; can't but own he is rather agreeable; and as to his proposals, they are greater than we could desire; but we are prudent and careful, say nothing without the Earl's approbation.

Simon. Oh, that will be easily had.   360

Mech. Not so easily; and now comes your part: but first, how goes the world with you, Simon?

Simon. Never worse! The ten bags of tea, and the cargo of brandy, them peering rascals took from me in Sussex, has quite broken my back.

Mech. Poor Simon! Why then I am afraid there's an end of your traffic.

Simon. Totally: for now those fellows have got the Isle of Man in their hands, I have no chance to get home, Mrs. Mechlin.

Mech. Then you are entirely at leisure?

Simon. As a Bath turnspit in the month of July.

Mech. You are then, Simon, an old family servant in waiting here on the lady; but dispatched to the North with a view to negotiate the treaty, you are just returned with the noble peer's resolution. Prepare you a suitable equipage, I will provide you with a couple of letters, one for the lover and one for the lady—   374

Simon. The contents—

Mech. Oh, you may read them within: now with regard to any questions,

I will furnish you with suitable answers; but you have a bungler to deal with, so your cards will be easily played.

Enter Jenny.

Jenny. Miss Dolly, Ma'am, in a hackney coach at the corner; may she come in?   380

Mech. Are the servants out of the way?

Jenny. Oh, she is so muffled up and disguised, that she'll run no danger from them.

Mech. Be sure keep good watch at the door, Jenny.

Jenny. Oh, never fear, Ma'am.   [*Exit* Jenny.

Mech. Simon, take those two letters that are under the furthermost cushion in the window, run home, get a dirty pair of boots on, a great coat, and a whip, and be here with them in half an hour at farthest.

Simon. I will not fail. But have you no farther directions?

Mech. Time enough. I shall be in the way, for it is me that must introduce you above.   [*Exit* Simon.

So, things seem now in a pretty good train; a few hours, it is to be hoped, will make me easy for life. To say truth, I begin to be tired of my trade. To be sure the profits are great; but then, so are the risks that I run: besides, my private practice begins to be smoked. Ladies are supposed to come here with different designs than merely to look at my goods: some of my best customers too, are got out of my channel, and manage their matters at home by their maids. Those asylums, they gave a dreadful blow to my business. Time has been, when a gentleman wanted a friend, I could supply him with choice in an hour; but the market is spoiled, and a body might as soon procure a hare or a partridge as a pretty—   401

Enter Dolly.

—So, niece, are all things prepared? Have you got the papers from Harpy?

Dolly. Here they are, Ma'am.

Mech. Let me see—oh, the marriage articles for Fungus to sign. Have you got the contract about you?

Dolly. You know, aunt, I left it with you.

Mech. True, I had forgot: but where is the bond that I—here it is; this, Dolly, you must sign and seal before witness.

Dolly. To what end, aunt?

Mech. Only, child, a trifling acknowledgment for all the trouble I have taken; a little hint to your husband, that he may reimburse your poor aunt, for your clothes, board, lodging, and breeding.   412

395 smoked] Here meaning 'seen through', 'found out'.   398 asylums] Secure refuges or retreats, i.e. their homes.

Dolly. I hope my aunt does not suspect that I can ever be wanting—

Mech. No, my dear, not in the least: but it is best, Polly, in order to prevent all retrospection, that we settle accounts before you change your condition.

Dolly. But, Ma'am, may not I see the contents?

Mech. The contents, love, of what use will that be to you? Sign and seal, that's enough.

Dolly. But, aunt, I choose to see what I sign.   420

Mech. To see! What, then you suspect me?

Dolly. No, Ma'am; but a little caution—

Mech. Caution! Here's an impudent baggage! How dare you dispute my commands? Have not I made you, raised you from nothing, and won't a word from my mouth reduce you again?

Dolly. Madam, I—

Mech. Answer me, hussy, was not you a beggar's brat at my door? Did not I, out of compassion, take you into my house, call you my niece, and give you suitable breeding?

Dolly. True, Madam.   430

Mech. And what return did you make me? You was scarce got into your teens, you forward slut, but you brought me a child almost as big as yourself; and a delightful father you chose for it! Doctor Catgut, the meagre musician, that sick monkey-face maker of crotchets, that eternal trotter after all the little draggle-tailed girls of town. Oh, you low slut, had it been by a gentleman, it would not have vexed me, but a fiddler!

Dolly. For Heaven's sake.

Mech. After that you eloped, commenced stroller, and in a couple of years, returned to town in your original trim, with scarce a rag to your back.

Dolly. Pray, Ma'am—   440

Mech. Did not I, notwithstanding, receive you again? Have not I tortured my brains for your good? Found you a husband as rich as a Jew, just brought all my matters to bear, and now you refuse to sign a paltry paper?

Dolly. Pray, Madam, give it me, I will sign, execute, do all that you bid me.

Mech. You will; yes, so you had best. And what's become of the child, have you done as I ordered?

Dolly. The doctor was not at home; but the nurse left the child in the kitchen.

Mech. You heard nothing from him?   450

Dolly. Not a word.

Mech. Then he is meditating some mischief, I warrant. However, let our good stars secure us today, and a fig for what may happen tomorrow. It is a little unlucky though, that Mr. Fungus has chosen the doctor for his master of music; but as yet he has not been here, and, if possible, we must prevent him.

Enter Jenny, *hastily.*

Jenny. Mr. Fungus, the tallow-chandler, Ma'am, is crossing the way; shall I say you are at home?

Mech. His brother has servants enough, let some of them answer. Hide, Dolly.   [*Exit* Dolly *and* Jenny.—*One knock at the door.*

Ay, that's the true tap of the trader; this old brother of ours, though, is smoky and shrewd, and though an odd, a sensible fellow, we must guard against him: if he gets but an inkling, but the slightest suspicion, our project is marred.—[*A noise without.*] What the deuce is the matter! As I live, a squabble between him and La Fleur, the French footman we hired this morning. This may make mirth, I'll listen a little.   [*Retires.*

Enter Mr. Isaac Fungus, *driving in* La Fleur.

Isaac. What, is there nobody in the house that can give me an answer; where's my brother, you rascal?   468

La F. Je n'entends pas.

Isaac. Pas, what the devil is that; answer yes or no, is my brother at home? Don't shrug up your shoulders at me, you—oh, here comes a rational being.   472

Enter Mrs. Mechlin.

Madam Mechlin, how fares it? This here lantern-jawed rascal won't give me an answer, and indeed would scarce let me into the house.

La F. Ce gros bourgeois a fait une tapage de diable.

Mech. Fy donc, c'est le frère de monsieur.

La F. Le frère! Mon Dieu!

Isaac. What is all this? What the devil linguo is the fellow a-talking?

Mech. This is a footman from France that your brother has taken.

Isaac. From France! And is that the best of his breeding? I thought we had taught them better manners abroad, than to come here and insult us at home. People make such a rout about smuggling their Frenchified goods, their men do us more mischief. If we could but hinder the importing of them—

Mech. Ay, you are a true Briton, I see that, Mr. Isaac.   484

Isaac. I warrant me: is brother Zachary at home?

Mech. Above stairs, Sir.

Isaac. Any company with him?

Mech. Not any to hinder your visit. La Fleur, *ouvrez la porte.*

462 smoky] Perceptive.   465 La Fleur] Possibly a reference to the character in Sterne's *Tristram Shandy.*

Isaac. Get along you—Mrs. Mechlin, your servant.—I can't think what the devil makes your quality so fond of the mounsiers; for my part I don't see— march and be hanged to you—you sooty-faced—   491

[*Exeunt* I. Fungus *and* La Fleur.

Mech. Come Dolly, you now may appear.

Enter Jenny.

Jenny. Mr. Paduasoy, Ma'am, the Spitalfields weaver; he has been waiting this hour, and says he has some people at home—

Mech. Let him enter; in a couple of minutes I'll follow you, Dolly.

[*Exit* Jenny.

Enter Paduasoy.

Mech. Mr. Paduasoy, you may load yourself home with those silks, they won't do for my market.

Pad. Why, what's the matter, Madam?

Mech. Matter! You are a pretty fellow indeed, you a tradesman; but it's lucky I know you, things might have been worse; let us settle accounts, Mr. Paduasoy; you'll see no more of my money.   501

Pad. I shall be sorry for that, Mrs. Mechlin.

Mech. Sorry! Answer me one question; am not I the best customer that ever you had?

Pad. I confess it.

Mech. Have not I mortgaged my precious soul, by swearing to my quality customers that the stuff from your looms was the produce of Lyons?

Pad. Granted.

Mech. And unless that had been believed, could you have sold them a yard, nay a nail?   510

Pad. I believe not.

Mech. Very well. Did not, Sir, I procure you more money for your cursed goods, when sold as the manufacture of France, than as mere English they could have ever produced you?

Pad. I never denied it.

Mech. Then are not you a pretty fellow, to blow up and ruin my reputation at once?

Pad. Me, Madam!

Mech. Yes, you.

Pad. As how?   520

Mech. Did not you tell me these pieces of silk were entire, and the only ones you had made of that pattern?

Pad. I did.

510 nail] Two and a quarter inches.

Mech. Now mind. Last Monday I left them as just landed, upon a pretence to secure them from seizure, at the old Countess of Furbelow's, by whose means, I was sure, at my own price, to get rid of them both; and who should come in last night at the ball at the Mansion House, where my Lady unluckily happened to be, with a full suit of the blue pattern upon her back, but Mrs. Deputy Dowlass, dizened out like a duchess.

Pad. Mrs. Deputy Dowlass! Is it possible?   530

Mech. There is no denying the fact: but that was not all; if indeed Mrs. Deputy had behaved like a gentlewoman, and swore they had been sent her from Paris, why there the thing would have died: but see what it is to have to do with mechanics, the fool owned she had them from you. I should be glad to see any of my customers at a loss for a lie. But those trumpery traders, Mr. Paduasoy, you'll never gain any credit by them.

Pad. This must be a trick of my wife's; I know the women are intimate, but this piece of intelligence will make a hot house. None of my fault indeed, Mrs. Mechlin; I hope, Ma'am, this won't make any difference?

Mech. Difference! I don't believe I shall be able to smuggle a gown for you these six months. What is in that bundle?   541

Pad. Some India handkerchiefs, that you promised to procure of a supercargo at Woolwich, for Sir Thomas Callico's lady.

Mech. Are you pretty forward with the light sprigged waistcoats from Italy?

Pad. They will be out of the loom in a week.

Mech. You need not put any Genoa velvets in hand till the end of the autumn; but you may make me immediately a fresh sortment of foreign ribbons for summer.

Pad. Any other commands, Mrs. Mechlin?

Mech. Not at present, I think.   550

Pad. I wish you, Madam, a very good morning.

Mech. Mr. Paduasoy, Lord! I had liked to have forgot. You must write an anonymous letter to the Custom-house, and send me some old silks to be seized; I must treat the town with a bonfire: it will make a fine paragraph for the papers; and at the same time advertise the public where such things may be had.

Pad. I shan't fail, Madam.   [*Exit* Paduasoy.

Mech. Who says now that I am not a friend to my country! I think the Society for the Encouragement of Arts, should vote me a premium. I am sure I am one of the greatest encouragers of our own manufactures.   560

[*Exit* Mrs. Mechlin.

END of the First Act.

559 Society for the Encouragement of Arts] The Society of Arts encouraged British agriculture and industry with medals and other prizes.

ACT II

SCENE *First Continues*.

Enter Commissary [Zach.] Fungus, Isaac Fungus, *and* Mrs. Mechlin.

Zach. Brother Isaac, you are a blockhead, I tell you. But first answer me this; can knowledge do a man any harm?

Isaac. No, sarting; what is befitting a man for to learn.

Zach. To learn! And how should you know what is befitting a gentleman to learn? Stick to your trade, master tallow-chandler.

Isaac. Now, brother Zachary, can you say in your conscience, as how, it is decent to be learning to dance, when you ha' almost lost the use of your legs?

Zach. Lost the use of my legs! To see but the malice of men! Do but ax Mrs. Mechlin; now, Ma'am, does not Mr. Dukes say, that, considering my time, I have made a wonderful progress?   10

Isaac. Your time, brother Zac!

Zach. Ay, my time, brother Isaac. Why, I ha'nt been at it passing a couple of months, and we have at our school two aldermen and a sergeant-at-law, that were full half a year before they could get out of hand.

Mech. Very true, Sir.

Zach. There now, Mrs. Mechlin can vouch it. And pray, Ma'am, does not master allow, that of my age, I am the most hopeful scholar he has?

Mech. I can't but say, Mr. Isaac, that the squire has made a most prodigious improvement.

Zach. Do you hear that? I wish we had but a kit, I would show you what I could do: one, two, three, ha. One, two, three, ha. There are risings and sinkings.   22

Mech. Ay, marry, as light as a cork.

Zach. A'n't it? Why, before next winter is over, he says, he'll fit me for dancing in public; and who knows but in Lent, you may see me ramble at a Ridotto with an opera singer.

Mech. And I warrant he acquits himself as well as the best.

Isaac. Mercy on me! And pray brother, that thing like a sword in your hand, what may the use of that implement be?

Zach. This? Oh, this is a foil.

Isaac. A foil.   30

Zach. Ay, a little instrument, by which, we who are gentlemen, are instructed to kill one another.

3 sarting] Certain, certainly.   20 kit] A small fiddle used by dancing-masters.
26 Ridotto] A ball.

Isaac. To kill! Marry, Heaven forbid; I hope you have no such bloody intentions. Why, brother Zac, you was used to be a peaceable man.

Zach. Ay, that was when I was a paltry mechanic, and afraid of the law, but now I am another guess person; I have been in camps, cantoons, and entrenchments: have marched over bridges and breaches; I have seen the Ezel and Wezell; I'm got as rich as a Jew, and if any man dares to affront me, I'll let him know that my trade has been fighting. 40

Isaac. Rich as a Jew! Ah, Zac, Zac, but if you had not had another guess trade than fighting, I doubt whether you would have returned altogether so rich: but now you have got all this wealth, why not sit down and enjoy it in quiet?

Zach. Hark ye, Isaac, do you purtend to know life? Are you acquainted with the *beaux d'esprits* of the age?

Isaac. I don't understand you.

Zach. No, I believe not; then how should you know what belongs to gentility?

Isaac. And why not as well as you, brother Zac? I hope I am every whit as well born? 51

Zach. Ay, Isaac, but the breeding is all; consider I have been a gentleman above five years and three-quarters, and I think should know a little what belongs to the business; hey, Mrs. Mechlin?

Mech. Very true, Sir.

Zach. And as to this foil, do you know, Isaac, in what the art of fencing consists?

Isaac. How should I?

Zach. Why, it is short; there are but two rules; the first is, to give your antagonist as many thrusts as you can; the second, to be careful and receive none yourself. 61

Isaac. But how is this to be done?

Zach. Oh, easy enough: for do you see, if you can but divert your adversary's point from the line of your body, it is impossible he ever should hit you; and all this is done by a little turn of the wrist, either this way, or that way. But I'll show you: John, bring me a foil. Mrs. Mechlin, it will be worth your observing. Here, brother Isaac. [*Offers him a foil.*

Isaac. Not I.

Zach. These bourgeois are so frightful. Mrs. Mechlin, will you, Ma'am, do me the favour to push at me a little? Mind, brother, when she thrusts at me in carte, I do so; and when she pushes in tierce, I do so; and by this means a

37 guess] Kind of. 37 cantoons] Cantons, soldiers' quarters. 39 Ezel and Wezell] Ezel is the Russian name for Saare, an Estonian island which Russia occupied in 1710. Wezell is a north Belgian town in Antwerp province. 71 carte . . . tierce] Respectively fourth (quarte) and third positions in fencing.

man is sure to avoid being killed. But it may not be amiss, brother Isaac, to give you the progress of a regular quarrel; and then you will see what sort of a thing a gentleman is. Now I have been told, do see, brother Isaac, by a friend who has a regard for my honour, that Captain Jenkins, or Hopkins, or Wilkins, or what captain you please, has in public company called me a cuckold—   77

Isaac. A cuckold! But how can that be? Because why, brother Zac, you be'nt married.

Zach. But as I am just going to be married, that may very well happen, you know.   81

Mech. True.

Zach. Yes, yes, the thing is natural enough. Well, the captain has said, I am a cuckold. Upon which, the first time I set eyes on Captain Wilkins, either at Vauxhall, or at Ranelagh, I accost him, in a courteous, genteel-like manner—

Isaac. And that's more than he merits.

Zach. Your patience, dear Isaac—in a courteous, gentlemanlike manner; Captain Hopkins, your servant.

Isaac. Why, you called him but now Captain Wilkins.

Zach. Pshaw! You blockhead, I tell you the name does not signify nothing. —Your servant; shall I crave your ear for a moment? The captain politely replies, your commands, good Mr. Fungus? Then we walk side by side— come here, Mrs. Mechlin.—[*They walk up and down.*] For some time as civil as can be. Mind, brother Isaac.   94

Isaac. I do, I do.

Zach. Hey! No, t'other side, Mrs. Mechlin.—That's right—I hear, Captain Wilkins—

Isaac. I knew it was Wilkins.

Zach. Zounds! Isaac, be quiet—Wilkins, that you have taken some liberties about and concerning of me, which, damme, I don't understand—

Isaac. Don't swear, brother Zachary.   101

Zach. Did ever mortal hear the like of this fellow!

Isaac. But you are grown such a reprobate since you went to the wars—

Zach. Mrs. Mechlin, stop the tongue of that blockhead; why, dunce, I am speaking by rule, and Mrs. Mechlin can tell you that duels and damme's always go together.

Mech. Oh, always.

Zach. Which, damme, I don't understand. Liberties with you, cries the captain, where, when, and in what manner? Last Friday night, in company at the St. Alban's, you called me a buck, and moreover said, that my horns were exalted. Now, Sir, I know very well what was your meaning by that, and therefore demand satisfaction. That, Sir, is what I never deny to a gentle-man; but as to you, Mr. Fungus, I can't consent to give you that rank. How,

Sir, do you deny my gentility! Oh, that affront must be answered this instant —draw, Sir. Now push, Mrs. Mechlin. [*They fence.*] There I parry tierce, there I parry carte, there I parry—hold, hold, have a care, zooks! Mrs. Mechlin.   117

Isaac. Ha, ha, ha! I think you have met with your match; well pushed, Mrs. Mechlin.

Zach. Ay, but instead of pushing in tierce, she pushed me in carte, and came so thick with her thrusts, that it was not in nature to parry them.

Isaac. Well, well, I am fully convinced of your skill; but I think, brother Zac, you hinted an intention of marrying. Is that your design?   123

Zach. Undoubtedly.

Isaac. And when?

Zach. Why this evening.

Isaac. So sudden! And pray is it a secret to whom?

Zach. A secret, no, I am proud of the match; she brings me all that I want, her veins full of good blood; such a family! Such an alliance! Zooks, she has a pedigree as long as the Mall, brother Isaac, with large trees on each side, and all the boughs loaded with lords.   131

Isaac. But has the lady no name?

Zach. Name! Ay, such a name, Lord, we have nothing like it in London: none of your stunted little dwarfish words of one syllable; your Watts, and your Potts, and your Trotts; this rumbles through the throat like a cart with broad wheels. Mrs. Mechlin, you can pronounce it better than me.

Mech. Lady Sacharissa Mackirkincroft.

Zach. Kirkincroft! There are a mouthful of syllables for you. Lineally descended from Hercules Alexander Charlemagne Hannibal, Earl of Glendower, prime minister to King Malcolm the First.   140

Isaac. And are all the parties agreed?

Zach. I can't say quite all; for the right honourable peer that is to be my papa, who (by the bye) is as proud as the Devil, has flatly renounced the alliance, calls me here in his letter Plebeian, and says if we have any children, they will turn out very little better than pie balls.

Isaac. And what does the gentlewoman say?

Zach. The gentlewoman! Oh, the gentlewoman (who between ourselves) is pretty near as high as her father; but, however, my person has proved too hard for her pride, and I take the affair to be as good as concluded.

Isaac. It is resolved?   150

Zach. Fixed.

Isaac. I am sorry for it.

Zach. Why so? Come, come, brother Isaac, don't be uneasy, I have a shrewd guess at your grievance; but though you may not be suffered to see

145 pie balls] i.e. piebalds.

Lady Scracarissa at first, yet who knows before long I may have interest enough with her to bring it about; and in the meantime you may dine when you will with the steward.

Isaac. You are exceedingly kind.

Zach. Mrs. Mechlin, you don't think my Lady will gainsay it?

Mech. By no means; it is wonderful, considering her rank, how mild and condescending she is: why, but yesterday, says her Ladyship to me, 'Though, Mrs. Mechlin, it can't be supposed that I should admit any of the Fungus family into my presence—' 163

Zach. No, no, to be sure; not at first, as I said.

Mech. 'Yet his brother, or any other relation, may dine with the servants every day.'

Zach. Do you hear, Isaac, there's your true, inherent nobility, so humble and affable; but people of real rank never have any pride; that is only for upstarts.

Isaac. Wonderfully gracious; but here, brother Zac, you mistake me: it is not for myself I am sorry. 171

Zach. Whom then?

Isaac. For you. Don't you think that your wife will despise you?

Zach. No.

Isaac. Can you suppose that you will live together a month?

Zach. Yes.

Isaac. Why, can you bear to walk about your own house like a paltry dependant?

Zach. No.

Isaac. To have yourself and your orders contemned by your servants?

Zach. No. 181

Isaac. To see your property devoured by your Lady's beggarly cousins, who, notwithstanding, won't vouchsafe you a nod?

Zach. No.

Isaac. Can you be blind at her bidding, run at her sending, come at her calling, dine by yourself when she has bettermost company, and sleep six nights a week in the garret?

Zach. No.

Isaac. Why, will you dare to disobey, have the impudence to dispute the sovereign will and pleasure of a lady like her? 190

Zach. Ay, marry will I.

Isaac. And don't you expect a whole clan of Andrew Ferraros, with their naked points at your throat?

Zach. No.

192 Andrew Ferraros] Andrea Ferrara was a celebrated sixteenth-century Venetian swordmaker.

Isaac. Then you don't know half you will have to go through.

Zach. Look you, brother, I know what you would be at; you don't mean I should marry at all.

Isaac. Indeed, brother Zachary, you wrong me; I should with pleasure see you equally matched, that is, to one of your own rank and condition.

Zach. You would? I don't doubt it, but that is a pleasure you will never have. Look you, Isaac, I have made up my mind; it is a lady I like, and a lady I will have; and if you say any more, I'll not be contented with that, for dammee, I'll marry a duchess.   203

Enter La Fleur.

La F. Le maitre pour donner d'eloquence.

Zach. What does the puppy say, Mrs. Mechlin, for you know I can't *parler vous.*

Mech. The gentleman from the city, that is to make you a speaker.

Zach. Odzooks! A special fine fellow, let's have him.

Mech. Faites-le entrer.   [*Exit* La Fleur.

Isaac. Brother, as you are busy, I will take another—   210

Zach. No, no, this is the finest fellow of all, it is he that is to make me a man; and hark ye, brother, if I should chance to rise in the state, no more words, your business is done.

Isaac. What, I reckon some Member of Parliament.

Zach. A Member; Lord help you, brother Isaac, this man is a whole senate himself. Why, it is the famous orationer that has published the book.

Isaac. What, Mr. Gruel?

Zach. The same.

Isaac. Yes, I have seen his name in the news.

Zach. His knowledge is wonderful; he has told me such secrets: why do you know, Isaac, by what means 'tis we speak?   221

Isaac. Speak! Why we speak with our mouths.

Zach. No, we don't.

Isaac. No!

Zach. No. He says we speak by means of the tongue, the teeth, and the throat; and without them we should only bellow.

Isaac. But surely the mouth—

Zach. The mouth, I tell you, is little or nothing, only just a cavity for the air to pass through.

Isaac. Indeed!   230

Zach. That's all; and when the cavity's small, little sounds will come out; when large, the great ones proceed; observe now in whistling and bawling.—

217 Mr. Gruel] Most probably a caricature of Richard Brinsley Sheridan's father Thomas, who had published *A Course of Lectures on Elocution* in 1763.

[*Whistles and bawls.*]—Do you see? Oh, he is a miraculous man.

Isaac. But of what use is all this?

Zach. But it's knowledge, a'n't it; and of what signification is that, you fool! And then as to use, why he can make me speak in any manner he pleases; as a lawyer, a merchant, a country gentleman; whatever the subject requires.— But here he is.

Enter Mr. Gruel.

Mr. Gruel, your servant; I have been holding forth in your praise.

Gruel. I make no doubt, Mr. Fungus, but to your declamation, or recitation (as Quintilian more properly terms it), I shall be indebted for much future praise, inasmuch as the reputation of the scholar does (as I may say) confer, or rather as it were reflect, a marvellous kind of lustre on the fame of the master himself.   244

Zach. There, Isaac! Didst ever hear the like? He talks just as if it were all out of a book; what would you give to be able to utter such words?

Isaac. And what should I do with them? Them holiday terms would not pass in my shop; there's no buying and selling with them.

Gruel. Your observation is pithy and pertinent; different stations different idioms demand, polished periods accord ill with the mouths of mechanics; but as that tribe is permitted to circulate a baser kind of coin, for the ease and convenience of inferior traffic, so it is indulged with a vernacular or vicious vulgar phraseology, to carry on their interlocutory commerce; but I doubt, Sir, I soar above the region of your comprehension?   254

Isaac. Why, if you would come down a step or two, I can't say but I should understand you the better.

Zach. And I too.

Gruel. Then to the familiar I fall: if the gentleman has any ambition to shine at a vestry, a common-hall, or even a convivial club, I can supply him with ample materials.   260

Isaac. No, I have no such desire.

Gruel. Not to lose time: your brother here (for such I find the gentleman is), in other respects a common man like yourself—

Zach. No better.

Gruel. Observe how altered by means of my art: are you prepared in the speech on the great importance of trade?

Zach. Pretty well, I believe.

Gruel. Let your gesticulations be chaste, and your muscular movements consistent.

Zach. Never fear—   270

Enter Jenny, *and whispers* Mrs. Mechlin.

Mrs. Mechlin, you'll stay?

Mech. A little business, I'll return in an instant.   [*Exit* Mrs. Mechlin.

Gruel. A little here to the left, if you please, Sir, there you will only catch his profile—that's right—now you will have the full force of his face; one, two, three; now off you go.

Zach. When I consider the vast importance of this day's debate; when I revolve the various vicissitudes that this soil has sustained; when I ponder what our painted progenitors were; and what we, their civilized successors, are; when I reflect, that they fed on crab-apples and chestnuts—

Gruel. Pignuts, good Sir, if you please.   280

Zach. You are right; crab-apples and pignuts; and that we feast on green peas, and on custards: when I trace in the recording historical page, that their floods gave them nothing but frogs, and now though we have fish by land carriage, I am lost in amazement at the prodigious power of commerce. Hail commerce! Daughter of industry, consort to credit, parent of opulence, full sister to liberty, and great-grandmother to the art of navigation—

Isaac. Why this gentlewoman has a pedigree as long as your wife's, brother Zac.

Zach. Prithee Isaac be quiet—art of navigation—a—a—'vigation.—Zooks, that fellow has put me quite out.   290

Gruel. It matters not; this day's performance has largely fulfilled your yesterday's promise.

Zach. But I ha'n't half done, the best is to come; let me just give him that part about turnpegs—for the sloughs, the mires, the ruts, the impassable bogs, that the languid, but generous, steed travelled through; he now pricks up his ears, he neighs, he canters, he capers through a whole region of turnpegs.

Enter Mrs. Mechlin.

Mech. Your riding-master is below.

Zach. Gadso! Then here we must end. You'll pardon me, good Mr. Gruel; for as I want to be a finished gentleman as soon as I can, it is impossible for me to stick long to any one thing.   301

Gruel. Sir, though your exit is rather abrupt, yet the multiplicity of your avocations, do (as I may say), in some measure, cicatrise the otherwise mortal wound on this occasion sustained by decorum.

Zach. Cicatrise! I could hear him all day. He is a wonderful man. Well, Mr. Gruel, tomorrow we will at it again.

Gruel. You will find me prompt at your slightest volition.

Zach. I wish, brother Isaac, I could have stayed; you should have heard me oration away like a lawyer, about pleadings and presidents, but all in good time.—   [*Exit* Zac. Fungus.

294 turnpegs] Turnpikes on the new toll highways.

Mech. This gentleman, Sir, will gain you vast credit.   311

Gruel. Yes, Ma'am, the capabilities of the gentleman, I confess, are enormous; and as to you I am indebted for this promising pupil, you will permit me to expunge the obligation by an instantaneous and gratis lecture on that species of eloquence peculiar to ladies.

Mech. Oh, Sir, I have no sort of occasion—

Gruel. As to that biped, man (for such I define him to be), a male or masculine manner belongs—

Mech. Any other time, good Mr. Gruel.

Gruel. So to that biped, woman, she participating of his general nature, the word *homo*, in Latin, being promiscuously used as woman or man—

Mech. For Heaven's sake—   322

Gruel. But being cast in a more tender and delicate mould—

Mech. Sir, I have twenty people in waiting—

Gruel. The soft, supple, insinuating graces—

Mech. I must insist—

Gruel. Do appertain (as I may say), in a more peculiar, or particular, manner;—

Mech. Nay, then—

Gruel. Her rank, in the order of entities,—   330

Mech. I must thrust you out of my house.

Gruel. Not calling her forth—

Mech. Was there ever such a—   [*Pushing him out.*

Re-enter Gruel.

Gruel. To those eminent, hazardous, and (as I may say), perilous conflicts, which so often—

Mech. Get downstairs, and be hanged to you. [*Pushes him out.*] There he goes, as I live, from the top to the bottom; I hope I ha'n't done him a mischief: you aren't hurt, Mr. Gruel?—No, all's safe; I hear him going on with his speech; an impertinent puppy.

Isaac. Impertinent, indeed; I wonder all those people don't turn your head, Mrs. Mechlin.   341

Mech. Oh, I am pretty well used to 'em. But who comes here! Mr. Isaac, if you will step into the next room I have something to communicate that well deserves your attention.   [*Exit* Isaac Fungus.

Enter Simon.

Simon. Doctor Catgut at the foot of the stairs.

Mech. The devil he is! What can have brought him at this time of day? Watch, Simon, that nobody comes up whilst he is here.   [*Exit* Simon.
I hope he has not heard of the pretty present we sent him today.

Enter Dr. Catgut.

Cat. Madam Mechlin, your humble; I have, Ma'am, received a couple of compliments from your mansion this morning; one I find from a lodger of yours, the other I presume from your niece; but for the last, I rather suppose I am indebted to you.   352

Mech. Me! Indeed, Doctor, you are widely mistaken; I assure you, Sir, since your business broke out, I have never set eyes on her once.

Cat. Then I am falsely informed.

Mech. But after all you must own it is but what you deserve; I wonder, Doctor, you don't leave off these tricks.

Cat. Why what can I do, Mrs. Mechlin? My constitution requires it.

Mech. Indeed, I should not have thought it.

Cat. Then the dear little devils are so desperately fond.   360

Mech. Without doubt.

Cat. And for frolic, flirtation, diligence, dress and address—

Mech. To be sure.

Cat. For what you call genuine gallantry, few men, I flatter myself, will be found that can match me.

Mech. Oh, that's a point given up.

Cat. Hark ye, Molly Mechlin, let me perish, child, you look divinely today.

Mech. Indeed!

Cat. But that I have two or three affairs on my hands, I should be positively tempted to trifle with thee a little.   371

Mech. Ay, but Doctor, consider I am not of a trifling age, it would be only losing your time.

Cat. Ha, so coy! But apropos, Molly, this lodger of yours; who is he, and what does he want?

Mech. You have heard of the great Mr. Fungus?

Cat. Well!

Mech. Being informed of your skill and abilities, he has sent for you to teach him to sing.

Cat. Me teach him to sing! What, does the scoundrel mean to affront me?

Mech. Affront you!   381

Cat. Why don't you know, child, that I quitted that paltry profession?

Mech. Not I.

Cat. Oh, entirely renounced it.

Mech. Then what may you follow at present?

---

348 s.d. Dr. Catgut] A caricature of Thomas Augustine Arne (1710–88), composer of 'Rule, Britannia' and a number of operas. He was made Doctor of Music by Oxford University on 6 July 1759.

Cat. Me! Nothing. I am a poet, my dear.

Mech. A poet!

Cat. A poet. The Muses; you know I was always fond of the ladies: I suppose you have heard of Shakespeare, and Shadwell, of Tom Brown, and of Milton, and Hudibras?   390

Mech. I have.

Cat. I shall blast all their laurels, by gad; I have just given the public a taste, but there's a bellyful for them in my larder at home.

Mech. Upon my word, you surprise me; but pray, is poetry a trade to be learned?

Cat. Doubtless. Capital as I am, I have not acquired it above a couple of years.

Mech. And could you communicate your art to another?

Cat. To be sure. Why I have here in my pocket, my dear, a whole folio of rhymes, from Z quite to great A. Let us see, A. Ay, here it begins, A, ass, pass, grass, mass, lass, and so quite through the alphabet down to Z. Zounds, grounds, mounds, pounds, hounds.   402

Mech. And what do you do with those rhymes?

Cat. Oh, we supply them.

Mech. Supply them?

Cat. Ay, fill them up, as I will show you. Last week, in a ramble to Dulwich, I made these rhymes into a duet for a new comic opera I have on the stocks. Mind, for I look upon the words as a model for that sort of writing. First she.—

> There to see the sluggish ass,   410
> Through the meadows as we pass,
> Eating up the farmer's grass,
> Blithe and merry, by the mass,
> As a lively country lass.

Mech. Very pretty.

Cat. A'n't it. Then he replies,

> Hear the farmer cry out, zounds!
> As he trudges through the grounds,
> Yonder beast has broke my mounds;
> If the parish has no pounds,   420
> Kill, and give him to the hounds.

386 a poet] Arne was librettist for the operettas *Thomas and Sally* (1760) and *Love in a Village* (1762). 389 Shadwell] Thomas Shadwell (1642?–92), poet and dramatist, was satirized by Dryden as the 'true-blue Protestant poet'; he succeeded Dryden as Poet Laureate in 1688. 389 Tom Brown] Sir Thomas Browne (1605–82), author of *Religio Medici*. 390 Hudibras] A long verse satire (published 1663–78) by Samuel Butler (1612–80)

Then *da capo*, both join in repeating the last stanza; and this tacked to a tolerable tune, will run you for a couple of months. You observe?

Mech. Clearly. As our gentleman is desirous to learn all kinds of things, I can't help thinking but he will take a fancy to this.

Cat. In that case, he may command me, my dear; and I promise you, in a couple of months, he shall know as much of the matter as I do.

Mech. At present he is a little engaged, but as soon as the honeymoon is over—

Cat. Honeymoon! Why, is he going to be married?   430

Mech. This evening, I fancy.

Cat. The finest opportunity for an introduction, in nature; I have by me, Ma'am Mechlin, of my own composition, such an epithalmium.

Mech. Thalmium, what's that?

Cat. A kind of an elegy, that we poets compose at the solemnization of weddings.

Mech. Oh, ho!

Cat. It is set to music already, for I still compose for myself.

Mech. You do?

Cat. Yes. What think you now of providing a band, and serenading the squire tonight? It will be a pretty extempore compliment.   441

Mech. The prettiest thought in the world. But I hear Mr. Fungus's bell. You'll excuse me, dear Doctor, you may suppose we are busy.

Cat. No apology then, I'll about it this instant.

Mech. As soon as you please; anything to get you out of the way.

[Aside and exit.

Cat. Your obsequious, good Madam Mechlin. But notwithstanding all your fine speeches, I shrewdly suspect my blessed bargain at home was a present from you; and what shall I do with it? These little embarrasses we men of intrigue are eternally subject to. There will be no sending it back. She will never let it enter the house.—Hey! Gad, a lucky thought is come into my head—this serenade is finely contrived.—Madam Mechlin shall have her cousin again, for I will return her by-blow in the body of a double bass viol; so the bawd shall have a concert as well as the squire.   453

[Exit Dr. Catgut.

END of the Second Act.

ACT III

SCENE *continues.*

Enter Harpy, Young Loveit, *and* Jenny.

Harpy. Tell your mistress my name is Harpy; she knows me, and how precious my time is.

Jenny. Mr. Harpy, the attorney of Furnival's Inn?   [*Exit* Jenny.

Harpy. The same. Ay, ay, young gentleman, this is your woman; I warrant your business is done. You knew Kitty Williams, that married Mr. Abednego Potiphar, the Jew broker?

Y. Love. I did.

Harpy. And Robin Rainbow, the happy husband of the widow Champansy, from the isle of St. Kitts?

Y. Love. I have seen him.   10

Harpy. All owing to her. Her success in that branch of business is wonderful! Why, I dare believe, since last summer, she has not sent off less than forty couple to Edinburgh.

Y. Love. Indeed! She must be very adroit.

Harpy. Adroit! You shall judge, I will tell you a case: you know the large brick house at Peckham, with a turret at top?

Y. Love. Well.

Harpy. There lived Miss Cicely Mite, the only daughter of old Mite the cheesemonger, at the corner of Newgate Street, just turned of fourteen, and under the wing of an old maiden aunt, as watchful as a dragon—but hush—I hear Mrs. Mechlin. I'll take another season to finish my tale.   21

Y. Love. But, Mr. Harpy, as these kind of women are a good deal given to gossiping, I would rather my real name was a secret till there is a sort of necessity.

Harpy. Gossiping! She, Lord help you, she is as close as a Catholic confessor.

Y. Love. That may be, but you must give me leave to insist.

Harpy. Well, well, as you please.

Enter Mrs. Mechlin.

Your very humble servant, good Madam Mechlin; I have taken the liberty to introduce a gentleman, a friend of mine, to crave your assistance.   30

Mech. Any friend of yours, Mr. Harpy; won't you be seated, Sir.

Y. Love. Ma'am.   [*They sit down.*

13 Edinburgh] Where marriage laws were more lenient than in England.

Mech. And pray, Sir, how can I serve you?

Harpy. Why, Ma'am, the gentleman's situation is—but, Sir, you had better state your case to Mrs. Mechlin yourself.

Y. Love. Why, you are to know, Ma'am, that I am just escaped from the University, where (I need not tell you) you are greatly esteemed.

Mech. Very obliging. I must own, Sir, I have had a very great respect for that learned body, ever since they made a near and dear friend of mine a doctor of music. 40

Y. Love. Yes, Ma'am, I remember the gentleman.

Mech. Do you know him, Sir? I expect him here every minute to instruct a lodger of mine.

Y. Love. Not intimately. Just arrived, but last night; upon my coming to town I found my father deceased, and all his fortune devised to his relict, my mother.

Mech. What, the whole!

Y. Love. Every shilling. That is, for her life.

Mech. And to what sum may it amount?

Y. Love. Why, my mother is eternally telling me, that after her, I shall inherit fifty or sixty thousand at least. 51

Mech. Upon my word, a capital sum.

Y. Love. But of what use, my dear Mrs. Mechlin, since she refuses to advance me a guinea upon the credit of it, and while the grass grows—you know the proverb.

Mech. What, I suppose you want something for present subsistence.

Y. Love. Just my situation.

Mech. Have you thought of nothing for yourself?

Y. Love. I am resolved to be guided by you.

Mech. What do you think of a wife? 60

Y. Love. A wife!

Mech. Come, come, don't despise my advice; when a young man's finances are low, a wife is a much better resource than a usurer; and there are in this town a number of kind-hearted widows, that take a pleasure in repairing the injuries done by fortune to handsome young fellows.

Harpy. Mrs. Mechlin has reason.

Y. Love. But, dear Ma'am, what can I do with a wife?

Mech. Do! Why, like other young fellows who marry ladies a little stricken in years: make her your banker and steward. If you say but the word, before night I'll give you a widow with two thousand a year in her pocket.

Y. Love. Two thousand a year! A pretty employment, if the residence could but be dispensed with. 72

Mech. What do you mean by residence? Do you think a gentleman, like a pitiful trader, is to be eternally tacked to his wife's petticoat? When she is in town, be you in the country; as she shifts do you shift. Why, you need not be with her above thirty days in the year; and let me tell you, you won't find a more easy condition: twelve month's subsistence for one month's labour!

Y. Love. Two thousand a year, you are sure?

Mech. The least penny.

Y. Love. Well, Madam, you shall dispose of me, just as you please.

Mech. Very well, if you will call in half an hour at farthest, I believe we shall finish the business.   82

Y. Love. In half an hour?

Mech. Precisely. Oh, dispatch is the very life and soul of my trade. Mr. Harpy will tell you my terms; you will find them reasonable enough.

Harpy. Oh, I am sure we shall have no dispute about those.

Y. Love. No, no. [*Going.*]

Mech. Oh, but Mr. Harpy, it may be proper to mention that the gentle-woman, the party, is upward of sixty.

Y. Love. With all my heart; it is the purse, not the person I want. Sixty! She is quite a girl; I wish with all my soul she was ninety.   91

Mech. Get you gone, you are a devil, I see that.

Y. Love. Well, for half an hour, sweet Mrs. Mechlin, adieu.

[*Exeunt* Young Loveit *and* Harpy.

Mech. Soh! I have provided for my dowager from Devonshire Square, and now to cater for my commissary. Here he comes.

Enter [Zach.] Fungus *and* Bridoun.

Zach. So, in six weeks—oh, Mrs. Mechlin, any news from the lady?

Mech. I expect her here every moment. She is conscious that in this step she descends from her dignity; but being desirous to screen you from the fury of her noble relations, she is determined to let them see that the act and deed is entirely her own.   100

Zach. Very kind, very obliging, indeed. But, Mrs. Mechlin, as the family is so furious, I reckon we shall never be reconciled.

Mech. I don't know that. When you have bought commissions for her three younger brothers, discharged the mortgage on the paternal estate, and portioned off eight or nine of her sisters, it is not impossible but My Lord may be prevailed on to suffer your name.

Zach. Do you think so?

Mech. But then a work of time, Mr. Fungus.

Zach. Ay, ay, I know very well things of that kind are not brought about in a hurry.   110

Mech. But I must prepare matters for the lady's reception.

Zach. By all means. The jewels are sent to Her Ladyship?

Mech. To be sure.

Zach. And the ring for Her Ladyship, and Her Ladyship's licence?

Mech. Ay, ay, and Her Ladyship's parson too; all are prepared.

Zach. Parson! Why, won't Her Ladyship please to be married at Powl's?

Mech. Lord, Mr. Fungus, do you think a lady of her rank and condition would bear to be seen in public at once with a person like you?

Zach. That's true, I—

Mech. No, no; I have sent to Dr. Tickletext, and the business will be done in the parlour below.   121

Zach. As you and Her Ladyship pleases, good Mrs. Mechlin.

Mech. You will get dressed as soon as you can.

Zach. I shall only take a short lesson from Mr. Bridoun, and then wait Her Ladyship's pleasure. Mrs. Mechlin, may my brother be by?

Mech. Ay, ay, provided his being so is kept a secret from her.

Zach. Never fear.—   [*Exit* Mrs. Mechlin.
Well, Mr. Bridoun, and you think I am mended a little.—

Brid. A great deal.

Zach. And that in a month or six weeks I may be able to prance upon a long-tailed horse in Hyde Park, without any danger of falling?   131

Brid. Without doubt.

Zach. It will be vast pleasant, in the heat of the day, to canter along the King's Road, side by side with the ladies, in the thick of the dust; but that I must not hope for this summer.

Brid. I don't know that, if you follow it close.

Zach. Never fear, I shan't be sparing of—but come, come, let us get to our business—John, have the carpenters brought home my new horse?

Enter John.

John. It is here, Sir, upon the top of the stairs.

Zach. Then fetch it in, in an instant.   [*Exit* John.
What a deal of time and trouble there goes, Mr. Bridoun, to the making a gentleman. And do your gentlemen born now (for I reckon you have had of all sorts) take as much pains as we do?   143

Brid. To be sure; but they begin at an earlier age.

Zach. There is something in that; I did not know but they might be apter, more cuterer now in catching their larning.

Brid. Dispositions do certainly differ.

Zach. Ay, ay, something in nater, I warrant, as they say the children of blackamoors will swim as soon as they come into the world.

Enter servants with a wooden horse.

Oh, here he is, ods me! It is a stately fine beast.   150

116 Powl's] St. Paul's.

Brid. Here my lads, place it here—very well, where's your switch, Mr. Fungus?

Zach. I have it.

Brid. Now let me see you vault nimbly into your seat. Zounds! You are got on the wrong side, Mr. Fungus.

Zach. I am so indeed, but we'll soon rectify that. Now we are right: may I have leave to lay hold of the mane?

Brid. If you can't mount him without.

Zach. I will try; but this steed is so devilish tall—Mr. Bridoun, you don't think he'll throw me?   160

Brid. Never fear.

Zach. Well, if he should he can't kick, that's one comfort, however.

Brid. Now mind your position.

Zach. Stay till I recover my wind.

Brid. Let your head be erect.

Zach. There.

Brid. And your shoulders fall easily back.

Zach. Ho—there.

Brid. Your switch perpendicular in your right hand—your right—that is it, your left to the bridle.   170

Zach. There.

Brid. Your knees in, and your toes out.

Zach. There.

Brid. Are you ready?

Zach. When you will.

Brid. Off you go.

Zach. Don't let him gallop at first.

Brid. Very well: preserve your position.

Zach. I warrant.

Brid. Does he carry you easy?   180

Zach. All the world like a cradle. But, Mr. Bridoun, I go at a wonderful rate.

Brid. Mind your knees.

Zach. Ay, ay, I can't think but this here horse stands still very near as fast as another can gallop.

Brid. Mind your toes.

Zach. Ho, stop the horse. Zounds! I'm out of the stirrups, I can't sit him no longer; there I go—   [*Falls off.*

Brid. I hope you aren't hurt?

Zach. My left hip has a little contusion.   190

Brid. A trifle, quite an accident; it might happen to the very best rider in England.

Zach. Indeed!

Brid. We have such things happen every day at the menage; but you are vastly improved.

Zach. Why, I am grown bolder a little; and, Mr. Bridoun, when do you think I may venture to ride a live horse?

Brid. The very instant you are able to keep your seat on a dead one.

Enter Mrs. Mechlin.

Mech. Bless me, Mr. Fungus, how you are trifling your time! I expect Lady Sacharissa every moment, and see what a trim you are in.   200

Zach. I beg pardon, good Madam Mechlin. I'll be equipped in a couple of minutes; where will Her Ladyship please to receive?

Mech. In this room, to be sure; come, stir, stir.

Zach. I have had a little fall from my horse.—I'll go as fast as I—Mr. Bridoun, will you lend me a lift?   [*Exeunt* Fungus *and* Bridoun.

Mech. There—Jenny, show Mrs. Loveit in here—who's there?

Enter servants.

Pray move that piece of lumber out of the way. Come, come, make haste. Madam, if you'll step in here for a moment—   [*Exeunt servants.*

Enter Mrs. Loveit.

Love. So, so, Mrs. Mechlin; well, you see I am true to my time; and how have you throve, my good woman?   210

Mech. Beyond expectations.

Love. Indeed! And have you provided a party?

Mech. Ay, and such a party, you might search the town round before you could meet with his fellow: he'll suit you in every respect.

Love. As how, as how, my dear woman?

Mech. A gentleman by birth and by breeding, none of your whipper-snapper Jacks, but a countenance as comely, and a presence as portly: he has one fault indeed, if you can but overlook that.

Love. What is it?

Mech. His age.   220

Love. Age! How, how?

Mech. Why, he is rather under your mark, I am afraid; not above twenty at most.

Love. Well, well, so he answers in everything else, we must overlook that; for, Mrs. Mechlin, there is no expecting perfection below.

Mech. True, Ma'am.

Love. And where is he?

194 menage] Confused with 'manège': riding school.

Mech. I look for him every minute; if you will but step into the drawing-room, I have given him such a picture, that I am sure he is full as impatient as you.   230

Love. My dear woman, you are so kind and obliging: but, Mrs. Mechlin, how do I look? Don't flatter me, do you think my figure will strike him?

Mech. Or he must be blind.

Love. You may just hint black don't become me, that I am a little paler of late; the loss of a husband one loves will cause an alteration, you know.

Mech. True; oh, he will make an allowance for that.

Love. But things will come round in a trice.   [*Exit* Mrs. Loveit.

Enter Simon.

Simon. Madam, Miss Dolly is dizened out and everything ready.

Mech. Let her wait for the commissary here; I will introduce him the instant he is dressed.   [*Exit* Mrs. Mechlin.

Simon. Miss Dolly, you may come in, your aunt will be here in an instant.

Enter Dolly *and* Jenny.

Dolly. Hush, Simon, hush, to your post.   242

Simon. I am gone—   [*Exit* Simon

Dolly. Well, Jenny, and have I the true quality air?

Jenny. As perfectly, Ma'am, as if you had been bred to the business; and for figure, I defy the first of them all. For my part, I think Mr. Fungus very well off; when the secret comes out I don't see what right he has to be angry.

Dolly. Oh, when once he is noosed, let him struggle as much as he will, the cord will be drawn only the tighter.

Jenny. Ay, ay, we may trust to your management. I hope, Miss, I shall have the honour to follow your fortunes; there will be no bearing this house, when once you have left it.   252

Dolly. No, Jenny, it would be barbarous to rob my aunt of so useful a second; besides, for mistress and maid, we rather know one another a little too well.

Jenny. Indeed! But here comes Mr. Fungus; remember distance and dignity.

Dolly. I warrant you, wench.

Jenny. So, I see what I have to hope. Our young filly seems to be secure of her match; but I may jostle her the wrong side the post: we will have a trial, however, but I must see and find out the brother.   [*Aside, and exit*.

Enter [Zach.] Fungus *and* Mrs. Mechlin.

Zach. Yes, scarlet is vastly becoming, and takes very much with the ladies; quite proper too, as I have been in the army.   263

Mech. Stay where you are till you are announced to the lady. Mr. Fungus begs leave to throw himself at Your Ladyship's feet.

Dolly. The mon may dra nigh.

Mech. Approach.

Zach. One, two, three, ha! Will that do?

Mech. Pretty well.

Zach. May I begin to make love?   270

Mech. When you will.

Zach. Now stand my friend, Mr. Gruel. But she has such a deal of dignity that she dashes me quite.

Mech. Courage.

Zach. Here, hold the paper to prompt me in case I should stumble.—Madam, or, may it please Your Ladyship, when I preponderate the grander of your high ginnyalogy, and the mercantile meanness of my dingy descent; when I consider that your ancestors, like Admiral Anson, sailed all round the world in the ark; and that it is a matter of doubt, whether I ever had any forefathers or no; I totter, I tremble, at the thoughts of my towering ambition.—Ah—a, is not Phaeton next?   281

Mech. Hey! [*Looking at the paper.*] No, Luna.

Zach. Right; ambition—dignity how debased, distance how great; it is as if the link should demand an alliance with Luna; or the bushy bramble court the boughs of the stately Scotch fir; it is as if—what's next?

Mech. Next—hey! I have lost the place, I am afraid—come, come, enough has been said; you have showed the sense you entertain of the honour. Upon these occasions, a third person is fittest to cut matters short. Your Ladyship hears that—

Dolly. Yes, yes, I ken weel enough what the mon would be at. Mrs. Mechlin has speard sike things in your great commendations, Mr. Fungus, that I canno' but say I cliked a fancy to you from the very beginning.

Zach. Much obliged to Mrs. Mechlin, indeed, please Your La'ship.

Dolly. You ken I am of as auncient a family as any North Briton can boast.

Zach. I know it full well, please Your La'ship.   295

Dolly. But after the ceremony it will be proper to withdraw from town for a short space o' time.

Zach. Please Your La'ship, what Your La'ship pleases.

Dolly. In order to gi' that gossip, Scandal, just time to tire her tongue.

Zach. True, Your La'ship.   300

Dolly. I mun expect that the folk will mak' free wi' my character in choosing sike a consort as you.

Zach. And with me too, please Your La'ship.

278 Admiral Anson] George, Lord Anson (1697–1762), admiral of the fleet, circumnavigated the globe 1740–4.   284 link] Torch.

Dolly. Wi' you, mon!

Mech. Hold your tongue.

Dolly. Donna you think the honour will dra' mickle envy upon you?

Zach. Oh, to be sure, please Your La'ship. I did not mean that.

Dolly. Weel, I say, we'll gang into the country.

Zach. As soon as Your La'ship pleases; I have a sweet house hard by
Reading.   310

Dolly. You ha'; that's right.

Zach. One of the most pleasantest places that can be again.

Dolly. Ha' you a good prospect?

Zach. Twenty stagecoaches drive every day by the door, besides carts and
gentlemen's carriages.

Dolly. Ah, that will—

Mech. Oh, Your Ladyship will find all things prepared: in the next room
the attorney waits with the writings.

Zach. The honour of Your La'ship's hand—

Dolly. Maister Fungus, you're a little too hasty.   [*Exit* Dolly.

Mech. Not till after the nuptials; you must not expect to be too familiar at
first.   322

Zach. Pray, when do [you] think we shall bring the bedding about?

Mech. About the latter end of the year, when the winter sets in.

Zach. Not before!

Enter Young Loveit.

Y. Love. I hope, Madam Mechlin, I have not exceeded my hour; but I
expected Mr. Harpy would call.

Mech. He is in the next room with a lady. Oh, Mr. Fungus, this gentleman
is ambitious of obtaining the nuptial benediction from the same hands after
you.   330

Zach. He's heartily welcome: what, and is his wife a woman of quality too?

Mech. No, no, a cit; but monstrously rich: but your lady will wonder—

Zach. Ay, ay, but you'll follow; for I shan't know what to say to her when
we are alone.   [*Exit* Fungus.

Mech. I will send you, Sir, your spouse in an instant: the gentlewoman is a
widow, so you may throw in what raptures you please.

Y. Love. Never fear.   [*Exit* Mrs. Mechlin.
—And yet this scene is so new, how to acquit myself—let me recollect—some
piece of a play now.—'Vouchsafe, divine perfection.'—No, that won't do for
a dowager; it is too humble and whining. But see, the door opens, so I have
no time for rehearsal—I have it—'Clasped in the folds of love I'll meet my
doom,/And act my—'—   342

Enter Mrs. Loveit.

Love. Hah!

Y. Love. By all that's monstrous, my mother!

Love. That rebel my son, as I live!

Y. Love. The quotation was quite apropos: had it been a little darker, I might have revived the story of Oedipus.

Love. So, Sirrah, what makes you from your studies?

Y. Love. A small hint I received of your inclinations brought me here, Ma'am, in order to prevent, if possible, my father's fortune from going out of the family.   351

Love. Your father! How dare you disturb his dear ashes; you know well enough how his dear memory melts me; and that at his very name my heart is ready to break.

Y. Love. Well said, my old matron from Ephesus.

Love. That is what you want, you disobedient unnatural monster; but complete, accomplish your cruelty: send me the same road your villainies forced your father to take.

Enter Mrs. Mechlin.

Mech. Hey-day! What the deuce have we here: our old lady in tears!

Love. Disappointed a little, that's all.   360

Mech. Pray Ma'am, what can occasion—

Love. Lord bless me, Mrs. Mechlin, what a blunder you have made.

Mech. A blunder! As how?

Love. Do you know who you have brought me?

Mech. Not perfectly.

Love. My own son! That's all.

Mech. Your son!

Love. Ay, that rebellious, unnatural—

Mech. Blunder indeed! But who could have thought it; why, by your account, Ma'am, I imagined your son was a child scarce out of his frocks.

Love. Here's company coming, so my reputation will be blasted for ever.

Mech. Never fear, leave the care on't to me.   372

Enter [Zach.] Fungus *and* Dolly.

Zach. What is the matter? You make such a noise, there is no such thing as minding the writings.

Mech. This worthy lady, an old friend of mine, not having set eyes on her son since the death of his father; and being apprised by me, that here she might meet with him, came with a true paternal affection to give him a little wholesome advice.

355 Ephesus] Proverbial for wealth and licentious conviviality. The priestess of Diana at Ephesus was believed to remarry annually.

Love. Well said, Mrs. Mechlin.

Mech. Which the young man returned in a way so brutal and barbarous, that his poor mother—be comforted Ma'am; you had better repose on my bed— 382

Love. Anywhere to get out of his sight.

Mech. Here Jenny—

Love. Do you think you can procure me another party?

Mech. Never doubt it.

Love. Ugh, ugh.— [*Coughing.*

Mech. Bear up a little, Ma'am. [*Exeunt.*

Zach. Fie upon you, you have thrown the old gentlewoman into the 'sterics. 390

Y. Love. Sir!

Zach. You a man, you are a scandal, a shame to your sect.

Enter Dr. Catgut.

Cat. Come, come, Mrs. Mechlin, are the couple prepared? The fiddles are tuned, the bows ready rosined, and the whole band—oh, you, Sir, are one party I reckon, but where is the—ah, Dolly, what are you here, my dear?

Dolly. Soh!

Zach. Dolly! Who the devil can this be?

Cat. As nice and as spruce too, the bridesmaid I warrant: why you look as blooming, you slut.

Zach. What can this be? Hark ye, Sir! 400

Cat. Well, Sir.

Zach. Don't you think you are rather too familiar with a lady of her rank and condition?

Cat. Rank and condition: what, Dolly?

Zach. Dolly! What a plague possesses the man; this is no Dolly, I tell you.

Cat. No!

Zach. No, this is the Lady Scracarissa Mackirkincroft.

Cat. Who?

Zach. Descended from the old, old, old Earl of Glendowery.

Cat. What, she, Dolly Mechlin? 410

Zach. Dolly Devil, the man's out of his wits, I believe.

Enter Mrs. Mechlin.

Oh, Mrs. Mechlin, will you set this matter to rights?

Mech. How, Dr. Catgut!

Zach. The strangest fellow here has danced upstairs, and has Dolly, Dolly, Dollyed my lady; who the plague can he be?

Cat. Oh, apropos, Molly Mechlin, what, is this the man that is to be married? The marriage will never hold good; why he is more frantic and madder—

Zach. Mad! John, fetch me the foils; I'll carte and tierce you, you scoundrel. 420

Enter Isaac Fungus *and* Jenny.

Isaac. Where's brother? It a'n't over; you be'n't married, I hope.

Zach. No, I believe not; why, what is the—

Isaac. Pretty hands you are got into. Your servant, good Madam. What, this is the person, I warrant; ay, how pretty the puppet is painted; do you know who she is?

Zach. Who she is? Without doubt.

Isaac. No, you don't, brother Zac. Only the spawn of that Devil incarnate, dressed out as—

Zach. But hark ye, Isaac, are—don't be in a hurry—are you sure—

Isaac. Sure—the girl of the house, abhorring their scandalous project, has freely confessed the whole scheme. Jenny, stand forth, and answer boldly to what I shall ask. Is not this wench the woman's niece of the house?

Jenny. I fancy she will hardly deny it. 433

Isaac. And is not this mistress of yours a most profligate—

Mech. Come, come, Master Isaac, I will save you the trouble, and cut this matter short in an instant; well then, this girl, this Dolly, is my niece; and what then?

Zach. And aren't you ashamed!

Y. Love. She ashamed! I would have told you, but I could not get you to listen; why, she brought me here to marry my mother. 440

Zach. Marry your mother! Lord have mercy on us, what a monster! To draw a young man in to be guilty of incence. But hark ye, brother Isaac—

[*They retire.*

Cat. Gads my life, what a sweet project I have helped to destroy; but come, Dolly, I'll piece thy broken fortunes again; thou hast a good pretty voice, I'll teach thee a thrill and a shake, perch thee amongst the boughs at one of the gardens; and then as a mistress, which, as the world goes, is a much better station than that of a wife, not the proudest of them all—

Mech. Mistress! No, no, we have not managed our matters so badly. Hark ye, Mr. Commissary.

Zach. Well, what do you want? 450

Mech. Do you propose to consummate your nuptials?

Zach. That's a pretty question, indeed.

Mech. You have no objection then to paying the penalty, the contract here that Mr. Harpy has drawn.

Zach. The contract, hey, brother Isaac.

Isaac. Let me see it.

Mech. Soft you there, my maker of candles, it is as well where it is; but you need not doubt of its goodness: I promise you the best advice has been taken.

Zach. What a damned fiend, what a harpy!

Mech. And why so, my good Master Fungus; is it because I have practised that trade by retail which you have carried on in the gross? What injury do I do the world? I feed on their follies, 'tis true; and the game, the plunder, is fair; but the fangs of you, and your tribe,   463

> A whole people have felt, and for ages will feel:
> To their candour and justice I make my appeal;
> Though a poor humble scourge in a national cause,
> As I trust I deserve, I demand your applause.

FINIS